Men at Home

Men at Home

❋

Imagining Liberation
in Colonial
and Postcolonial India

GYANENDRA PANDEY

Duke University Press
Durham and London
2025

Project Editor: Liz Smith
Cover design by Dave Rainey
Typeset in Garamond Premier Pro by Copperline Book Services

Library of Congress Cataloging-in-Publication Data
Names: Pandey, Gyanendra, [date] author.
Title: Men at home : imagining liberation in colonial and
postcolonial India / Gyanendra Pandey.
Description: Durham : Duke University Press, 2025. |
Includes bibliographical references and index.
Identifiers: LCCN 2024017459 (print)
LCCN 2024017460 (ebook)
ISBN 9781478031383 (paperback)
ISBN 9781478028154 (hardback)
ISBN 9781478060376 (ebook)
Subjects: LCSH: Men—India—Attitudes. | Masculinity—
Social aspects—India. | Home—India. | Families—India. |
Postcolonialism—South Asia. | India—Social life and customs. |
India—Civilization—1947– | BISAC: SOCIAL SCIENCE / Ethnic
Studies / Asian Studies | POLITICAL SCIENCE / Colonialism &
Post-Colonialism
Classification: LCC HQ1090.7.I4 P36 2025 (print) |
LCC HQ1090.7.I4 (ebook) | DDC 305.610954—dc23/eng/20240922
LC record available at https://lccn.loc.gov/2024017459
LC ebook record available at https://lccn.loc.gov/2024017460

Cover art: Gathering of family members on wedding of Hameeda Omar, December 25, 1935. Family photograph generously provided by family of Begum Hameeda Husain Raipuri (née Omar). Jamshed Omar brought the original photo from "Neeli chatri," Aligarh, India, while leaving for Pakistan in 1948.

Sitting on chairs L to R: Said Omar, Munawwar (Begum Said Omar), Begum Mohammad Abdullah, Mohammad Abdullah (father of Zafar, Muzaffar, and Aftab Omar), Zafar Omar, Begum Zafar Omar, Hamida Omar. *Standing first row L to R:* Hameed Omar, Ayesha Omar, Bi (Begum Aftab Omar), Khadija Omar, Shoukat Omar, Jamila (Begum Shoukat Omar), Akhtar Hussain Raipuri. *Standing second row L to R:* Zahid Omar, Mahmoud Omar (with Jamshed Omar in her arms), Rashida Omar. *Sitting on ground L to R:* Aziz Omar, Ahsan Omar, Khalil Omar, Zakia Omar, Khurshid Omar, Anis Omar, Amna Omar (Munna, sister of Ayesha and Ahsan Omar).

To—

The savants of "World History,"
men and women,
who articulated dreams of
a more egalitarian society,
And the toilers of the "everyday,"
women and men,
who struggled to make it.

Contents

Dramatis Personae

Readers will note that I include men's and women's autobiographies as almost independent actors in the following listing of dramatis personae. I explain the reasoning in chapter 1.

❋ ❋ ❋

AMBEDKAR, BHIM RAO (1891–1956): *Babasaheb* to his legions of followers, distinguished scholar and political leader, founding father of the Dalit movement, first law minister of the government of independent India, and chief draftsman of the Indian constitution of 1950. His voluminous writings on economics, politics, religion, and law include a few autobiographical fragments and extensive commentary on the life and conditions of the poorest castes and classes in the Indian subcontinent. His life, he said, was an open book, documented in the abundance of writing about him by colleagues, followers, and biographers.

His second wife, SAVITA AMBEDKAR (1909–2003), a doctor whom he married in 1948 and who was his companion and primary caretaker throughout the last years of his life, wrote a detailed autobiography of their years together, which provides fascinating information on his life and activities in the home.

❋ ❋ ❋

BACHCHAN, HARIVANSH RAI (1907–2003): renowned Hindi poet, educator, and translator, special officer in the central government of independent India, and nominated member of the upper house of Parliament, 1966–1972. Wrote a four-volume autobiography on his personal life, published over two decades from 1969 to 1991.

His second wife, TEJI BACHCHAN (1914–2007), also appears as an important figure in the following analysis. She gave up her teaching position at a Lahore college to marry and support him in his career, and looked after their home and children, though she continued some work in theater, other artistic ventures, and social work.

❀ ❀ ❀

BAISANTRI, KAUSALYA (1926–2011): Dalit student activist in high school, forced into the role of middle-class housewife and mother after her marriage in 1947. Her autobiography published in 1999 details the life and struggles of her working-class parents and grandparents in and around Nagpur, the industrial city where she and her siblings grew up.

❀ ❀ ❀

GANDHI, MOHANDAS KARAMCHAND ("Mahatma") (1869–1948): acknowledged leader of the last phase of the Indian national movement, *Bapu* (father) to his millions of followers. Discusses his personal life, including his relationship with his wife and children, in remarkable detail in his autobiography, originally published between 1927 and 1929, as well as in other writings and speeches.

❀ ❀ ❀

JADHAV, NARENDRA (1950–): well-known economist and public intellectual, rose to become chief adviser to the governor of the Reserve Bank of India, vice-chancellor of a leading university, and member of the National Planning Commission and upper house of India's parliament. His family memoir, broadcast over the radio and published in several recensions through the 1990s and 2000s, documents the life of three generations, focusing especially on his parents, Damodar and Sonubai Jadhav, as they moved from hard labor and poverty in the fields of Nasik district to the railways and slums of Bombay, where their children entered into middle-class status and professions after the 1960s.

❀ ❀ ❀

KAMBLE, BABY (1929–2012): *Baby tai* (Aunt Baby) in her later years; distinguished Dalit writer, activist, and overworked housewife. Her autobiography, among the earliest by a Dalit woman, written in hiding over twenty years and published in the 1980s, describes the lives and homes of the laboring poor in the small towns and villages of western India from the 1930s and 1940s onward.

❀ ❀ ❀

MIRZA, AKBAR (1909–1971): member of the British colonial police service who transferred to the Pakistan police in 1947.

His wife, KHURSHID MIRZA (1918–1989), wrote a lively and detailed account of their life together in an autobiography published in the 1980s. An actor, singer, and dancer in Bombay films in her early twenties, she gave up her career for her husband and children; she became a leading radio and television artiste later in Pakistan, gaining considerable prominence in the years after Akbar's death in 1971.

❊ ❊ ❊

MOON, VASANT (1932–2002): civil servant and distinguished editor of the multivolume collected works of Dr. B. R. Ambedkar, commissioned by the government of Maharashtra. He grew up in a working-class neighborhood in the industrial city of Nagpur. His 1990s autobiography is a celebration of Dalit life and struggles in the neighborhood where he was born, and of his working-class mother, Purnabai, who raised him as a single parent.

❊ ❊ ❊

PRASAD, RAJENDRA (1884–1963): devoted Gandhian, prominent leader of the Indian National Congress, lawyer, legislator, and first president of the republic of independent India. Voluminous autobiography published in 1947, with brief but important comments on his marriage and domestic life.

❊ ❊ ❊

PREMCHAND (1880–1936): Dhanpat Rai, known by his pen name Premchand, "storyteller of the Independence movement," probably the most important Hindi-Urdu writer of the early twentieth century, devoted Gandhian and socialist. There is little by way of direct autobiographical statement in Premchand's extraordinary oeuvre of short stories, novels, and essays, which document the lives of the upper as well as the middle and lower classes in the villages and towns of northern India.

His second wife, SHIVRANI DEVI PREMCHAND (1888–1976), provides a wonderfully evocative account of their life together in a memoir written a few years after his death.

❊ ❊ ❊

RAIPURI, AKHTAR HUSAIN (1912–1992): radical leftist intellectual and writer, prominent national and international educationist after his move to Pakistan in 1947. Wrote a detailed autobiography centered on his intellectual and political commitments.

His wife, HAMEEDA AKHTAR HUSAIN RAIPURI (1920–2009), became a well-loved writer after his death, largely on account of her colorful autobiography, which focuses more on their life in the home.

❀ ❀ ❀

RAM, JAGJIVAN (1908–1986): among the most prominent Dalit leaders of the twentieth century, Congress leader, minister in provincial and central governments of India for several decades from the 1930s, and deputy prime minister of the country in 1977–1978.

His second wife, INDRANI JAGJIVAN RAM (1911–2002), a schoolteacher who gave up her job after their marriage, published a three-volume memoir in the 1990s celebrating her husband's career and her life with him.

❀ ❀ ❀

SANKRITYAYAN, RAHUL (1893–1963): Kedarnath Pandey, renamed Rahul Sankrityayan when he became a Buddhist priest; outstanding scholar and writer known as *Mahapandit* (great scholar), religious reformer and political activist, Congress worker, communist, organizer of peasant movements, and advocate for Hindi language and literature. His enormous body of work includes numerous autobiographical writings in the form of fiction and history, and a six-volume autobiography—over two thousand pages in its latest published form. The first four volumes of the autobiography are dated 1944, 1950, 1951, and 1967 (the last published posthumously).

His third wife, KAMALA SANKRITYAYAN (1920–2009), compiled and edited the fifth and sixth volumes of his autobiography after his death. She added other details of their life together in several of her own writings, memoirs, and reminiscences, as she established herself as a prominent educationist and writer in Hindi and Nepali.

❀ ❀ ❀

SINGH, AMAR (1878–1942): *Thakur* (lord or estate-holder) of Kanota, in Rajasthan, western India, and officer in the Jaipur and then the British Indian Army. Wrote a daily diary in English for forty-four years from 1898 to 1942, preserved in eighty-nine bound volumes, about eight hundred pages each, in the Kanota archive. A condensed version of part of this trove, with considerable detail on domestic life and arrangements, was published in 2000.

❀ ❀ ❀

VALMIKI, OMPRAKASH (1950–2013): prominent Hindi writer and midlevel officer in the Indian government's federal bureaucracy, from a poor Dalit background in rural north India. Published an acclaimed autobiography in 1997, as well as other autobiographical statements in his short stories, plays, poems, and historical writings.

MAP 1 Indian subcontinent before Partition and Independence in 1947

MAP 2 Indian subcontinent after Partition and Independence in 1947: Administrative divisions, circa 1960

Prelude

FRAGMENTS OF FAMILY

This book is an essay on men's existence in the South Asian domestic world, and on their self-contradictory articulation in that world of ideas of freedom, or liberation, for themselves and their loved ones: women, children, family, community, nation, and more.

The work begins by situating men firmly in the domestic arena—a domain they, and others, often treat as incidental to their lives and being. Nevertheless, men spend a good deal of their time in this secluded familial space and are plainly dependent on it. The study proceeds through an exploration of the discourses surrounding the mysterious absence/presence of men in—and from—a large part of their own existence, and the expectations and behavior that flow from the resulting rhetoric.

The title of this prelude underscores the conundrum. "Fragment," as I use the term, is not simply the dictionary's "piece, broken off." Rather, it is an interruption, a disruption, an unexpected departure in a conversation or line of thinking: an answer to a question that has not been posed in the conversation, or in the received reflections or inherited common sense of a specific question.[1] Men in the home are a fragment in both senses of the term: a *part* of, and an *interruption* in, a widely received understanding of family life.

Startling changes occur in ideas of the home and the family in South Asia, and in ideals of the good modern man and woman, between the later nineteenth century and the middle decades of the twentieth—the anti-colonial moment in India's colonial and postcolonial history. Parallel shifts take place over much of the world in the industrial and postindustrial age. Yet, the context and the fallout have their quite distinct, colonial and postcolonial, inflections in the Indian subcontinent.[a]

[a] I use India and South Asia interchangeably in these pages, since much of the investigation deals with areas in the northern, central, and western regions of the undivided subcontinent, before and after its partition and the establishment of the independent nations of India and Pakistan in 1947 (and the separation of Bangladesh from Pakistan in 1971).

Consider the advent of notions or ideals of (and aspirations to), among other things, "industrial time" and the small, consanguine, loving family—greatly modified as these are in the urban as well as rural Indian context. Industrial time—factory or clock time—is an emphatic feature of this new age, even as it coexists with the more fluid time of light and dark, agricultural seasons, and the ritual calendar. It is especially marked in urban areas, where the clock tower, the factory siren, and other accessories of modern states and entrepreneurship shape timetables for much of the population. However, it extends forcefully into the countryside, to apparently noncapitalist sectors of the society, through the interventions of police, bureaucracy, modern law, and medical institutions; the influence of schools and colleges; and even social service and civic reform.

Similar "deviations" characterize the second symbol of South Asian modernity I have mentioned: understandings of the fundamental unit of domestic life. While the nuclear family—the small, intimate unit of a loving husband, wife, and children—emerges as an ideal, this smaller modern family often includes older generations (grandparents and sometimes great-grandparents), as well as cognate units like "nuclear" families of male siblings, living under the same roof or in adjacent dwellings.

Other radical departures may be noted in the domestic order. Fatherhood emerges in transformed guise. It is attached now to an individual male, the biological father, who in theory has primary responsibility for the maintenance of his immediate family and the training of sons. Fathers become educators. Education is equated with school certificates and college degrees, as cleanliness is with tailored clothes, shoes, soap, and hair oil: objectified and separated from a rather different sense of learning in a wide variety of ways in the community and environment of one's birth (kith and kin, human and nonhuman neighbors, physical surroundings).[2]

The notion of "inner" and "outer" worlds, the "private" retreat inside domestic space and "public" activities in the world outside, comes to be more sharply etched. This is accompanied by a thickening and concretization—one might say, externalization and objectification—of the inner and outer, the home and the world. The wider community, collective gatherings, and storytelling sessions recede as places where inheritance, tradition, and knowledge are passed on in the course of other social engagements. Notions of fostering, nurturing, and training the young are redefined, as is the understanding of men's and women's role in history.

Given the heft of these developments, the following chapters underline the importance attached to formal schooling, to cleanliness in dress and appearance, and to the roles of men and women in child- and homecare—all seen as signs of the modern and the future. I focus on conjugal relations, central to new ideas of family and home, and detail the daily attrition and constant negotiation that accompany the reentrenchment of domestic hierarchies. One of my aims is to draw attention to the physical, psychological, and emotional costs incurred by men and women, the axiomatically privileged and the routinely disenfranchised alike.

There has been considerable writing and commentary on the question of the modern South Asian domestic order and its enduring hierarchies and discrimination. Why, then, another investigation of the theme? I offer a few reasons. First, whether they are well-recognized, statistically documented, targeted, critiqued, and repeatedly condemned, or not, the discriminatory structures and the violence attendant on gendered hierarchies, male privilege, and women's subordination are still in place—doggedly persistent and deeply damaging. They are compounded by every man-made and natural disaster, from the climate crisis, to COVID-19, to war and displacement and famine. At the same time, they are regularly brushed under the carpet in the name of "sacred" inheritances that families, communities, and nations tout as needing protection from alien assaults. Or, alternatively, by the logic that such commonplace discrimination and violence is not a crisis of nation or state, not an event in World History, but a matter of secondary importance.[3] Such issues, regrettable as they might be, can only be tackled over time, it is said: best of all, through quick economic growth and expanding opportunities and education around the globe.

I believe the present work is necessary also because, for all the commentary on familial hierarchies and oppressions, there has been little investigation of the real-life, flesh-and-blood meaning of being embedded in structures of discrimination and denial in privatized, domestic spaces. This is true not only for women, servants, poorer relatives, and hangers-on, the drudges of the inner world, reflective not only of the humiliation, physical distancing, indignity, and invisibility that they suffer daily: it is true also for those in power in this domain, the upholders of family and national "honor" fulfilling their "duty" through open acts of violence if necessary.

❊ ❊ ❊

This is a "personal" book in terms of the questions it asks about family, community, culture, and history in contemporary South Asia. I have in some ways lived with the inquiry all my adult life, though it has taken concentrated research over the last decade to bring it to fruition. The exploration flows from observations and questions I had from childhood onward, growing up in a home with a present/absent father and exposed to many homes that were structurally not very different from ours, however diverse they were in terms of the strictness, ebullience, forcefulness, or timidity of the men who were supposedly heads of these modern households, centered on the "nuclear"—yet often three-generational—family.[b]

My father had little time for hands-on care of children or other domestic duties. He appeared as a distant authority figure, a spectral presence with "more important things to do": absent even when physically present, a haunting shadow even when absent. A hush fell on the rest of us when he walked into a room, though we waited eagerly to see what gifts he had brought when he returned from an official tour or other engagement out of town. Often, they were fruits and sweets he himself was fond of, from places especially known for them. The shadow of authority surrounding him was accompanied, as well, by his boisterous laughter and storytelling (he was a fiction writer as well as a bureaucrat), as he held court in an outer drawing room where a homosocial company of friends, acquaintances, and sundry male relatives, close and not so close, assembled frequently.

As schoolboys, my older brother and I were often invited to meet these visitors, and then invited to go away and play or do something else. My mother and younger sisters were free to wander in the garden, and to go out for specific ends—to school, to shops, and to friends' houses. There were also invitations for lunches and dinners or other outings with family friends in which all of us participated. But for much of their time at home, my mother and sisters kept to the inner rooms and courtyard, adjoining the front rooms—for these weren't great mansions. The "women" met important visitors infrequently, my mother ate last, and my mother and sisters were expected to be withdrawn, the seclusion and watchful eyes of the elders growing keener once my sisters reached the age of puberty.

Questions that arose in my mind in childhood and adolescence multiplied in my years as a college student and university teacher. Extended research, as well as conversations with colleagues, students, and interlocutors from diverse castes, classes, communities, and countries, led to the conviction that closer investigation of the history of domestic interactions was necessary for a more realistic understanding of modernity, democracy, and dreams of the future in colonial and postcolonial India, and of the social conservatism that survives in the subcontinent even in what appear at first sight as politically and intellectually enlightened circles.

❁ ❁ ❁

[b] One might even call it the "extended nuclear family." The photograph that appears on the cover, marking the wedding of two protagonists whom I center in chapter 4, Hameeda and Akhtar Husain Raipuri, points nicely to the paradoxical character of this modern South Asian family. For a further comment on the cover photograph, and its contents and framing, see footnote a in chapter 4.

Another word on "beginnings"—moments that are always indistinct and uncertain. A decade or so ago, I re-read Shivrani Devi's memoir of her life with her husband, Premchand, perhaps the biggest name among the founders of modern Urdu/Hindi literature and hailed as "the storyteller of India's Independence movement." That renewed encounter with Shivrani Devi's *Premchand Ghar Mein* (Premchand in the home)[4] convinced me more than ever of the need for a study of *Hindustani Aadmi Ghar Mein* (Indian men in the home)—a theme I had been mulling over for some time.

Premchand's second wife's reconstruction of the thirty years she spent with him differs startlingly from the single summary comment Premchand left on their life together. Hers is an uplifting account of two sensitive and committed human beings discovering each other—warts, foibles, exceptional qualities, strengths, weaknesses, all: drawing close together, sharing interests and activities, doing everything they could for one another and for others in their domestic circle. His is a brief and unexpectedly dry statement in a letter written in English in 1935, the year before he died. Following the death of his first wife, he says, "I married a *'Bal Vidhwa'* [child widow] and am fairly happy with her. She has picked up some literary taste and sometimes writes stories. She is a fearless, bold, uncompromising, sincere lady, amenable to a fault and awfully impulsive. She joined [Gandhi's] N[on] Co-op[eration] movement and went to jail. I am happy with her, not claiming what she cannot give."[5]

I have much more to say about Shivrani Devi and Premchand in the chapters that follow. For the moment, I mention Shivrani Devi's memoir on their marriage as one intimation of a beginning.

Another beginning occurred when I was nearing the end of a first draft of the book. As I worked on what I hoped would be a close-to-finished version of one of the concluding chapters, I stopped short on encountering a term I had read—and passed by—several times before in my engagement with the distinguished Dalit writer Baby Kamble's 1986 autobiography in Marathi, *Jina Amucha*, and its English translation, *The Prisons We Broke*.[6] The term, *navrapana* (husbandness, from *navra*, husband), condenses multiple dimensions of the history of male privilege, and the expected but not always welcome assertion of manly behavior and male priority, in a single edgy concept. Kamble used it to explain why she had kept her autobiographical writings secret from family members for twenty years. She had to do this, she said to the scholar who translated her memoir into English, because of her husband: "He was a good man, but like all the men of his time and generation, he considered a woman an inferior being." Her comment on this common mindset and behavior was sharp: "Husbandness [is] the same in every man.... Their male ego [gives men] some sense of identity."[7]

I had not come across anything like Kamble's conceptualization in Hindi, Urdu, or other Indian languages I know—or, for that matter, in English. There is common talk in north India of *mardangi* and *aadmi bano* for manliness and being-a-man. Haughty male behavior is characterized as *zamindarana adab*, the bearing and behavior of a ruler or aristocrat, and sometimes as *sahabi-pan*, behaving like a Sahib or overlord, like the British rulers of India. Notably outspoken, brash, or "independent" men might also be described as suffused with devil-may-care life: full of *dillagi* (fun-loving, jocular), *rangeela* (colorful), *aazad-khayal* (freethinking). Rarely are they encapsulated in terms of their readily observable attitudes toward and interactions with a constant presence in their lives, their wives: that is, in terms of an everyday relationship that has come to occupy a central place in most discourses on family life in India.

Contrary to the experience of women, it is unusual to have man, and man's behavior, reduced to one aspect of his being: in this instance, "husbandness." Women are regularly defined through a relationship, usually one in a confined domestic world, as wife, mother, or daughter who will soon be a wife and mother. Wifehood itself is subsumed in motherhood, for the maternal instinct is taken to be the "essential" quality of woman. The world is different for the other half of humanity, represented as being complete in themselves, almost from birth: the male of the species growing into himself. There is extensive talk of boyhood, manhood, fatherhood, alongside other "essential" attributes, which can encompass head of household, property owner, breadwinner, professional, laborer. Certainly not qualities that can be condensed into something as reductive—primal and "primitive"—as husbandhood.

The status and authority of woman in an Indian home derived commonly from motherhood, from becoming a mother, or better still, in much of the world, the mother of sons. In the case of men in modern South Asia, that authority comes earlier, but it is not given from birth. It is captured perhaps in the relationship of husband and wife—"a man" in charge of his "little community," even if that is a community of two, or a few (a wife/wives and in time children). Yet, we must remember that in traditional multigenerational families, age and other factors often trumped "gender" (reckoned as man/woman).[8] The biological father did not even have primary authority over his children; that privilege was reserved for the grandfather and granduncle, or, if that generation had retired, the father's older brothers and cousins, along with family elders more generally.[9] Consider the implications of Baby Kamble's *navrapana* (husbandness, husbandly authority and behavior) in that context.

Navra, in Marathi, refers to a bridegroom or husband. The dictionary suggests it derives from the root *nav*, new, suggesting a "new man," reborn as in many societies on the attainment of maturity, on becoming adult and independent, a stage signaled in India by marriage. *Navri,* "new woman," is also used for a bride, wife, or girl of marriageable age, but usually for a short while, no more than a few months following marriage, after which the common term for wife or woman of the home, *bai-ko* (*patni, gharwali* in Hindi), supervenes.[10] For the modern South Asian man, this moment in the passage from adolescence to adulthood marks the onset of new responsibilities and authority in his bit of the domestic world—and perhaps beyond. The male, now recognized as a grown-up, gains manly status in husbandhood. Conceptually, a shift occurs in the location of this individual from the realm of nature and nurture to that of politics, responsibility, and authority. And many men claim the latter as their primary, if not sole, arena of work.

It takes the doughty, down-to-earth, insurrectionist language of a Marathi Dalit woman, freshly energized and assertive in the era of the anti-Brahmanical movement inspired by Ambedkar, to deploy an idea so "ordinary," arresting, and rich in its ability to capture the banality of men's claims to God-given privilege and power. A banality daily on display in men's comportment and behavior in the mundane, unremarked, everyday domain of the domestic—the supposedly sequestered and invisible space of family and home.

The concept *navrapana* (husbandness or husbandly authority), with its implicit critique of male arrogance in the assertion of men's rights as men, opens up the question of male comportment, claims to manliness, and men's vulnerability—central themes of my study—in unexpected ways. Throughout this book, I use men's physical and psychological being in the home as an entry point for investigation of their privileged place in the domestic world and of their simultaneous denial of any serious responsibility in that space. Baby Kamble sees husbandness as emblematic of this privilege. I will argue that across castes, classes, and communities in modern South Asia, male authority has been signaled in what she calls husbandness. The privilege of boyhood mutates into the authority of man with the onset of marriage, the stage of householdership (the *grihastha ashram*) and the responsibilities that stage implies.

A central thread of the present study emerges more sharply from my belated recognition of the implications of Kamble's insight.

❀ ❀ ❀

This book is not a history of nation, state, and institutional politics—the well-established subjects of World History—viewed from an unusual vantage point. It is better seen as a history of *ordinary life* among *ordinary people* (with both phrases appearing under the sign of a question mark), told from the location of the home—or what I shall for convenience, in the interest of flexibility and in recognition of its uncertain boundaries, simply call *domestic space* in modern South Asia. If the changed perspective and object of inquiry say something about the limits of World History, or of what a richer world history might be—a history of how people lived, and what it felt like to live in their times and conditions—that is a welcome bonus.

I have framed the inquiry under the mundane rubric of men in the home, since that bland formulation engages questions of male entitlement, authority, and hierarchy in a relatively accessible and open-ended way. Perhaps it will also invite in readers who are daunted by the theoretical language that is often key to close analysis of issues of gender, patriarchy, and masculinity. That said, let me turn to a more substantive discussion of historical and historiographical legacies, and the ascribed, claimed, or asserted place of men in the history of domestic life in modern South Asia.

❋

Part I

❋

Legacies

❋

❋

❋

1. The Indian Modern

If people of a certain country, who have hitherto not been in the habit of wearing
much clothing, boots, etc., adopt European clothing, they are supposed to
have become civilized out of savagery. — M. K. GANDHI

❋ ❋ ❋

I begin this chapter with a handful of snapshots of domestic life in colonial and
postcolonial South Asia. These serve to focus many of the issues I engage in this
book, and several contradictions of the Indian modern that are still inadequately
acknowledged. I go on to illustrate some unusual features of South Asian modernity through a consideration of two discrete issues that appear rather different
from one another, and yet intersect. The first is the persistence of extreme forms
of gender and caste discrimination; the second, a theme that is less frequently
addressed—the local understanding of the relation between private and public,
personal and political, all too often equated with an intimate, domestic arena
and a wider, civic one. That relationship is represented in Indian languages by
a vocabulary not easily translated into the modern bourgeois notion of discrete
domains of private and public, familial and worldly: I point to some of the im-

plications. The chapter concludes with a brief discussion of the vibrant scholarly debates on this range of issues, and how the present work seeks to build on and hopefully expand those debates.

Snapshots of the Domestic

I. THE HOME AND THE WORLD

> *My husband was very eager to take me out of purdah.... When he brought in Miss Gilby, to teach me and be my companion, he stuck to his resolve in spite of... all the wagging tongues at home and outside.... One day I said to him: "What do I want with the outside world?... If the outside world has gone on so long without me, it may go on for some time longer."*

These words in Rabindranath Tagore's 1915 novel, *Ghare Baire*, are attributed to Bimala, the sensitive, traditional wife of a reformist, liberal-minded landowner who believes in education and equal rights for women.[1]

We meet the third protagonist of Tagore's novel, a visiting Swadeshi activist, as he addresses a meeting in the landlord's temple courtyard. Bimala and other women listen from behind a screen in the adjacent hall. Carried away by his nationalist rhetoric, Bimala pushes the screen to the side. She makes eye contact with the speaker and feels transformed: "*I was no longer the lady of the Rajah's house, but the sole representative of Bengal's womanhood. And he was the champion of Bengal.... I said within myself that his language had caught fire from my eyes; for we women are not only the deities of the household fire, but the flame of the soul itself.*"[2]

She now accedes to her husband's long-expressed desire, and hesitantly comes out of purdah to meet the visitor who is staying in the men's (which is also the visitors') section of their mansion. Drawn into the debate between the radical young activist and her soft-spoken, reflective husband, she expresses her budding patriotic feelings: "*I am only human.... I would have good things for my country.... I would smite and slay to avenge her insults.... I would make my country a Person, and call her Mother, Goddess, Durga—for whom I would redden the earth with sacrificial offerings.*"

> "*Hurrah!*" says the visiting firebrand, besotted by Bimala's looks and her quiet manner of articulating her views. He goes on to anoint her as that "*Person*," that "*Mother, Goddess*": "*Today you have given me the message of my country. Such fire I have never beheld in any man. I shall be able to spread the fire of enthusiasm in my country by borrowing it from you. No, do not be ashamed.... You are the Queen Bee of our hive, and we the workers shall rally around you. You shall be our centre, our inspiration.*"[3]

2. ANOTHER HOME, ANOTHER WORLD

In her 1994 collection, *Sangati*, real-life stories presented in fictionalized musings, the noted Dalit writer Bama tells the story of a little girl aged 11, "*so small and shrunken . . . you'd take her for seven or eight.*" Maikkanni's mother was very young when she ran away and married her father. The man deserted her when Maikkanni was born, but continued to come and go as he willed, and left her pregnant each time. "*Now she's pregnant for the seventh time,*" Bama writes. "*After this one, she says, she'll go in for birth control. . . . The day Maikkanni learnt to walk, she started to work as well. Her mother had to go out to work in the fields. It was Maikkanni who looked after all the tasks at home. . . .* [In time, she was sweeping, cooking, collecting water, washing clothes, going to the shops . . .]"

> *Whenever her mother has a baby, Maikkanni goes off to our neighbouring town to work in the match factory because her mother cannot go to work in the fields then. At that time, they managed entirely on what Maikkanni earned. I used to feel really sorry for that child. . . . But . . . she used to say, "Who does my mother have, except me? My father has left us. I must see to everything."*[4]

3. MORALITY

(A) *Of the Rich*

Laila, the protagonist of Attia Hosain's 1961 novel, *Sunlight on a Broken Column*, is an educated, progressive young woman, born and raised in an unapologetically patriarchal, old-world, aristocratic Muslim household.[5] Laila has a close and empathetic relationship with Nandi, a young maidservant, the "Untouchable" washerman's daughter, who was her favorite playmate when they were younger. One day, Nandi is found in the garage with a male servant. Her outraged father beats the girl mercilessly. Stopped by his wife, he drags the girl to the big house for justice. Nandi pleads she had only gone to return a washed shirt to the driver. Laila's aunt turns the matter over to an elder kinsman, saying "*this is a matter for a man to deal with.*"

> *Uncle Mohsin prodded Nandi with his silver-topped stick contemptuously. "This slut of a girl is a liar, a wanton. Nandi looked up with fear-crazed eyes, looked round at that cruelly silent, staring ring of trappers and cried out: "A slut? A wanton? And who are you to say it who would have made me one had I let you?"*

Mohsin raises his stick to beat her. As he aims a second blow, Laila moves forward, takes the blow on her body, and runs out with the words "*I hate you, I hate you.*" The next day, her loving aunt summons her and asks her to apologize to

Uncle Mohsin when he comes. *"But what wrong have I done?"* Laila bursts out. *"To respect your elders is your duty.... My child... [y]ou have a great responsibility. You must never forget the traditions of your family.... Never forget the family into which you were born."*

(B) *And the Not-So-Rich*

The autobiography of the renowned Hindi poet, teacher, and translator Harivansh Rai Bachchan (Srivastava; 1907–2003), written over two decades from the 1960s to the 1980s, provides a detailed account of his family life and intimate relations. Volume 1 describes his parents' struggles to produce and maintain the family they wanted, and the circumstances of his own birth and infancy in that context.[6]

Bachchan's parents longed for a son. The birth of a daughter after the early deaths of their first two children did not quench their thirst for a male child. The couple sought, and were deluged with, advice on ways to ensure the survival of one. Following one injunction, based on widespread belief in rewards gained through major sacrifices, they nominally "sold" their next child, the baby boy, Bachchan, to the midwife who delivered him. Thus, for the sum of five paise—no more than a penny, one might say—a poor woman from the lowly (Untouchable) leatherworking caste of Chamars became the child's mother: *Chamarin Amma* (or Chamar Mother), which the little boy soon reduced to Chhamma. Chhamma had lost her own child a little earlier, shortly after its birth. She never had another. Bachchan ("little child"), the endearment that the poet took as his surname in later life, stayed in his respectable, lower-middle-class parents' home. He fed for a while on Chhamma's breast milk. The prayers of the Rai/Srivastava household were rewarded: Bachchan survived, lived a long life in good health, and earned considerable fame.

Throughout her days of nursing Bachchan, Chhamma visited the home as a servant. Bachchan recalls that she was given a special present each year on his birthday. Five colored baskets made of cow dung were placed in the courtyard, filled with five kinds of grain. The family priest was present, with other dependents: the barber, the water-drawer, the odd-jobs man. Chhamma was there too. Wearing the new, embroidered *dhoti* (or cotton dress) she'd been given, she would stand at the side of the door, shrinking into herself so no one was polluted by her touch.

When the birthday boy emerged, oiled, bathed, and dressed in new clothes, he was told to kick the baskets. The grains that fell on the floor would go to Chhamma, the remainder to the other attendants. As the child moved forward, Chhamma entreated him to *"kick hard, my son. Harder... still harder."* As he grew, Bachchan learned to kick harder, and, spreading out an old dhoti to collect the grain, Chhamma blessed him — "*a little in words,*" he writes, "*a little more through her glances.*"

Chhamma passed away while Bachchan was still a child. Her wish, to have her titular "son" perform the purificatory ritual of putting a few drops of water from the river Ganga in her mouth when she died, was granted. When her body was taken away the following day, Bachchan writes, "*someone picked me up and touched my shoulder to her bier,*" symbolically fulfilling the Hindu custom of having a son carry the parent's body to the funeral.

4. THE DIFFERENCE BETWEEN GODS AND MEN

Gods are greater than humans precisely because they do not have to worry about cooking/housework.

Rahul Sankrityayan, *Mahapandit* (Great Scholar, as he was known) — extraordinary researcher, writer, cultural and political activist, Buddhist, communist, and peasant leader — makes this comment in a short, three-and-a-half-page chapter entitled "*Noon-tel-lakdi*" (literally, salt-oil-wood) in the third volume of his six-volume autobiography, referring to the mundane tasks he had to share when he lived with his Russian wife and son in Leningrad between 1945 and 1947.[7]

5. BRINGING UP CHILDREN

(A) *Among the Elite*

The celebrated feminist writer Ismat Chughtai (1911–1991) reports a discussion she had as a teenager with Begum Waheed Jahan (1884–1939), the progressive founder-principal of the Girls' High School in Aligarh where Chughtai studied. When the youngster mentioned what people said about the principal's neglect of her children — "*Your sisters had to nurture them*" — the elder responded:

> *Ai hai! So who rears children in your Khwaja family* [referring to noble and honorable families like her own and the girl's]? *Ayah, dada or dadi or nani, khala, phuphi* [nurses, grandparents, aunts]. *Mothers have little to do with nursing children in our world. The first child goes to the paternal grandmother, the second to the maternal, then to paternal and maternal aunts. And don't we have a nurse for every child? That leaves the cooking, for which there are cooks.*[8]

Chughtai's comments on her own natal family, which was steeped in the aristocratic culture of the north Indian Muslim elite, though her father came from an urban business family and served as a judge in the princely states of western India, are no less sharp. She writes as follows of her parents' ten children, four daughters and six sons: "*We children were left to the care and kindness of servants, to whom we were intensely attached. . . . There is no other social section as unfortunate as the domestic servant. Especially in India, where poverty and unemployment have forced vast numbers of people to become the underlings and slaves of a small elite.*"[9]

(B) *Among the Working Classes*

Kausalya Baisantri (1926–2011), a Dalit student activist in high school, later forced into the prescribed role of "obedient" (ideal, middle-class) housewife and mother, writes of the homes in the industrial city of Nagpur in central India, where she and her siblings grew up. The residents of the Khalasi Lines *basti* (neighborhood) where they lived were largely Dalits, at the time still called Untouchables—predominantly her own subcaste of Mahars, but including Mangs and Chamars, leatherworking subcastes from western and northern India, and low-caste aboriginal communities from different places, all of which were ranked lower than the Mahars. Most of the houses were small, made of mud, bamboo, bits of wood, and sometimes cheap bricks. There were a few makeshift huts of grass, but not many, and perhaps five or six brick houses belonging to the richest inhabitants. The forty or fifty households living in the *basti* shared one tap. People lined up as early as 3 a.m. for the water that would come for a while at dawn, and there were frequent fights in the long lines. They had three rows of common toilets, with eight lavatories, always overflowing: there was "shit" everywhere, notes Kausalya, and "*no place to put one's foot.*"

Nevertheless, even in these conditions, there was a palpable sense of home and a community of belonging, upheld especially by the women. Parents went to work even when children were ill. They left younger children in the care of whoever was available: an older sibling, if no adult was around. When no family member was available, since older children also worked, mothers would take infants to their workplace and lay them down in the shade of a tree or building. "*The mother would check and feed the child periodically. Or she might lay the child in a* [flimsy] *cloth hammock, and ask a nearby child—sometimes as young as five—to keep an eye on him or her. . . . On occasion, mothers gave the child a bit of opium, to make him/her sleep longer.*"[10]

The small, not entirely random, sample of snapshots presented above, one that could easily be multiplied and disaggregated further, should suffice to indicate the chasm that separates the lives and conditions of different sections of society in modern South Asia. The gulf is evident not only in terms of mate-

rial resources, though that is surely its foundation. It is seen also in more rar-
efied discourses on morality, respectability, duty, and honor, and hence on the
appropriate place and conduct of men, women, and children in the domestic
world—and beyond. These discourses are suffused with the importance of status and inheritance, themselves largely determined by the caste, class, community, and biological sex one is born into. The following two sections outline a
few of the consequences.

"Feudality without Feudalism"

India is a modern country with decidedly feudal values.[11] It remains to this day a
notoriously status-conscious society, deeply marked by caste and gender discrimination. Notions of purity and pollution affect social interactions throughout the
subcontinent, across diverse religions and communities, higher classes and lower.
Not only "clean" caste Hindus but also Christians, Muslims, Sikhs, and others
practice casteist distancing from less privileged members of their communities. So
do lower castes and subcastes, nominally classified as Hindu and slotted into a single broad category in the overall hierarchy—say, Dalits, or, more broadly, groups
listed as Scheduled Castes and Tribes (or ex-Untouchables) in the Indian constitution of 1950—refusing marriage, inter-dining, and other kinds of close interaction
with those they see as more polluted than themselves. This is what the renowned
Dalit leader Babasaheb Ambedkar described as a system of graded inequality.[12]

For those at the bottom of the social order, the humiliation is unceasing. In
the countryside, the lowly live on "the other side of the tracks," as they called it
in the American South. Omprakash Valmiki (1950–2013), well-known Hindi
writer and midlevel officer in the Indian government's federal bureaucracy, published an acclaimed autobiography in 1997. In it, he described living conditions
in the north Indian village where he was born and raised. The Chuhras, the
caste of sweepers into which he was born, lived on one side of a small pond that
separated Valmiki's depressed caste locality from the rest of the village. "Right
in front of Chandrabhan Taga [a landowner]'s *gher* [or cowshed] was a small
pond, which had created a distance between the Chuhra habitation and the rest
of the village.... The pond was like a deep pit, across which stood the high walls
of the ... [landowners]' brick-built homes." The fear of pollution from contact
with Untouchables was overwhelming. "While contact with dogs and cats, cows
and buffalos was fine, the mere touch of a Chuhra was a sin."[13] Dogs, cats, and
cows were given names and individuality by the upper castes. The Dalits had no
such luck. Older and younger Chuhras were addressed by abusive caste names,
applied to an entire collective and signifying base origin: "*Oe Chuhre!*," "*Abe*

Chuhre!," or "*Chuhre-ke* [you, born-of-a-Chuhra]!" —the equivalent of the N-word in the United States.

Over much of the country, such practices continue in the twenty-first century. In urban areas, including large metropolitan cities, Dalit men, women, and children descend into poisonous underground gutters and climb mountains of garbage to clear vast accumulations of waste and sewage with their bare hands. Privileged universities have in recent years been the site of increasing slights and discrimination against Dalit students by "clean caste" students, teachers, administrators, and staff. Obstacles the targeted students face in trying to access scholarships and funds promised to them have driven some to suicide.

Gender discrimination, and the abuse and violence attendant on it, is equally pervasive. The National Family Health Survey of November 2021 reported that a large percentage of women they spoke with justified a husband's beating of his wife if he suspected she was unfaithful, disrespected her in-laws, argued with her husband, refused to have sex with him, went out of the house without informing him—or, more generally, neglected the home or the children, and even if she "doesn't cook good food." States and territories throughout the Indian Union—from densely populated and relatively prosperous states in southern India, to isolated, mountainous territories in the North and Northeast, areas with high and low levels of literacy, abundant or scattered signs of technological advancement and globalization—were implicated. Over 75 percent of women justified men beating their wives in three states, Telangana, Andhra Pradesh, and Karnataka. Manipur, a small and relatively secluded mountainous state in the Northeast, with substantial ethnic and religious diversity, was not far behind. From 42 to 52 percent of women from West Bengal, Maharashtra, Jammu and Kashmir, and Kerala justified men beating their wives. At least for the purposes of the survey, a smaller percentage of men owned up to approving such behavior.[14]

The double burden of women, widely commented on and consistently underplayed throughout the world, is amplified in the subcontinent by a fundamental contradiction at the heart of the position of the girl-child/woman.[15] The female child, elevated as mother and goddess among Hindus, is at the same time an unwanted, if inescapable, factor in the aspiration to preserve and perpetuate the family line. An extreme example is found in a brief autobiographical account written in his prison cell by Ram Prasad Bismil (1897–1927), scion of a respectable small-business family in northern India, founder and member of the Hindustan Republic Association (later renamed the Hindustan Socialist Republican Army), shortly before he was hanged to death for alleged involvement in a revolutionary terrorist plot against the British. In it, he described the fate of girls in his natal home.

My mother gave birth to five sisters and three brothers after me. My grand-mother pleaded fervently that, in accordance with family custom, the girls should be killed. Mother refused, and saved her daughters. In our lineage, this was the first time that girls were allowed to live. Unfortunately, two of the sisters and two brothers died. The remaining brother, who is 10 now [in 1927], and three sisters survived. My mother ensured that the three girls were sent to school, and married off with fanfare. Before this, no girl in the family had ever married, since they weren't kept alive.[16]

Indeed, the burdens that the girl-child/woman supposedly brought on a household, burdens that the girls and women in fact shouldered, were accepted and expressed in numerous other ways across wide swathes of the society. That revivalist Hindu nationalists of the late nineteenth century could define conjugality as a binding "system of non-consensual, indissoluble, infant marriage" is a blatant demonstration of the point. The colonial regime separated criminal law (governing land, territory, and public space and activities) from civil law (matters of family, household, marriage, and inheritance, which were left officially to the different religious communities), a historian writes, allowing "the household generally, and conjugality specifically" to be seen as the one "independent space left to the colonized." Infant marriage and cohabitation after a girl's first menstruation were deemed essential to the preservation of lineage and property, and conjugality came to be defined in extremist terms: "the woman needed to be strictly faithful even if her husband abandoned her, remarried many times, and even if the marriage was not consummated, and even if he died."[17]

Such views were strongly challenged in the century that followed. There was an outcry against female infanticide, ideas of obligatory infant marriage came to be frowned upon, and notions of consent, equal rights, and companionate marriage gained currency in the early and middle decades of the twentieth century in the context of a powerful, widespread, and multifaceted anti-colonial struggle. Then, and since, South Asian family ideals have contended with an increasingly popular discourse of romantic love, independence, privacy, individual rights, and expanded (if not equal) opportunities for the education, employment, and advancement of all boys and girls, men and women, high and low.

Many old questions acquired new dimensions, and fresh aspirations and struggles emerged, as men and women at all levels of the social ladder moved into new public spaces and more crowded urban neighborhoods. How, for example, could men and elders provide schooling to girls and young women without letting them forget "their traditions"? And how could upper- and middle-caste elites keep the "unclean" in their place and maintain the sanitation barrier when they moved into smaller modern houses, including flats (apartments) in multi-storied buildings in the cities?

The generations born after Partition and Independence in the 1940s have not readily accepted the ideals of "ancient tradition," or facile talk of the need to preserve the prestige of community and inheritance. In the bigger, cosmopolitan cities, and in small towns and rural areas too, girls and women from working-class families and lower- and upper-middle-class backgrounds have opposed their subordination and the oppression inside and outside their homes. They have fought for better education and jobs, greater financial security, and increased freedom of movement. There is no stopping this shift, however punishing or brutal the reactions from beloved kith and kin, as well as from a callous and reactionary police and public. Many young men and boys have joined the women in their struggle, although as a rule they have been distinctly more accommodating of inherited arrangements and "traditions" so advantageous to them.

The old regime lives on in the new, or at any rate claims to. In the following pages, I explore this mix of "old" world and "new"—both imagined and both contested, and everywhere, ever only partially and unstably realized.

The World in the Home

The poet and Nobel laureate Rabindranath Tagore's phrase *Ghare Baire*—"inside and outside," "the home and the world"—has often been used as shorthand to describe the parameters of inquiry into the remapping of an inner, domestic world, and with it the conventionally recognized public and political world, in modern South Asia.[18] In Tagore's formulation, the terms *ghar* and *bahar* ("the home" and "outside" in Bengali, Hindi, Urdu, and other north Indian languages) seem to refer to distinct domains that align with modern, bourgeois notions of activities described as public and private, and are contained within conceptually well-demarcated spheres. Yet, for most people in South Asia and the rest of the world, the boundaries of "home" and "world" require immediate qualification.

Much research and writing on the domestic world in modern South Asia has focused on the *bhadralok, bade log*, "big people" or "respectable" classes—in part because the history of the propertied and privileged is better documented, in part because the terms of the modernist debate were laid down by men and women from these classes. The emphasis on elite groups has marginalized the lives and experiences of the working masses: the people whose toil made for the comforts of the privileged, and whose own material conditions made for homes and worlds of a different order than those of the well-to-do—homes and worlds that were constituted, arranged, and lived in differently.[19]

Let me illustrate the proposition by reference to early twentieth-century comments on the lives, homes, and workspaces of the laboring poor in Bombay: huts and hovels, tenements and gullies, so overcrowded and "filthy" they could, according to several observers, hardly be called "homes."[20] Domestic activities extended beyond the four walls of these homes, if they had walls, into the neighborhood and into the formal workplace: fields and factories, building sites, the homes of employers. Children were brought up differently; childhood was different. "On account of insufficient space the natural sex function of the married couples takes place with the full consciousness of other inmates in the same room."[21] Neighbors and older children, some of them barely out of infancy themselves, looked after younger children. Many men, as well as women and children, slept out in the open. In smaller industrial towns too, a community of fifty or more households might share three taps and eight lavatories.

Homes here spilled over into neighborhoods in a much more obvious, self-evident way than for the middle and upper classes. As a corollary, paid work, even if it brought in a pittance, was not confined to the workplace; the toil for income occupied domestic space and time insistently. The bourgeois sense of home as sanctuary, and the world as risk or special opportunity, scarcely retains its proffered commonsense meaning in such a setting.

Given the variations, and the inadequacy of modernist claims regarding autonomous domains of public and private life, our object of inquiry is perhaps better described as the world-in-the-home, where the world and the home implicitly bleed into and constitute one another. The slight shift also helps bring the inquiry more into line with the distinct conceptualization of the domestic world that appears in many Indian languages. The home, *ghar*, is also described as *ghar-sansar*, literally, the "home-world," or more idiomatically, the wider community that makes up the family and home. In many instances, indeed, it is referred to as *sansar*: literally translated, "the world."

The world-in-the-home, *ghar-sansar*, refers of course to structures of power, hierarchical relations and interactions among men, women, children, and other putative members of the domestic circle. It gestures at the same time to "worldly"—that is to say, public, politically and culturally vital—activities carried on by both women and men in the space of family and home. The proposition may be elaborated, both in terms of the spatiality associated with the distribution of men's and women's activities, and in relation to the temporality undergirding this distribution of space: the "unequal" time-space of modernization under conditions of colonial capitalism.

The "combined and unequal development" that modernization, capitalism, and imperialism have brought—not only between countries and continents, but *within* countries and regions and local communities, as they are counted, classified, dislocated, and disciplined—shows in the history of the domestic sphere as in other domains. The clash between colonial and anti-colonial modernity produced a twofold sense of time and space, allotted to the two halves of the population. Men's time was designated World Historical time, the time of the future; men's space, the space of politics and History, of striving for social, cultural, and economic transformation and the good society. Women's time became "everyday time," the time of the present, of the monotony and daily grind of routine existence; women's space, the space of nature, nurture, and care for the survival and reproduction of individuals and communities.[22]

In the age of industrial capitalism, with the increased prosperity and leisure it brought, or promised, this distribution of time and space has been seen as the chief marker of difference between the "home," described as the realm of women and children and other (natural) caregivers and caretakers, and the "world," described as the domain of mature, thinking men. The nineteenth- and twentieth-century reinterpretation of the life stages set out in classical Hindu philosophy provides an unexpected illustration of the tendency. A scheme that was—as such schemes often are—symbolic, followed only in extreme circumstances, now came to be invoked rather more literally for important segments of the population, albeit in transformed and truncated form.

Of the three major paths to salvation elaborated in Hindu philosophy—*gyan* (knowledge), *karma* (action), and *bhakti* (devotion)—Dayanand Saraswati (1824–1883), founder and fount of the reformist Arya Samaj, focused on *gyan*, the path of knowledge, which for him encompassed scientificity and rationalism. The eminent propagator of Hinduism in late nineteenth-century North America, Swami Vivekananda (1863–1902), and the firebrand nationalist leader Lokmanya Tilak (1856–1920) emphasized *karma*, action or selfless service. Mahatma (Mohandas Karamchand) Gandhi (1869–1948), exceptionally for a political leader in his time, privileged *bhakti* or devotion, love for the divine.

For all of these visionaries, however, there was a new immediacy—a concern with the welfare of the individual as part of the community, country, and humanity here and now. Thus, Dayanand: "I hold that *tirthas* [pilgrimages] are good works, such as speaking the truth, acquisition of knowledge, company of the wise and the good, practice of . . . yoga, life of activity, spreading knowledge for the good of society." Vivekananda, one commentator notes, "was intensely interested in social problems, declared himself a socialist, and wanted to 'make a European society with India's religion.'"[23]

The changed ethos affected the lives of different segments of society in fascinatingly different ways. *Brahmacharya*—the ascetic stage of learning, studying, seeking knowledge and enlightenment—became the sign of a nobler search, a higher order of being. This remained for a long time the preserve of boys and men, especially of the privileged classes: the male student, turned householder, turned retiree, who could continue, to the end of life, to search for fulfilment, liberation, enlightenment—now frequently equated with Reason and Science.[24] In the same breath, the divide between intellectual and physical labor, a primary marker of the division between the well-to-do and the poor, the "respectable" and the "base," intensified.

For the lower classes, and for women of all classes, there could be no easy escape from acts of continuous physical labor and service. The *grihastha ashram*—the time of the householder with prescribed duties to kin and community—fully encompassed the lives of girls and women. From infancy, through the stage of informal or formal learning, through marriage, motherhood, nursing, and caring for children and family, and through "retirement," the girl-child/woman inhabited, trained for, lived in, and prepared younger girls/women for motherhood and homemaking.

Yet, men and women of all classes and communities—Hindus, Muslims, Sikhs, Christians, Dalits, and others—necessarily inhabited both "public" and "private" domains. They were creatures of the home and the world alike, the time of "world history" as well as the time of mundane survival and care. As infants and children, men obviously depended on the home. That dependence was also evident in the contradictory temporality of men's behavior as adults. Among the middle and upper classes at least, "world historical" time was fractured at the threshold of the domestic. The "future" was already present in men's contentment with things as they were in the domestic world—in terms of their commitment to inherited values and prescriptions.

Amid the dislocations, opportunities, aspirations, and contradictions of colonial and postcolonial South Asian lives, then, notions of the "new man," "new woman," and ideal modern family regularly came apart—sometimes at the very moment when they appeared to be reaching fruition. One might adapt and add to a phrase from E. P. Thompson to underscore the point: the new Indian man, the new Indian woman, and the ideal Indian family were present at their simultaneous *making* and *unmaking*.[25]

Historiography

Over the last two decades and more, feminist historians, anthropologists, and literary scholars have undertaken a wide range of critical investigations into the record of domestic life in modern South Asia. They have noted that colonialism and the broader "imperial social formation" provided the context for the construction of family ideals as well as national identities and cultures among the colonizers and colonized alike.[26] They have pointed to the diverse regional and class circumstances that made for divergent positions and conflicts over modernist aspirations, variations in family types and domestic arrangements, and women's continuous negotiations of existing and emerging prescriptions.

The corpus of academic writings on India includes considerable work on the interrelated processes of nation-building and (middle-class) family formation, refigured notions of masculinity and femininity in these domains, and the mutual constitution of the new man and new woman. Partha Chatterjee's argument about men spiritualizing the domestic space; Sumit Sarkar's analysis of Ramakrishna's advice to men on how to handle domesticity; Judith Walsh's work on Hindu men's advice to women; Gail Minault and Ruby Lal's parallel investigations on prescriptions and constraints among elite Muslim families; Tanika Sarkar and Mytheli Sreenivas on the new conjugal family and the homology established between family and nation among middle- and upper-class Hindus; Rochona Majumdar on modern marriage; and Swapna Banerjee on *Fathers in a Motherland* are but a few notable contributions on elite and middle-class families.[27]

Collectively, these writings reconstruct the vibrant debate in colonial and postcolonial India around the structure and ideals of the family. While the extent and quality of change on the ground remains a matter of debate, the proliferation of discourses on the family, the importance of the conjugal couple, and the advocacy of greater consultation and companionship is not in doubt. Tanika Sarkar suggests that, given the constraints of colonialism, the "Indian woman" in an idealized, monogamous conjugal marriage took the place of the (male) economic entrepreneur as the sign of modernity.[28] Judith Walsh, Gail Minault, Ruby Lal, and Swapna Banerjee point to the increasing centrality of men in the new domestic order: fathers and husbands as "managers and mentors," preparing their sons to be good citizens and leaders, and guiding their wives, daughters, and other women in "the 'art' of marriage, what it takes to maintain a good household and good relationships with kinsfolk and elders and what constitutes the appropriate training and upbringing of children."[29] Mytheli Sreenivas writes of how the husband-wife dyad came to be seen as "the central axis of affect and property ownership within families" and became "foundational to the quality of all other family relations."[30]

Thus, as Mrinalini Sinha puts it, "the domestic . . . emerge[d] in the context of colonial Indian conditions as a preferred site for the self-constitution of men qua men," and man as the legislator of domestic as well as national manners.[31] Not surprisingly, the spurt of inquiries included pathbreaking work on colonial and anti-colonial masculinities.[32] Early investigations of men and masculinity in modern India detailed the militaristic aspect of the Indian rejoinder to colonial propositions about emasculated natives: the turn to gymnasia and physical training, beef and football, a past of newly discovered warriors and a present of Western-style military drills, for the promotion of manhood and "manly" activities.[33] Studies concerned with masculinity have expanded in many other directions since then.

A leading contributor to the history of bodybuilding, wrestling, warrior monks, and soldiers, Joseph Alter notes in a 2019 review that scholars are now far more attentive to "the broader implications of masculinity relative to class, caste, ethnicity and region, as well as in relation to a spectrum of embodied experiences and sexualities."[34] In an important illustration of new lines of inquiry, Sanjay Srivastava asks how a "general ethic of brahmacharya [asceticism] and 'self-control,'" promoted by Gandhi and the national movement, resulted in the installation of "semen anxiety" as an almost "irrevocable truth of the Indian (male) milieu." Indeed, he says, "the stoic father, whose sexual activity remains confined to the imperatives of reproduction, and whose daily routine is one of unremitting frugality and discipline, is . . . a stock figure of many twentieth century biographies."[35]

And yet, the physical absence of men remains a feature of the literature on the South Asian domestic world. The biological conditions of procreation and the social history of nurturing the young have combined to produce a strong predisposition to equate domesticity with the female of the species and "her" offspring. An ossified sense of the domestic world makes it almost counterintuitive to think of men in that space. Consequently, notwithstanding the many important theoretical interventions mentioned above, and the continued debates on the history of fatherhood and conjugality, South Asian scholarship on the family retains its principal concentration on women.

The figure of man hovers over the proceedings. However, men do not figure as fleshed out, calculating, feeling, jealous, overweening, vulnerable human beings. There has been little detailed investigation of the concrete lives and performances of men in the domestic sphere, even in the case of prominent leaders who declared themselves committed to social justice, including gender equality.

Gandhi is a small, but far from adequately studied, exception in this regard, in part because of his own reflections on his investment in the domestic.[36] Little exploration, in a word, of "the range of subject positions taken up by men and women in everyday life."[37] Whence my renewed attempt to center the issue of men in domestic space.

The Plan of This Work

My investigation of the history of men in South Asian homes, focused particularly on the comportment of husbands in their conjugal relationships, builds on an abundant, expanding, and still underutilized archive of autobiographies and memoirs, ethnographic accounts, and fiction, detailing and commenting on life in the intimate space of family and home. I comb through men's writings—among them, some exceptionally detailed autobiographies by reflective and, in their own reckoning, progressive men, writing about their personal lives—to ask how often, to what extent, and in what ways domestic conditions and relations figure in their memoirs. And I counterpose men's and women's writings throughout the book to emphasize how differently the same histories and experiences are recalled and represented in them.

By the twentieth century, many women were writing autobiographies, memoirs, critical essays, poetry, and fiction. In general, women's writings provide more detailed commentary on the domestic world and give us greater insight into the passion and emotions, expectations and frustrations, of men and women living together. This will come as no surprise. Nor should the use of these writings be considered a handicap in an attempt to excavate the history of men in domestic space. For the women's writings reflect a different training, another sensibility and sensitivity at work than the men's—less mansplaining, more womansfeeling. If much of the information comes from women, it is an appropriate corrective, given that historians have for so long relied on men's writings (didactic literature, moral and medical treatises, fiction, and more) for most of what they say about women's being and thought—and social life in general![38]

Throughout this study, I read autobiographies as performative acts—performing the self, or perhaps better, performing the desired or anticipated self—and analyze, in that light, what they aver, admit, evade, or obscure about life experiences. These writings are especially useful, not for their retelling of *what actually happened*, though that is the rhetoric they use, but for how the authors see and present themselves: the claimed or desired selves they seek to perform. Both people and autobiographies are *actors* in this sense. One might even suggest, outrageously, that the autobiography is the performer here, and "real," lived lives the performance. Both lived and remembered lives are conditioned, fundamentally, by how we present ourselves—itself a function of what we believe we are, or would be if given the chance: and it is not easy to disentangle the living of life from the telling of it.[39]

I would push the point further. Memory, the fount of all autobiographical writing and recollection—perhaps of all archives—is not, as it is sometimes taken to be, an unmediated truth, the "insider's" account, as compared for example to history, the "outsider's" account, characterized appropriately as "a discourse drafted from other discourses."[40] Except in the case of memories carried deep in the body, and expressed often involuntarily in and by the body, memory too is a second-order discourse. The enunciation of memory is conditioned by many factors other than the experience of the subject: inherited languages and frameworks of understanding, power equations in the contexts that call forth a memory, presumed audiences, fears and expectations. It does not flow, naturally, unmediated, from some authentic experience or "real life."

In almost all the graphic, visual, and verbal articulations of memory available to us, the rememberer steps outside the remembered to render it communicable. The articulation of memory, like the writing of autobiography, is a performative act. I suggest this is true even when the remembrance of past conditions, feelings, sensations, is recorded by a person for herself or himself—say, in daily journals or notes. Memoirists perform the self that they believe they are, or wish to be in the eyes of the world, however that world is conceived. Hence, my reading of autobiographies as records of desired or anticipated selves.

This makes the different narratives found in men's and women's autobiographies, which are the central sources for this study, all the more significant. In instance after instance, women's writings provide the more detailed commentary on the values and conduct of husbands and wives, and the texture of life in the home. Juxtaposed with the women's recollections, even the fleeting comments that men make on their domestic lives shine a light on men's aspirations and commitments in this era of emergent modernity.

To take account of the divergences in domestic lives, inheritances, and practices across the Indian subcontinent, I attend to three large, varied, and internally differentiated social groupings—even if they are often described as cohesive. Two of the three are privileged groups of Hindus and Muslims: individuals and families from elite, "respectable" classes (*ashraf, bhadralok, bade log,* "big people") who do not soil their hands with physical labor and are sharply distinguished from the mass of the working people, the base and lowly (*ajlaf, chotolok, chote log,* "small people") who have no choice but physical labor—in part because they are denied access to "cleaner" intellectual and cultural pursuits. Coming from educated and largely urban middle and upper-middle classes, some of these authors write about themselves and the domestic worlds they inhabit as if these are, at least in their fundamentals, what they should be. The "future" is already present in the hidden realms of the domestic, as I suggested above.

The third assemblage—Dalits, formerly known as Untouchables—provides a critically important counterpoint to the first two. The Dalit memoirs I turn to, like those of the higher-status Hindu and Muslim examples, come from the pens of educated and broadly middle-class individuals. Among the Dalits—over 16 percent of the Indian population, over 25 percent if we add the even more impoverished and marginalized Scheduled Tribes to the Scheduled Castes—this means a relatively small set of newly educated, upwardly mobile, and assertive professionals, intellectuals, and activists.[41]

The absence of autobiographical writings from men and women still in working-class occupations is a limitation.[42] However, Dalit artists and intellectuals—producing poetry, fiction, memoirs, paintings, and more—write pointedly about the lives of their forebears, and more broadly about the oppressed and laboring poor at large. Those on whose backs the nation's (and the national elites') resources, honor, and opportunities have been built. Individuals and families sometimes still in search of stable homes—and indeed a homeland they can "own."[43]

Whereas the elites talk of new citizens and a new society and nation in the making, for which existing forms of family, community, and domestic life provide a sacred inheritance and strength, stigmatized working people cannot see existing inheritances as satisfactory at any level. The temporality that emerges in Dalit writings is insistently that of World History, the society of the future. The search for stable homes, livelihood, and community is a search for dignity, identity, and self-respect. In documenting the imagination of this future, Dalit autobiographies add significant new dimensions to the record of domestic life amid the persistent social and economic iniquities of modern South Asia.

The autobiographical sources differ in other ways as well. The men's writings fall into several categories. Many are detailed political autobiographies, retrospective accounts by politically or culturally successful men writing about their public lives, which only touch incidentally on affairs in the domestic arena. A few are extraordinarily detailed, almost diary-like offerings published in multiple volumes, with important elements of candid introspection about intimate personal affairs and engagements. These make for another genre, in which the authors themselves and an intimate circle of close associates, as well as wider circles of admirers and followers, are likely audiences. The Dalit memoirs are clearly intended for the burgeoning population of younger, educated Dalit activists, but also—especially when translated into English—for a wider audience of potential allies and supporters, national and international.

Among the more comfortable upper castes and classes, women's memoirs sometimes appeared after the deaths of husbands who were well-known public figures. Even when written in honor and celebration of the husbands' lives and careers, they often detail the consequences of men's presence/absence in domestic space and reveal aspects of this world that the women themselves were not seeking to advertise. Similarly, women from lower castes and classes sometimes write of domestic arrangements and conflicts within the rather different frame of advancing lower-caste and lower-class struggles through "collective" autobiographies of their downtrodden communities. In what follows, I analyze such autobiographical accounts for what they tell us about the diverse perspectives of men and women in different sections of South Asian society: how the writers construe what was expected of them, or what they "ought to be and to do."[44]

Chapterization

This study consists of seven chapters, apart from a prelude and an epilogue. The chapters are arranged in three parts.

Part I, "Legacies," has two chapters. Chapter 1, "The Indian Modern," has attempted to delineate some significant aspects of the historical and historiographical inheritances that have necessitated as well as enabled contemporary inquiries into the domestic world, including the present investigation. Chapter 2, "Homes Our Fathers Built," presents in broad brushstrokes the architectural and physical surroundings in which men, women, and children of diverse classes and communities lived, made their homes, and sought to manage their domestic lives through the later nineteenth and the twentieth centuries.

Part II, "Practices," engages the themes of duty, discipline, and dignity to consider the range of men's practices in the domestic worlds of "respectable" elite groups, Hindu and Muslim, on the one hand, and of working people such as the Dalits, on the other. It consists of three chapters. Chapter 3, "Duty," examines the new stress on professionalism and dedication to "work" or "calling." Until the later nineteenth century, ideas of respectability had derided "work" (*pesha*, also translated as service or occupation) as *infra dig*: occupations undertaken by lower classes and "deviant" groups like "singing girls," courtesans, and sex workers—all clubbed together as "prostitutes" in the colonial period—not something the elites with their aristocratic inheritances and aspirations had to stoop to. Leading activists and reformers in the twentieth century made a deliberate effort to elevate the idea of work or profession as a noble activity. Work is the theme here: work as fulfilment of duty to self and to others. The chapter considers what work meant for the leading public men advocating it and considers the implications for domestic relationships in this "traditional" modern world: a "modern" located in a specific time/place, as it is everywhere.

Chapter 4, "Discipline," turns to the next generation of professionals and their dedication to the making of a new and better world before and after the Partition and Independence of British India in 1947. Their professionalism functions in a somewhat changed context of urbanity, specialization, and history-in-the making. It demands commitment, not to say sacrifice, for the cause—by bureaucrats, intellectuals, and poets. The "family" is already different here, the element of individual choice and the focus on the nuclear family greater. Nevertheless, modern middle-class men display considerable hesitancy in accepting the idea of women as equals, and therefore of living with—sharing, understanding, and negotiating with—mature, thinking women as partners. Male initiative remains a dominant theme, accompanied by fresh arenas of male bonding and displays of male longing for, and fear of, women and marriage. Fraught selves and fraught relationships.

Chapters 3 and 4 also exemplify the inability of men to recognize that it is the drudges of the domestic world—women and girls in their families, and often poorer relatives and servants—who give them the liberty to venture forth in the world, pursue their callings, or simply enjoy their leisure time. Men, women, and children of elite groups betray a similar blindness in their failure to acknowledge the labor of working people, inside and outside their homes, that allows them their privileges, leisure, and dreams of advancement.

Chapter 5, "Dignity," turns to the lives of the working poor. Labor and education are the themes here. Labor, which women of all classes perform in the domestic world, is an all-consuming activity for the protagonists of this chapter—inside the intimate circle of family, as well as beyond it. Labor is love: a love performed in the colonial and postcolonial periods not only for survival but also to seek avenues of escape from the wretched conditions of their birth and inheritance. Among subordinated castes and classes, this labor is increasingly focused in the late colonial and postcolonial period on the dream of education and freedom for future generations. The chapter considers how changes in social, economic, and political circumstances, and a new striving for social mobility and self-respect, affect domestic life among long subordinated and stigmatized communities. What opportunities are available to male and female members of Dalit households? What expectations and requirements remain in place or are even reinforced?

Part III, "History in a Visceral Register," consists of two chapters. I have pointed in the present chapter to evidence of remorseless oppression within the circle of family, kith and kin, and beyond it. The crushing evidence must give us pause. There is not only an epistemological question here: How do we know what we know? There is also a question of anti-epistemology: How do we not see what is plain for all to see? I asked a similar question in my study of race, caste, and difference in India and the United States: "How, out of what archive are we to write a history of... gestures" so deep-rooted that they may not be noticed even by the perpetrators: "the spat-out, half-suppressed, [almost unconscious] ... gesture of disdain, contempt and disgust, the pause and the recoil, the refusal to touch, what in India is called Untouchability."[45] I return pointedly to the question of touching and not touching, seeing and yet not seeing, in the two chapters in Part III, which seek to pull together several threads of my exploration of diverse aspects of men's being and behavior in the domestic arena.

Chapter 6, "The Things Men Touched," analyzes three dimensions of men's conduct through a consideration of work performed, languages used, and moods expressed in the domestic arena. Chapter 7, "The Nature of Men," turns to the justifications that progressive men provided for what they touched and did, or did not do, in this space. The two chapters may be thought of as focusing respectively on men's *activities* (things *seen*) and men's *thinking* (things *unseen*), although there is no real divide between the two: thinking clearly informs activities, and things that can be seen often go unseen.

The epilogue adds a few reflections out of my own and my natal family's experiences. These should serve to indicate how traces of the broader history outlined in the pages of this book appear in unexpected ways, in unexpected places, and continue to mark the lives of recent generations—my parents,' mine, and indeed those that follow.

I believe the diverse histories I bring together illuminate something of the desired, expected, anticipated—in a word, lived experiences of men and women in the modern Indian home and family. I hope they capture something of the *feel* of marriage, intimacy, and togetherness, including the effects of the humiliating and constant assertion of gender, caste, and class power in domestic interactions. By that route, I hope they also raise further questions about the meaning of honor and shame, rights and responsibilities, citizenship and belonging in the domestic—and wider public—worlds of colonial and postcolonial South Asia.

2. Homes Our Fathers Built

Never forget the family into which you were born.
— ATTIA HOSAIN

❊ ❊ ❊

Men build houses, or order their building; women make homes. Houses are physical structures, bricks and mortar, wood and straw, providing shelter, retreat, privacy. Homes are emotional spaces: demanding, embracing, nurturing, alienating, stifling. Physical structures often tell us little if divorced from a knowledge of the way in which they were desired, imagined, conceptualized—and lived in. Hence, lived experience must be a part of this outline of the houses men built through the later nineteenth century and the first two-thirds of the twentieth, roughly the period under study in this book.

Conceptions of house and home changed significantly during this period. Fascinating details of these changes appear in the autobiographies of both "clean caste" middle- and upper-class men, and of writers from Dalit backgrounds.

"The soft focus of legend crispens into the tighter narrative of remembered and contemporary relatives," Rupert Snell remarks in analyzing one of these auto-biographies.[1] I depart a little from Snell's view of how and when legend becomes fact. It is somewhere between the "legendary" and the "observed," I suggest, or what one might call the seen and the unseen—both idealized—that the "facts" of family life emerge. The ideals, or mythologies, are evocatively detailed in many autobiographical and fictional accounts; the facts are traces that may be gathered in passing comments about lives imagined and lived.

I begin my reflections in this chapter with the autobiography of the poet, translator, and teacher Harivansh Rai Bachchan (1907–2003), the source of snapshot 3(b) in chapter 1. Bachchan's four-volume autobiography provides a summary account of the common sense of domestic life across several classes and generations in nineteenth- and twentieth-century South Asia: a widely disseminated narrative of the shared duties and responsibilities of family life. He sees his mother and father, Surasti (a colloquial form of the name of the goddess Saraswati) and Pratap Narain, who married in the 1890s and lived together till their deaths in the 1940s, as fine examples of the ideal man and woman. It was the man's responsibility to bring in an income and provide for the family, he writes, the woman's to run the home. More: "Pratap Narain was imbued with appropriate manliness, Surasti with appropriate womanly tenderness. One was born to rule, the other to be ruled—not perforce, but of her own desire."[2]

For Bachchan, ideas of domestic order were not altogether different in his own time, judging from his lovingly detailed account of his second marriage with Teji Suri, a highly educated and independent woman whom he married in 1942. The poet describes Teji as the love of his life, the first "real" woman he met: many-sided, rounded, thinking, deliberative, creative, individual, no one's possession, and wanting no one as hers.[3] She gave him everything he could have wanted from a spouse, he notes, including two sons. And yet, in his lyrical reminiscence, an interesting theme returns.

Teji gave up her teaching position to marry Bachchan and support him in his career, although she remained engaged in theater and other creative endeavors, as well as social work, in later life. She took care of all household tasks because, as Bachchan announces, he was completely ignorant in that respect "then" as "now"—from 1942 when they married until 1970, when the second volume of his autobiography was completed. Teji bought whatever was needed for the house—from coal and vegetables to radios, refrigerators, and cars. "Her taking over of all these responsibilities made possible the little writing and studying I have done." She looked after the children and their education as a matter of course. "My sole domestic responsibility was financial." And for this, he says, his university salary, plus royalties and honorariums from his books and poetry readings, were quite sufficient.[4]

In a highly publicized memoir about his Dalit family, the well-known economist and public intellectual Narendra Jadhav reinforces this stereotype of men's and women's roles and responsibilities in the home.[5] The memoir documents the family's journey over the half century from the 1910s to the 1960s, from hard labor and poverty in the fields of Nasik district and the railways and slums of Bombay, in western India, to distinguished middle-class status and professional achievement. Narendra's older brothers became prominent civil servants; he himself, chief adviser to the governor of the Reserve Bank of India, vice-chancellor of a leading university, and member of the powerful National Planning Commission as well as the upper house of India's parliament.

Few people with such a background achieved the same kind of social mobility over two generations. What made the Jadhav family an exception, as Narendra has it, was an extraordinary and indomitable father. "Given the economic, social and cultural circumstances in which we grew up, the other boys and girls of the locality fared as one might expect. The sole difference [between them and us] was this, that we had Dada [their name for their father] with us!" A believer in rational thought, education, and the rewards of individual effort, he was not only the breadwinner but also the visionary, planner, motivator. "Dada's self-confidence was extraordinary. 'Get me a long enough stick, I'll flatten this circular earth and show you,' so he would announce like an Archimedes."[6]

By comparison, Narendra presents the women in the family as superstitious, narrow, insecure. Running the household and looking after the needs of the man of the house and the children, they appear confined to the home, both in body and mind, although like other working people they went out to work and indeed participated in working-class and labor protests in the 1920s and later. His mother was "the quintessential farmer's daughter," writes Narendra, collecting and selling produce to supplement her husband's income from work in the Bombay Port Trust railways, and keeping chickens and goats in their tiny one-roomed accommodation.[7]

The "facts" of family life appear in these accounts as eternal verities, self-evident truths about gender inclinations and roles in the home and the world. The houses that men built or came to live in were meant to reinscribe these values, and the attendant distribution of rights and responsibilities. Yet, the different burdens of men and women, and the asymmetry in available resources across class and caste, affected domestic arrangements. To contextualize the individual and family histories examined in the pages that follow, this chapter sketches a handful of recurrent features in the physical layout of elite homes, indicating something of the hierarchies and orders they symbolized, before turning to living conditions among lower-class working people and the constraints these diverse arrangements imposed on domestic life and relationships.

Three Generations of "Respectability"

Many aspirations found among modern South Asian elite groups are captured in Bachchan's description of the homes his father, grandfather, and great-grandfather lived in. Bachchan's great-grandfather was a Nayab Kotwal or Deputy Inspector of Police under the East India Company, before formal British rule was established after 1857. He was posted in Allahabad, the prominent administrative and pilgrimage center at the confluence of the Ganga and the Jamuna, two of the largest and most sacred rivers of northern India. The memoirist conjures him up as a six-footer built of iron, skilled at wrestling, horse riding, *lathi*, and swordplay, a keeper of pet falcons, a spendthrift, and a philanderer. In keeping with this image, he built a grand four-sectioned house, which his sister, still alive in her nineties in Bachchan's childhood, called a "fort." As the collective family memory had it, one section of the house was enough for the police inspector and his immediate family: his wife, their two children, his sister Radha, and her daughter Maharani. He gave the second section to a cousin brother, a third to a Brahmin man he revered; the fourth part lay vacant, along with the open land behind it. This was the house in which Bachchan's great-grandfather, his grandfather, and for the better part of his life, his father lived.

Bachchan's nineteenth-century progenitors came from a line of small landowners who sought service opportunities to supplement the family income. The family encompassed a wide kinship network. Bachchan recalls from his early years that the family house in Allahabad was never closed to visitors from Babupatti, the ancestral village thirty-five miles to the north in the adjoining district of Pratapgarh, colloquially Partabgarh. An annual Hindu festival that centered on a ritual bath at the spot where the Ganga and Jamuna met provided a striking illustration of the strength of these ancestral ties and open doors.

The day before the most auspicious time for the ritual dip, at the peak of the cold north Indian winter, many men, women, and children traipsed barefoot from the village, in coarse clothes laden with food supplies and offerings: radishes and sugarcane they had grown, peas and parched gram, sweets made with sesame seeds, and pickles of many kinds. The Brahmins and close relatives were accommodated inside the house; others spread out on the veranda. Separate units lit cooking fires on the open ground in front of the house. Before dawn, at an auspicious hour, the visitors set off for the river. They returned in the evening and left for the village the next day. Bachchan recalls this happening year after year, as long as the hereditary house stood in Chak Mohalla. Once more, "our severed links with the village were rejoined; from townsfolk, we became villagers, from Allahabadis, Partabgarhias."[8]

Bachchan's grandfather, Bholanath, was apparently very different from his larger-than-life policeman father, yet steeped in the same traditions of welcoming all, and keeping some—especially women and servants—at a distance. He too trained in wrestling, *lathi*, and swordplay, but preferred the Arabic, Persian, and Urdu learning he got from a personal tutor. It was a world of Persian and Urdu poetry, and male gatherings in which poetry recitation and "educated" conversation—and Bholanath—flourished. Bachchan describes his grandfather's cherished lifestyle. He sat in the *mardana* (outer, men's section) of the Allahabad home—in the veranda or a sitting room, depending on the weather and the hour—reclining on a large cushion placed on a bed, reading or writing. Near him, tied in a cloth bag, lay book manuscripts he had diligently transcribed, in an age when printed copies were not readily available. An inkpot lay by his side, a spittoon underneath the bed, and a large flat-bottomed *hookah* (water-pipe) on its other side: he smoked when he read or wrote.

Bholanath was already married and head of the household, but still unemployed, in 1857, when Allahabad became a center of British military actions and vengeance against Indian insurgents and many women of the neighborhood hid in their "fortress" home. Sometime afterward, he was appointed a jailer in the revamped British colonial administration and posted to a small town 275 miles west-southwest of Allahabad. However, he retired early to return to the life of a gentleman of leisure in his home city. He had his bed set up in the *mardana* once more, with his bag of handwritten texts, spectacles, pen and ink, spittoon, and hookah at hand. At times, the bag of books gave way to a chessboard, with Bholanath and an opponent ranged on its two sides, utterly absorbed. Their concentration was broken only when his wife signaled from the kitchen, clanging on some utensil, gently, then more loudly, or someone else—his son or an elderly aunt—was sent urgently to say that his meal was waiting. The women of the family would not eat until the men of the house had done so—a practice that continued through Bachchan's father, Pratap Narain's time, as we will see.

As it happened, the grandeur of the family's ancestral home had declined since the fabled time of Bachchan's great-grandfather. "Grandfather [Bholanath]'s life continued to be divided between books and chessboard," writes Bachchan.[9] His household was run on savings, without a regular job or earnings, and his grandmother's jewelry was pawned piece by piece. Bachchan's grandfather and father both experienced hard times and relative penury. Through it all, they insisted on maintaining the decorum of times gone by—not least, in the requirements and performance of men and women in the home.

Bholanath returned to Allahabad at the end of the 1880s in part to ensure that his son, Bachchan's father Pratap Narain, then thirteen, was properly educated. The daughter, Tulsa, aged fifteen, never went to school. Before Bholanath passed away, leaving his son as head of household, Pratap had matriculated, was married, and found himself in dire need of a job. His in-laws, long settled and well connected in the city, helped him find one at the English-owned Pioneer Press. Having witnessed the undisciplined ways of his father and his father's companions, Pratap vowed not to duplicate their lifestyle. He worked at the Pioneer Press for thirty-five years, impressing the management with his discipline and hard work, arriving punctually, staying late, and rising to the highest position available to Indians, who were confined to the printing and accounting sections: that of head clerk.

Bachchan cites his father's unwavering timetable to show how frugally he lived. Rising at 3 a.m., walking seven or eight miles to and from the river Ganga for a ritual bath, he ate his morning meal at 8:30 and left for work at 9, walking to the press roughly four miles away. If his wife was late with the meal, "he was incensed. Mother shook with fear—but he didn't even have the time to vent his rage."[10] Surasti would then finish cooking as quickly as possible, and find someone to take her husband's food to the office. Until the carrier returned to say that the man of the house had eaten, the four women at home (Pratap's wife, mother, paternal aunt, and grandmother) could not eat. On occasion, when no errand boy or man was found, they fasted all day, until Pratap Narain returned and ate.

In the early days, Bachchan's father often returned at 8 or 9 p.m. or later, ate, and went to sleep. Later, once he felt more secure in his job and the children were older, he began returning earlier. His daily routine reflected his views on the assigned responsibilities and duties of men and women, the men working to earn, the women looking after the home and family. The design of a new house he built in the late 1920s, when the ancestral home fell prey to "urban development," provides further evidence of the desired arrangement.

In designing the two-storied house, Bachchan observes, "Father kept in mind the needs of the new age." Yet, while more flexible and modest, it was conceptually not radically different from the old. The men's section, abutting the street, had two sitting areas, "perhaps with the thought that there should be separate arrangements for the older and younger men, who may not want to sit together." Pratap Narain had planned a covered veranda at the entrance, where the men and their visitors could sit, read, and converse; this was never built, presumably because the money ran out. The rear portion of the ground floor had two separate rooms for Pratap and Surasti, and spaces for other essential functions: a prayer room, store, kitchen, bathroom, inner courtyard ("who could conceive of an Indian home without a courtyard?"), and adjacent to that, "a small shelter where a cow could be tied if they got one."

On the upper level were two large and two small rooms, adjoining two terraces with partially covered roofs: one set for Bachchan and the girl/woman he'd recently married, one for his younger brother and the latter's (expected) future wife. The terraces provided each couple the opportunity to sleep beneath the stars or partially under cover, depending on the season. His younger sister had no designated room of her own: "she would go off to another [implicitly, her "real"] home someday."[11]

Let me set this account of one family's domestic arrangements and practices in the broader context of aristocratic ideals and modernist aspirations in late nineteenth- and twentieth-century South Asia.

Aristocratic Ideals

Through the eighteenth and nineteenth centuries, the dwellings of established and aspirant elites in the long-settled, landlord-dominated lands of India's riverine plains were modeled on that of a local *raja* (king or aristocrat). This was the case in urban, administrative, and commercial centers as well as in the agricultural countryside. Extended networks of kith and kin, friends, associates, visitors, guests, and servants of many descriptions floated through these aristocratic homes. But different groups were allowed very different degrees of access.

The universal aristocratic prescription of appropriate distance and inaccessibility was compounded in the Indian case by strict control on interaction between the sexes, as well as stringent caste restrictions. Domestic space was divided into an outer, men's area (*mardana*) and an inner, less accessible, women's domain (*zenana*), connected but largely separate. The diaries of Thakur Amar Singh (1878–1942) describe one example of the ideal.

Amar Singh was the scion of a prominent princely family in Rajasthan, third Thakur (lord or estate-holder) of Kanota in Jaipur district, and officer in the Jaipur and then the British Indian Army. The family's grand, three-storied *haveli* (or mansion) in Jaipur was built in 1874 by his grandfather Zorawar Singh, a senior minister in the Jaipur court. Within the cramped space of the walled city, it was something of an island, with a "self-contained economy," as the editors of his extraordinarily voluminous diaries have it.[12] The several open courtyards and verandas, adjoining closed rooms and sequestered spaces, "teem[ed] with people." Three generations of the Kanota clan were permanent residents: the widowed grandfather; the father with his wife and children, and father's brothers with their wives and children; and father's sons (including Amar Singh) with their wives and children. All had their individual man- or maidservants, some of them dependents working with the family for generations—purchased servants, as it were. By one informed estimate, the *haveli* housed over a hundred men, women, and children, though some of them (accountants, craftsmen, the family priest) slept elsewhere. Many servants slept on the verandas, to be available all the time.

The front area on the ground floor was reserved for business activities. One entrance from the main street led straight to large storerooms for grains, oils, pulses brought from the Kanota estate, sheds for cattle providing milk, and stables for horses. Through the main entrance, a little farther north, surrounding an open courtyard and the portico and verandas leading to it, were rooms for accountants, tailors, and craftsmen, a guest room for less intimate guests, and a shrine room where some more public prayers to the household goddesses were performed. Across the main street were elephant stables, a staff kitchen, and an office for domestic purchases.

The *zenana* or women's section lay beyond the entrance gate, portico, verandas, and outer courtyard—blocked off from public gaze. The outer courtyard was not visible from the street. Nor could visitors see the doors or staircases leading to the women's rooms and spaces from the outer entrance to the courtyard. The larger rooms on the lower floors were for the senior women. Until her death, Zorawar Singh's wife occupied the large, central room on the south side of the open, inner courtyard—beyond the strong room, record rooms, and other offices that separated the outer courtyard from the inner, and directly across from the long shared lounge for women on the courtyard's north side. The wives of younger brothers started out on the third floor, moving down to larger rooms on lower floors "as they acquire[d] sons, age, and importance." Amar Singh's mother, wife of Zorawar Singh's eldest son, the heir apparent, moved from her original quarters on the third floor to several on the second, until she reached the best room at the center of that floor, with an open terrace on one side and the courtyard floor on the other: a treasured space that allowed women to observe the "comings and goings outside and below."[13]

Spacious courtyards, verandas, and gardens hidden from public view, screens and walls and guarded areas, strict segregation and hierarchies of age, gender, and class were part of the dream "respectable" folk espoused through much of the late colonial period. The emphasis on invisibility and segregation showed clearly in the mansions of officials attached to the last Mughal emperor, living in nineteenth- and twentieth-century Delhi. They reappeared, often through vertical stratification and segregation on upper floors, as Delhi's old nobility declined; new entrepreneurs, traders, and professionals gained in wealth and influence; and many old houses and plots were abandoned or sold, divided up, and rebuilt, sometimes as smaller *havelis* with a single courtyard.[14] They were reproduced too in the dwellings of less privileged but "respectable" families in the countryside, Hindu as well as Muslim.

An official *Gazetteer* from 1912 described a typical dwelling of a *zamindar* (small, self-cultivating, independent landowner or peasant proprietor) in the districts of Punjab and Delhi, parts of the country not overwhelmingly dominated by great landlords. The housefront on the village main street was usually a blank wall ten to twelve feet high, with one door opening to a *dahlij* or porch. An inner door on one side of the porch, not visible from the street door, screened off the inner courtyard and spaces where the women and children of the house lived and passed much of their time.[15]

Such aristocratic aspirations affected elite homes and lives throughout the region where I did my research, from Bihar to Punjab in northern India, Madhya Pradesh and Rajasthan in central India, and to some extent Gujarat and Maharashtra in western India too. By the turn of the twentieth century, however, subtle and not-so-subtle changes were occurring in domestic architecture and living arrangements.

On the Brink of the Modern: The Punjab Story

Through the late colonial and early postcolonial period, increasing numbers of men and women seeking education, employment, and new opportunities moved to urban settings: not only burgeoning new trading and industrial centers, large and small, but also rurban towns and district headquarters that provided administrative, trading, and educational facilities, as well as older cities that had long been pilgrimage centers or hubs of trade, courts, and cultural activity.[16] A new political consciousness and reformist zeal introduced wider debates on individual and collective rights, autonomy, self-help, human dignity, and equality. All of this deepened and extended discourses about house building and the lived environment, especially among privileged groups aspiring to a new urban modernity. In his monograph on the making of modern Lahore—the old Mughal capital, later the headquarters of Maharaja Ranjit Singh's Sikh kingdom, which was annexed by the British in 1849 to become the administrative, trading, and cultural capital of British Punjab—William Glover provides a succinct account of new tendencies and contentions.

To colonial observers, Lahore, like all Indian cities and homes, represented a spectacle of chaos, dirt, and disease. Their "improvement" rhetoric focused on "narrow winding streets"; "evil smells" emanating from shops that also served as little manufactories; cattle, goats, donkeys, and "ravenous dogs . . . covered with disgusting sores" wandering freely in the midst of ruined and half-built houses; garbage and waste.[17] Veena Oldenberg has summarized the "three imperatives" that dominated the transformation of colonial Lucknow in the mid-nineteenth century: "safety, sanitation and loyalty."[18] Glover notes the persistence of discourses of urban sanitation and public health in the late nineteenth and early twentieth centuries. The voices of colonial "improvers" had now been joined by Indian reformers. Kashi Ram, Secretary of the Sanitation Committee, *Anjuman-i-Punjab,* wrote of urban populations inhabiting "narrow . . . tortuous lanes," "overcrowded, damp, ill-ventilated and dirty houses several stories high," with the air and ground fouled by excretions from humans and animals, overflowing privies, and stagnant sewage.[19]

By the turn of the twentieth century, there were distinct signs of efforts to improve drainage, sanitation, and the availability of daylight in buildings. However, Glover observes, most of these improvements concerned the "management of . . . interior[s]" rather than the layout of buildings: Glover's term is "outward appearance." Small windows, ventilators, and "grated apertures for admitting fresh air" appeared. There were moves toward greater specialization in room and space usage, which had long served for multiple activities. "Bedrooms" and "storerooms," "sitting rooms," "drawing rooms," and "ladies' sitting rooms" took the place of generic *kothis* (private rooms upstairs or toward the back of houses) and *kamras* ("rooms").[20] At the same time, older styles of building continued.

As a popular 1937 book on house plans, *Joshi's Modern Designs,* had it, a "passage [*andarooni rasta ya gulli*] is a necessity in modern buildings, as it keeps the suites of rooms independent of each other." The inner passage was a means of allowing movement and ensuring privacy, "strategies," in Glover's words, for "keeping different types of people [men and women, lower and upper castes and classes] separated from one another." The result could be achieved in other ways as well. Joshi presents the example of a three-storied home designed for a shopkeeper. Here, "only the frontage," where business was conducted on the street level, faced the street. A staircase on one side, "entirely partitioned from the shop," provided "strict privacy" for women who needed to go up or downstairs.[21]

Prakash Tandon (1911–2004), who became the first Indian general manager of Unilever's Indian branch, Hindustan Lever, describes a classic example of a new traditional/modern dwelling in the house built in the 1870s or '80s by his granduncle, one of the first modern pleaders in the Gujrat district of Punjab. The house stood just outside the Gujrat city walls, not far from the older community of lawyers, traders, merchants, and scribes in the city. Its sense of openness, the high ceilings, the arrangement of rooms according to their specialized functions, and the means of segregating its inhabitants, distinguished the building from the cramped houses of the elites inside the walled city, usually two to three stories high owing to the minimal possibilities of horizontal expansion. Yet, important elements of the courtyard house or *haveli* remained.

A high wall, closed on three sides, barricaded the house. The fourth side, opening onto the main road, had arches and "a high old-fashioned studded gate, barred at night from inside." Just inside the gate was a rectangular courtyard with rooms on two sides for the lawyer's clerk, servants, clients, distant relatives, and visitors from the village, as well as a stable and a shed for the house owner's *tonga* or horse-drawn carriage. The entrance to the courtyard faced a blank wall. At one end of this wall, at the left-hand corner of the courtyard farthest from the entrance, an inner gate led to the family quarters, through a dark vestibule or *deorhi*. Beyond the *deorhi* was another square courtyard with a kitchen and storerooms. Facing the latter, and invisible from the *deorhi*, were the family's living rooms. Opposite the blank wall on the right of the inner courtyard was the pleader's sitting room-cum-office, occupying the length of the left side. Another passage from the outer courtyard led directly to this room; thus visitors and clients entered without seeing the family quarters. Behind the house was a small sunken garden with fruit trees and flowers—oranges, mangoes, jasmine, and roses for the family.[22]

Similar hybrid structures emerged in Lahore. After the annexation of Punjab, the British built their civil station just south and southeast of Lahore's old city, dominated by the Mughal fort and its attendant habitations and markets. The area was already home to several Indian homes and neighborhoods; these now expanded rapidly. Between 1868 and 1881, the population of the civil station grew from 26,000 to 34,000. New migrants to the city and older residents moving out of the old city established new settlements. "Educated members of the native community" were keen to escape the unsanitary conditions of the old city, a local official declared in 1893; anyone who could afford it moved out.[23] While the new elite and middle-class Indian homes appeared to British observers as "chaotic" in conception, the trend toward the modern—always, by definition, a "traditional" modern, as I have said—was unmistakable.

By the 1920s, there were growing calls for planned development of Indian neighborhoods. An outstanding example of this was Lahore's Model Town, built in the 1930s and '40s by middle-class residents, many of them retired employees of the provincial and local governments. The underlying idea, Glover notes, was to combine the "restorative elements" of gardens and parks with the commercial, industrial, and professional services needed in a modern urban center. "Each segment or 'block' of Model Town had a park at its center, where buildings for public use were erected," including schools, a mosque, a Sikh temple, and Hindu temples in every second block. Model Town had its own hospitals, post office, police station, cooperative store, separate men's and women's clubs, and even a hall for wedding parties.[24] The first houses in Model Town, where Prakash Tandon's father moved after retirement, followed the traditional/modern pattern.

"Each house was divided into two parts by a huge vestibule in the middle," Tandon writes. One side had dining room, drawing room, and office; the other, bedrooms, dressing rooms, and bathrooms. "The front verandah . . . [where] male visitors were received . . . overlooked a lawn surrounded by flower-beds and cypresses." Toward the back was "an enclosed paved courtyard, the women's domain, with kitchen and storeroom," another veranda, servants' quarters, kitchen garden, and maybe a small orchard. "In its own way the house was like the British bungalows in front and grand-uncle's house at the back."[25]

Beyond Punjab

Other parts of India saw parallel developments: Bachchan's Allahabad, to which I return in the next section, six hundred miles east of the cities of Gujrat and Lahore in Punjab, as also Gandhi's state of Gujarat, western India, several hundred miles to the south. Here and elsewhere, middle-class bungalows, ordered along a different plan from the courtyard house, became increasingly popular in the early and mid-twentieth century. Many were built in geometrically arranged plots of uniform size, which were different from the earlier, inner-city *mohallas* and *pols,* socially and architecturally homogeneous neighborhoods with well-marked boundaries in old cities like Ahmedabad and Surat, Allahabad and Banaras—although some commonality of caste and status was reproduced in the new neighborhoods too.[26]

"European" and indigenous architectural features and spatial arrangements were commonly mixed in modern housing. Consider the two-storied mansion that Dr. B. R. Ambedkar built in Bombay in the early 1930s, when he was established as a leading lawyer and distinguished public figure. The house was built on a five-thousand-square-foot plot in Dadar that he acquired on long lease from the Bombay Improvement Trust. The ground floor had two sets of three rooms each, for the Dalit leader's family and his widowed sister-in-law's. The upper floor was given over entirely to Ambedkar's library and office, "which also doubled as his bedroom." "With towering columns and an emphasis on symmetry," writes one commentator, "the bungalow exuded the simple grandeur of ancient

Greek and Roman buildings, reflecting the American neoclassical architectural style Ambedkar had seen in Columbia [New York, where he studied from 1913 to 1916]."[27]

A similar mix of diverse inheritances is found in the building where Premchand's second wife, Shivrani Devi, lived for much of the 1950s and '60s. The four-storied complex in the crowded business district of Godowlia, in Banaras, housed the Banaras branch of Saraswati Press, the publishing enterprise that Premchand had established before his death. The work of organizing supplies, printing, publishing, and distribution happened on the street level. The second story, with its marble floor, was "posher." Sripat Rai, Premchand's eldest son and head of the publishing house, stayed here when he was in town, and "put up his friends, artists or writers visiting Banaras." One level up, "away from the hubbub," was where Shivrani Devi lived "with a goat and a servant." The top floor was not in use at the time. Through the wrought iron railings that ran all along the balconies on the upper floors, people could observe the comings and goings in the central courtyard below. On the other side, from the window of the "little dark room" where the goat lived at one end of the third floor, one could see the main street, "crowded with shops . . . [and] busy at all hours."[28]

By the 1960s and '70s, modern housing preferences, along with aspirations to a nuclear family structure and the decision of many couples to have no more than two or three children, gave middle-class families across the land greater privacy, and the women, a growing number of them now in salaried employment, greater freedom and say in the home. The bungalow in a suburban neighborhood, when the latter was laid out in the way of the colonial civil lines and cantonments, meant greater isolation, especially for women denied ready access to driving and public transport. In bigger bungalows, men might meet visitors in large spaces in the front of the house, complete with colonial furniture. Separate areas might be found at the back for the servants and for the housewives' supervisory activities.

In more crowded urban neighborhoods and new areas of urban expansion, often called "colonies," middle-class life, whether centered on a smaller or larger nuclear/multigenerational family, including servants and guests, extended into the neighborhood. Middle-class women, as well as men, children, and the family's servants, met and interacted at boys' and girls' schools, local playgrounds and parks, religious and other community centers, and festivals and celebrations, and in nearby bazaars, the stalls of passing vendors, sometimes a local theater or cinema. Women of neighboring households exchanged visits and shared food. Where houses were old-style and crowded together, rooftops served as places of congregation and conversation for women. The neighborhood was also a space in which upper-caste men and women sought to exercise moral authority and to discipline the behavior of lower castes and classes.

Many of these social practices continued when the middle classes moved into flats or apartments in double-, triple-, or multi-storied buildings, particularly in the bigger cities: conversations across balconies, the borrowing of vegetables and spices, the sharing of responsibilities for each other's children, including shepherding them to schools and other cultural activities. Women's homosocial gatherings and the middle-class disciplining of lower-class behavior have mutated further with the late twentieth- and early twenty-first-century rise of gated communities, with new features such as kitty parties, on the one hand, and semi-official (housing association) regulation of working people's entrances, dress, and deportment, on the other.

However, "traditional" social expectations reappeared alongside "modern" architectural arrangements in the vertical move that occurred with the rise of flats, now the most common form of middle-class dwelling in India's teeming towns and cities. Bombay, the industrial and commercial capital of modern India, where flats had become a feature of the urban landscape by the 1930s, provides an early example. In the first decade of the twentieth century, the official *Gazetteer of Bombay* reported that only the wealthiest Indians of the city lived in independent houses, with Parsi businessmen and entrepreneurs in "European-style" ones and "Bhatias, Banias and Jains" (Hindu business communities) in "traditional" houses that had separate women's quarters in the rear. Some of the richer, modern middle classes, both Muslim and Hindu, had moved into flats. A *divankhana* or reception room took up a large part of the front space in these. Beyond this were the kitchen, washing room, sleeping rooms, and women's quarters, which varied in size and number in proportion to the owner's wealth.[29]

Thirty years later, Hansa Mehta (1897–1995)—the distinguished Gandhian educationist and freedom fighter, member of the Bombay Legislative Council and subsequently of the Indian constituent assembly, President of the All-India Women's Conference in 1946, and India's delegate to the United Nations Commission on Human Rights in 1947—spoke of her problems with the different kinds of flats available in Bombay. In those called "Hindu flats," she said, the main room at the front was like a "durbar hall," extending across the entire length or breadth of the flat. The remaining rooms, which served as living spaces and bedrooms, were cramped: "One can hardly move in them." The European-style flats had their own drawbacks. The low ceilings were suffocating; the combined drawing-dining room hardly suited "Indian" manners. Was Mehta thinking of the upper-caste Hindu male practice of eating in silence in a separate, cleansed space? Worst of all, she noted, the flats had "hardly any provision for the servants' quarters." Their one redeeming feature was "good" sanitary arrangements, a reference to the presence of internal toilets and baths.[30]

Sanitation marked the boundary between the privileged and the lowly classes. The shifting of the toilet and bathroom "into the dwelling from its former exilic location outside," writes Nikhil Rao, minimizing contact with undesirable outsiders, was critical to the acceptance of flats, especially by the Hindu middle classes. The coming of electricity, and a "full flushing system" replacing the older basket privy that had to be removed manually, facilitated the "domestication" of the European-style apartment. Many flats had (and many still have) two entrances, one leading into the main living room, the other into a passage or lobby with direct access to the kitchen, bathroom, and toilet. In flats with only one entrance, the lobby still helped to preserve traditional divisions, frequently opening in two directions—to the family rooms and living space, on the one hand, and directly to the cleaning and cooking areas, on the other. Such a lobby served as a buffer, Rao observes, not to protect the home from the outside cold, as in many European countries, but to protect the respectable from other, "undesirable" and polluting, elements—such as servants and sweepers.[31]

Life for the Independence Generation

In a word, many old patterns changed, others re-insinuated themselves, in the modified *havelis* and bungalows of the late nineteenth and early to mid-twentieth centuries, and in apartment living. Once again, Harivanshrai Bachchan's description of the houses he lived in as an adult illustrates the proposition. Let me make the point through a focus on one aspect of domestic life in his various homes: sleeping arrangements for newly married couples, which provide a glimpse into the competing desires that ruled the lives of an Independence generation caught up in the throes of self-assertion, anti-colonial struggle, and militant nationalism.

Bachchan's first marriage occurred in 1926, when he was eighteen and still living with his parents in their ancestral house; his wife, Shyama, was fourteen. "In those days," writes Bachchan, "there were no separate rooms for married couples." He and his wife met each other alone only at night, and then stealthily. "When the household slept, or feigned sleep out of kindness for us . . . I would tiptoe to a closed room where Shyama would be waiting for me."[32] In the new house designed by Bachchan's father in 1927, as I have noted, arrangements were a little different. The upper level had separate units for the families of the two sons: one just married, the other hopefully to be married soon. Each unit had a large and two small rooms, plus an adjoining terrace where the couple could sleep under the open sky or under a partially covered roof—"depending on the season."[33]

As it happened, Shyama never got to enjoy the new arrangement. She stayed only a week after their marriage, before returning to her parents' home in another part of the city to care for her mother, who was diagnosed with tuberculosis, as well as her father and younger siblings. She returned to her husband's home after her mother died in 1929, but lived for the most part at her father's, since she had contracted TB and his financial circumstances and acquaintance with local doctors facilitated medical attention. She died in 1936.

Between Shyama's death and his marriage with Teji in 1942, Bachchan completed his MA in English, became a lecturer in the English department at Allahabad University, and moved into rented accommodation near the university: a bungalow-style cottage, followed by an independent house where his mother and younger sister moved in for a while on the death of his father in 1941. Bachchan describes the house as "a cross between an Indian home and a British bungalow." The two front rooms became a sitting room and study, the two rooms at the back, bedrooms: one for his mother and his younger sister who was with them for a while, the other for him. Ram, his deceased older sister's son, got a room on the roof. There was an inner courtyard, a veranda adjoining the bedrooms, separate little rooms for kitchen and storeroom, and in front of the house a sizable lawn bounded by a low wall.[34]

This was the house Teji came to after their marriage in January 1942. In the first months, before her mother-in-law returned to her husband's modified ancestral home, Teji spent much of the day getting to know her and talking about their two families. Over the next few years, Teji and Bachchan lived in different rented cottages and parts of bungalows and houses. A few relatives and dependents were always in tow. Bachchan's mother stayed with them often, until her death in 1945; and, for some months in 1947–48, when many of Teji's relatives fled from the widespread Partition violence in Punjab, their home took on the appearance of a small refugee camp.

It was only in July 1948, writes Bachchan, that "we found ourselves alone"—in 17 Clive Road. Teji and he had two sons by then. A young male relative (Bachchan's younger brother's brother-in-law) was "the only outsider," and he had been with them so long, studying at Allahabad University and helping Teji manage all the household work, that "he was really one of the family." "We were finally able to enjoy the peace, privacy and homely domesticity that had been so elusive in recent times."[35]

The layout of this dream house, and the sleeping arrangements, say something about ideals of domesticity and a competing desire for "freedom" among middle-class males of this generation. The house was spacious, with many rooms, mosaic floors, broad verandas, lawns, two garages, and separate accommodation for servants. The Bachchan family occupied one side of the ground floor, separated from the other ground-floor tenant by a gallery; a third tenant lived on the second story. Given its total of ten doors and windows, Bachchan named their section *Dashdwar* (ten gates or entrances), after a couplet from the great fifteenth–sixteenth-century mystic and poet Kabir. Teji had the drawing room painted an almond color, Bachchan's study green, the dining room white, the children's room pink, and their own bedroom blue. However, Bachchan did not always sleep in their bedroom. His need for concentration on his work, as well as his sensibility as a poet, inclined him, he says, to sleep on his own. "When I could not sleep outside under the open sky, I slept on the verandah, even in winter; . . . I feel stifled if I sleep where I cannot see the sky, the moon and stars."[36]

I will take the story no further, and do not know about the specific sleeping arrangements in Bachchan and Teji's later years. But we know that many of the features emphasized in the description of the Allahabad home they occupied between 1948 and 1954—broad verandas, spacious lawns, garages, and servants' quarters—were present in Bachchan's official house in Lutyens' Delhi, a stone's throw from the Prime Minister's residence, after Jawaharlal Nehru invited him to be a translator in the Government of India's External Affairs Ministry in 1955. This was also the case in the new, double-storied house the Bachchans built in the posh South Delhi colony of Gulmohar Park in the 1980s, when they were already known more as the parents of their elder son, the megastar of the Bombay films, Amitabh Bachchan. Amitabh's own palatial homes in Juhu Beach, Bombay, and elsewhere would retain many of these features.

All of Which Leaves Out Only the Majority

"Never forget the family into which you were born," Aunt Abida says to Laila. "Who could conceive of an Indian home without a courtyard?" asks Bachchan, writing about the new house his father built in Allahabad in 1927.

Where does the question of family honor, courtyards, inner toilets, and servants leave the laboring people with or without regular paid employment—the majority of India's population, crowded into urban slums and the least desirable parts of villages and rural estates? Here, I turn to other autobiographical, historical, and ethnographic accounts that speak more directly of the lives and homes of the Indian poor.

Living conditions for the lowest castes and classes in South Asia remained abysmal through the colonial period and beyond. The extract from Omprakash

Valmiki's autobiography cited in the section titled "Feudality without Feudalism" in chapter 1 indicates that this was the case for large parts of rural India long after Independence. In his birthplace, a hundred miles north-northeast of Delhi, Valmiki's caste of sweepers, the Chuhras, lived in a settlement separated from the rest of the village by a pond or deep pit. Their homes lay amid "narrow lanes with wandering pigs, dogs, children without a stitch on their bodies, everyday fights ... garbage strewn all over. Such a stench that one couldn't bear it." The neighborhood served as the public toilet for the villagers, upper caste and lower: "All the women of the village, young girls, older women, even the newly married brides, would sit in the open space behind [the Chuhra] homes ... to defecate. Not only at night, under cover of darkness, but in the light of day, purdah-observing Tyagi women [of the landowning caste], faces veiled with the ends of their saris, shawls covering their upper bodies, found relief in this open public lavatory. They sat [by the pond] exposing their private parts, without any possibility of modesty or shame."[37]

From the mid-twentieth century onward, scholars, activists, and investigative journalists have repeatedly reported similar, if increasingly contested, patterns of caste segregation and marginalization in villages throughout India.[38] Three examples, one from an American anthropologist writing about northern India in the 1950s, and two from Dalit activists documenting life in 1930s and '40s western India and 1960s and '70s southern India, respectively, will suffice to illustrate the point.

Oscar Lewis wrote in the early 1950s of conditions in a village fifteen miles from Delhi, connected to the nation's capital by a highway that lay two miles from the village. He was struck by the density and crowding of the village population, the shortage of space to house people and their animals, as well as the poverty. The 150 households in the village came from twelve castes: seventy-eight households of landowning farmers (Jats, as in Valmiki's village), fifteen of Brahmins, twenty of Chamars (traditionally leatherworkers), ten of sweepers, and smaller numbers of potters, watercarriers, washermen, carpenters, barbers, two calico-printer families, one blacksmith, and one merchant. The castes claimed different ethnicities, and each inhabited "more or less separate quarters" in the village. The lower castes lived on its outskirts and had no part in its formal organization, even though several lower-caste families were "ancient inhabitants." The Dalits had to draw water from separate wells, and when government officials came "to explain ... new community development projects," the Dalits stood to one side at the village meetings, "know[ing] their place."[39]

Baby Kamble (1929–2012), writing in the 1980s, portrayed conditions of Dalit existence in Pune and Satara districts in western India, still somewhat removed from the direct influence of urban development in her childhood and youth. In her grandparents' village, as she puts it in a searing if somewhat stylized portrait, there were fifteen or sixteen households of her Mahar caste. Caste distance was evident in the raised platforms around upper-caste houses, which ensured that the lower castes would deliver goods and receive their miserable recompense standing at a distance on a lower level. Three or four Mahar families, related to the head of the local Mahar community who received 16 percent of payments made for traditional services (removing animal carcasses for higher-caste villagers, carrying notices of death and other urgent messages to neighboring habitations, guarding the village, sweeping village roads, serving visiting officials), lived in tolerable housing. The rest inhabited makeshift huts of the poorest description. "The walls were nothing but stones arranged vertically with some mud coating." "Children looked as if they had rolled in mud, snot dripping from their noses in green gooey lines . . . their bodies . . . completely bare without a stitch on them. Each hut contained at least eight to ten naked children; some had as many as fifteen or twenty." The goddess Satwai, who supposedly determined the fate of every living creature, "had stamped hunger" on every Mahar forehead.[40]

A younger Dalit feminist, Bama Faustina Soosairaj (b. 1958), in turn, writes of her sense of suffocation and humiliation in the village in faraway Tamil Nādu, South India, where she grew up in the 1960s and '70s. Men and women of her Paraya community, both the elderly and the young, were expected to step out of the way, bow low, and act submissive in the presence of higher castes, and were forced to dangle goods on the end of a long string when offering them to upper castes, to guard against the danger of polluting them.[41]

The lived environment was different for working people in the new urban centers of the twentieth century, driven by administrative, commercial, and industrial growth. Bombay, which attracted migrant labor on a huge scale and occasioned an early debate into housing for manual workers, provides a dramatic example of the circumstances of the laboring poor in the "new" India. It demonstrates too that modern developments did not always provide significant relief from the poverty and stigma the subordinated castes and classes experienced in the countryside.

At the beginning of the nineteenth century, a visitor to the string of islands that would become Bombay, a city built around villages surrounded by hills and coasts and coconut plantations, noted that the richer "natives" had expansive dwellings. For, "if a man has twenty sons, they all continue to live under the same roof even when married." Their houses were well ventilated and surrounded by verandas, with the walls decorated in green and red, and in Hindu homes with fables from their mythology. By contrast, the lower classes lived in "small huts, mostly of clay and roofed with cadjan, a mat made of the leaves of the palmyra or cocoanut tree plaited together. Some of these huts are so small that they only admit of a man's sitting upright in them and barely shelter his feet when he lies down."[42]

In the early twentieth century, some of the poorest and most marginalized sections of the population still lived in huts and temporary shelters scattered around the city. However, shortage of space, population density, and commercial and industrial expansion caused an explosion in tenement and apartment living in Bombay after the First World War and, more dramatically, after Indian independence. Large numbers of blue-collar workers and the emerging lower middle classes (struggling office workers, clerks, small-time traders, and contractors) were accommodated in *chawls*: multi-room tenements housing multiple families, with shared verandas, water sources, toilets, and open spaces. Ambedkar and his family lived in a tenement through the 1910s and even the 1920s, that is, after Ambedkar's higher education and admission to the bar in New York and London, when his attempt to establish a law practice, or find secure employment as a professor, encountered open caste hostility. The family had two rooms (50 and 51) facing one another in Bombay Improvement Trust Chawl No. 1 in Parel: one with eight or ten members of the family crammed into it, the other used by Ambedkar as his library and office, from where he was occasionally called down to the street by visitors as unexpected as Shahu Maharaj, ruler of Kolhapur, social reformer and benefactor of the non-Brahmin and Dalit movements, and Maulana Shaukat Ali, the militant Muslim political leader and close ally of Gandhi.[43]

Fragile, makeshift structures, made of mud and thatch in some places, wood and brick and later reinforced concrete in others, tenements soon became a ubiquitous feature of mill districts in several cities of western India.[44] In Bombay, they were commonly double- or triple-storied blocks, with single and sometimes double rooms, perhaps ten by ten or ten by twelve feet, opening onto a veranda, a common space and passageway that sometimes connected to a separate central block of bathrooms and toilets. Originally, one scholar notes, each unit was designed to house a large group of working men, perhaps twenty or more, "sleep[ing] in rotation according to their mill shift."[45] In time, the *chawls* came to house entire families as more working men, women, and children settled in the city. Communal kitchens, shared toilet blocks where tenants lined up for their turn, and public taps where fights regularly broke out presented serious problems, especially for women from the countryside who were used to more open spaces and the privacy those spaces provided.

As its mills expanded in size and number, Bombay came to be divided between a residential southern area and the mill districts to the north. The latter were filled with "smoke, mean little alleys, ramshackle tenements erected for quick profit," Radha Kumar writes. The overcrowding was unbelievable: 72,000 persons per square mile in E ward, the smallest of the mill wards, which contained 44 percent of Bombay's tenements in 1931. Mazagaon, one of the two villages swept away by the establishment of twenty-seven mills in the ward, had eight or more families in each of its thirty-six one-room units. By one conservative estimate, "approximately twelve hundred people lived in these thirty-six rooms—or rather, stored their goods in them."[46] Many, especially the men and boys, slept outside on the pavement or the street—a feature of Bombay life from that day to this.

If conditions for workers living in tenements were deplorable, they were worse for numbers of the most depressed castes and classes, many of them designated Untouchables. These marginalized laborers still sought shelter in tin sheds "made of pieces of kerosene tins ... opened up, hammered out and fitted together" and *zavlis* or "huts made of the dry leaves of coconut or date palms"—without taps, toilets, or water. "Each big shed was divided by cloth drapings into four or six rooms and one family occupied each room," the Royal Commission on Labour in India noted in 1929. "None of the tin sheds were high enough for an adult to stand up in without hitting his head and dislodging pieces of tin."[47]

The material circumstances of Bombay's working people were replicated, with local variations, in other new industrial centers, railway junctions, and ports: Calcutta, Ahmedabad, Nagpur, Kanpur, Visakhapatnam, Calicut, and more. In 1927, a British Trades Union Congress Delegation visited what they called typical workers' "lines" or tenements in several places around the country. Here is an extract from their account:

> Each house, consisting of one dark room used for all purposes, living, cooking and sleeping, is 9 feet by 9 feet, with mud walls and loose-tiled roof, and has a small open compound in front, a corner of which is used as a latrine. There is no ventilation in the living room except by a broken roof or that obtained through the entrance door when open. Outside the dwelling is a long, narrow channel which receives the waste matter of all descriptions and where flies and other insects abound. Four to eight persons, including children, crowd together into such a room.[48]

Such houses, they declared, "whether they be the single-roomed or double-roomed dwellings built in 'lines' or tenements, or the single-roomed dwellings dotted about separately" in villages, small towns, and big cities, could hardly be called "homes." People living in these homes would obviously agree, in terms of the miserable character of their physical surroundings. Yet, they would point too to a palpable sense of home in the working people's neighborhoods and communities they inhabited. Again, autobiographical as well as academic works, written in diverse locations, provide moving testimony to the fact.

Working-Class Homes

Kausalya Baisantri, from whom I drew snapshot 5(b) in chapter 1, provides a stark account of the homes her grandparents and parents inhabited in Nagpur, the leading industrial city of central India. Sakhrabai, an elderly widow, had adopted Kausalya's father, the one surviving child of his parents, some time after the latter's deaths. The foster mother and adopted son fled to Nagpur to escape famine in the countryside: probably the great famine of 1905–1906. In Nagpur, they found themselves in a hut not far from the home of Kausalya's future maternal grandmother (her mother's mother). Later, Kausalya's father and his adoptive mother Sakhrabai moved to a different locality, using savings from Sakhrabai's police-inspector husband's earnings to buy and repair a broken down, two-roomed house made of mud and straw.

The maternal grandmother had seen and liked Kausalya's father. Having learned that the lad came from the same Mahar subcaste as her own family, she proposed that he should marry her daughter. The teenagers were married in the second decade of the twentieth century. Their first marital home was a room allotted to Kausalya's father in the servants' quarters behind the Central Provinces Club, where he had found work as an errand boy. Other menial servants— bearer, cook, gardener, washerman, sweeper—lived alongside. The families shared two toilets, one tap, and a small veranda, which also accommodated the club's kitchen. While living there, Kausalya's parents had four children: the eldest, a daughter born in 1918 or 1919, survived; the other three died in infancy.

A few years later, with Sakhrabai's support, the couple left the club and moved to the Khalasi Lines, or railway workers' colony, adjoining the Nagpur railway station. Here, they were closer to Kausalya's maternal grandmother, Aaji. With savings from the club and income from a job Kausalya's father obtained in a Goanese bakery, they bought a little land and built a small hut. Afterward, with a loan from a local moneylender and money given by Sakhrabai and Aaji, Kausalya's father and mother "built a firmer two-roomed home with their own hands," although this too was made of mud.

After Kausalya's birth in 1926, her mother found a job in the large Empress textile mills. Her father worked long hours at the bakery, and then as a *kabadi* or dealer in scraps and waste, bottles, tins, newspapers, to recycle, before he too found a job with Empress Mills, probably in the early 1940s. (The chronology is a little unclear in Kausalya's account.) "He was at home so little that we thought of him as a guest," writes Kausalya. Aaji, who lived nearby, worked as a casual laborer on daily wages. She or Kausalya's eldest sister, Janabai, seven or eight years older than Kausalya, looked after the baby when her mother went to work.[49]

These were conditions that her parents, who were lucky enough to get regular jobs in a factory, shared with a range of other oppressed working people—forty or fifty households, as Kausalya computes it, provided with one tap and eight overflowing lavatories. Yet, the circumstances could not erase working people's sense of home, community, and belonging.

Narendra Jadhav, whom I cited at the start of this chapter, writes of parallel circumstances in his parents' habitations in Bombay from the 1920s on. The women—initially his mother, his paternal grandmother, and a widowed aunt—ran the home, notwithstanding Narendra's declaration that it was his father who made the family and its future. In his recounting, his mother, Sonubai, described the house she came to live in as a young bride as follows. It was a small and dingy room, with one window opening onto a common balcony. A stove, and pots and pans, occupied one corner of the space, a small washing area another. There was hardly any room to move. The residents of the *chawl* shared common bathrooms and toilets outside. "The morning chores started with a rush for water," the women pushing and shoving to fill their buckets. "It was truly like communal living," Sonubai said; people were in and out of each other's houses and "knew all the details of what was going on."[50]

Their later home in the central Bombay neighborhood of Wadala, when the family was larger and financially a little more comfortable, was not radically different. There were nine people in the ten-by-ten room, Narendra tells us: his parents, his grandmother, and six children, two girls and four boys. The eldest, a boy, was born in 1938; the youngest, Narendra, in 1953. The family lived on the ground floor of a two-story *chawl*. The tiny kitchen opened onto a common balcony running around the building. There was a dim electric bulb in the balcony. The family members carried a kerosene lantern to light the way when they went to the bathrooms at the back.

Nevertheless, Narendra recalls his childhood home with fondness. "It was one big melting pot of communities: Muslims, Christians, north Indians, and south Indian construction workers . . . , but the majority of people in Wadala were [like his family] Dalits from Nashik and other places in Maharashtra." And no one who lived there wanted to move. "People who lived in Wadala even for a year would swear that they could never live anywhere else."[51] Wadala was home.

Working-class interlocutors living in a "de-industrializing" Bombay reiterate this sentiment at the end of the first decade of the twenty-first century. Manda, a textile mill worker, tells the anthropologist Maura Finkelstein of "how we used to live" and "how some of us continue to live today." The Bombay *chawl* where Manda and her husband live is cramped: "one room that serves as both bedroom and kitchen: a cupboard, a faucet, a woven mat on the floor. Piles . . . of pots and pans and dishes and utensils." When Finkelstein visits, she and Manda sit on the floor, while Manda's husband crouches in the doorway. "There is little room for him in the small space he shares with his wife. At night, he sleeps outside or with friends so that Manda can almost stretch her legs out at a right angle from her body within the room that is their home." That is the reason why they spend little time in the room when the researcher visits. Though Manda's one-room unit is "in and of itself . . . virtually uninhabitable," writes Finkelstein, "she shows me how chawl *life* is far more expansive than the tiny unit she cooks and sleeps in." As they walk, "Manda asserts her right to occupy the streets, to live in her chawl, to inhabit Lower Parel. She marks her territory through connection and conversation." "Home is not just four walls, but instead a neighborhood community. Manda is known here: she is aunt, sister, mother, friend."[52]

Middle- and upper-class men could choose to sleep under the stars. For the poor and downtrodden, it was not a matter of choice. Additionally, women across classes were pushed to sleep indoors, no matter how cramped the space, to protect them from the passer's gaze. These are conflicting legacies, occasionally converging, often diverging: of constraints that so many were born into, and comforts that all desired; of senses of home, and domestic concord, that had varied meanings for the individuals and families from privileged and unprivileged groups whom we dwell on at greater length in the pages that follow.

❋

Part II

❋

Practices

❋

❋

❋

3. Duty

Going around with your eyes bound ... playing the part of a devoted wife,
[y]ou were chained by the consequences of your own actions.
— IRAWATI KARVE

* * *

This chapter could be entitled "Work/Duty/Calling." Its central concern is with the call of national work that a generation of outstanding public men articulated through the later nineteenth and the early and mid-twentieth centuries. This was a major departure in thinking among the respectable, elite classes—for work was traditionally frowned on in these circles.

Calling as a secular professional ideal has a distinct history in India. Hindi and Urdu have no word for profession or calling. *Kaam* (work or job) or *pesha* (occupation or trade) would be the nearest equivalents. *Pesha* was the word traditionally used for a business, trade, or ongoing line of work, reserved in the main for the down-and-out and stigmatized: sex workers would be a paradigmatic example.[1] "Work" was what lower-class people did, artisans and laborers and toilers of all kinds: indeed, what they *had* to do. The upper castes and classes would not deign to work if they could help it. And if a calling occurred, it was of a religious kind—something reserved for the rarest and most exceptional of humankind.

Changing economic and social practices in modern times, and in the thinking that accompanied these, gradually established the dignity of white-collar work and made it possible to speak of professionals and their occupations as honorable and important. However, the idea of professionalism remains constricted. The position of school or college teacher, lawyer, doctor, engineer, or bureaucrat comes to be valued for the material security and social status it brings. But the idea of a professional remains tied to a class position or standing; it is rarely linked to thoroughness or competence in the performance of a task.

This is what new nationalist leaders and thinkers were up against. Their charge was to lift work from its lowly status and raise it to the level of a national service: *svadharma* in Hindi (self + duty), suggesting now a self-recognized individual calling rather than a socially prescribed individual *dharma*. In this, they succeeded remarkably. However, the other side of the coin was a new ambivalence about their place in a domestic world that was rapidly changing, while continuing to be an inescapable part of their lives.

The male protagonists of this chapter all made their names pursuing the dream of a resurgent, self-governing and self-confident new India. Yet, their marital histories tell a complicated story of their failure in the more intimate circles of family and kin to break with traditions that they consciously opposed. I begin with three figures from an upper-caste and middle- or upper-class background: Rajendra Prasad (1884–1963), devoted Gandhian and first president of the republic of independent India; Dhanpat Rai (1880–1936), known by his pen name Premchand, the renowned Hindi-Urdu writer whom I introduced in the prelude; and Kedarnath Pandey (1893–1963), who adopted the name Rahul Sankrityayan, scholar and activist extraordinaire, Buddhist, communist, organizer of peasant movements, prominent Congress worker, and campaigner for the establishment of Hindi as the national language of the land.

In the second half of the chapter, I counterpose these examples with sketches of two public figures from less privileged caste and class backgrounds: Babasaheb (Bhim Rao) Ambedkar (1891–1956) and Babu Jagjivan Ram (1908-1986), both counted among the most distinguished Dalit leaders of the twentieth century. Ambedkar is a contemporary of Rajendra Prasad, Rahul Sankrityayan, and Premchand; Jagjivan Ram belongs to the next generation. Collectively, their life stories testify to the hold of a widely accepted common sense of men's and women's domestic responsibilities and duties, and of the new urgency of men's *calling*, across generations as well as social backgrounds.

Bhadralok Leaders

The first three of my examples, born in relatively comfortable, upper-caste Hindu households tied in sundry ways to the demands of rural respectability, adopted urban professional careers and lifestyles.[2] This was a common trajectory for youth from a wide array of castes and classes throughout the twentieth century. Like Gandhi and others of similar social standing in this period, these three were married off at a tender age: Prasad and Sankrityayan were eleven or twelve, Premchand fifteen. Prasad, married in 1895 or '96, dutiful scion of a wealthy landed family, stayed in the marriage through his life. Premchand stayed in his childhood marriage for about ten years before abandoning his first wife; he then married a young woman who had been widowed as a child. The scholar-activist Rahul Sankrityayan escaped from his first marriage, in an early signal of revolt, a few years after its occurrence. He married again twice. His second, common-law marriage, a love match he made in Russia when he was forty-five, also ended in abandonment, chiefly on account of his commitment to the calling of political, literary, and cultural work in India. His third marriage, at the age of fifty-seven, was with a twenty-year-old woman of Nepalese origin from a far poorer social and economic background.

The three men differed in their political leanings. Prasad was a nationalist of conservative Hindu inclination; Premchand and Sankrityayan were committed to socialist thought and ideals. Nevertheless, all three favored education and expanded opportunities for men and women alike, and opposed child marriage, dowry, bigamy, the ill-treatment of widows, and other inimical practices. Prasad condemned customs like dowry and purdah, and supported education for girls, even as he endorsed traditional views of women's place in the home and of the woman as mother. Premchand wrote against inherited social ills, especially the unhappy condition of widows, perpetuated among respectable castes and classes by a refusal to let widows, even the little girls among them, remarry. When his first marriage broke down, he defied community elders to marry a woman widowed at the age of eleven. He spoke out strongly against the confinement of women and for universal education, although he gave in to orthodox views in the matter of his own daughter's schooling—as Prasad did on questions of dowry and purdah in his own extended family.

Sankrityayan, the most openly rebellious of the three, wrote copiously and frankly about his life in his different homes: in a six-volume autobiography (around two thousand printed pages), based on a detailed daily diary and reading much like one, and dozens of other autobiographical writings. Prasad and Premchand advanced arguments paralleling those of Sankrityayan: Prasad in his autobiographical writings and political statements, Premchand in the voluminous documentation of the freedom struggle in his short stories, novels, essays, and critiques. However, they wrote about their personal familial relations only briefly and indirectly. For Premchand, I am able to build a fuller picture through the lively account of their life together provided by his second wife, Shivrani Devi, in her moving tribute, *Premchand Ghar Mein*. Together, these varied writings and reflections tell us a great deal about three very different, reformist, thinking men's understanding of the needs of domestic order and intimate relations in their changing times.

I spell out aspects of Rajendra Prasad's marital life to illustrate the burden of tradition, often translated into the authority of elders; Premchand's idealistic marriage to a child widow to bring into focus the challenge of public, national work; and Sankrityayan's self-consciously chosen second and third marriages to discuss the men's dependence on networks of family. However, these different features mark the marriages of all three.

Gandhi has written angrily about his feelings on the tradition of child marriages in India. He was betrothed for a third time at the age of seven, and married at thirteen; two earlier betrothals had come to naught with the death of the chosen child brides. "I can see no moral argument in support of such a preposterously early marriage," he wrote.[3] Prasad, Premchand, and Sankrityayan all shared Gandhi's opposition to child marriage. However, they dealt with the issue and its fallout in rather different ways.

Sankrityayan comments on the oppression entailed in early marriage: "My family had no right to play with [literally, sell] my life at the innocent age of 11." From the age of fifteen, he attempted to escape from home. He succeeded in 1913 (at age twenty), and pledged soon after, as his parents and elders maneuvered to get him back from the Arya Samaji (Hindu reformist) educational centers where he had sought shelter, not to set foot inside the boundaries of his parents' home district until he was fifty. The "divorce" from Ramdulari Devi, he says in his autobiography, "unnecessary in the case of this innocent, involuntary marriage—was more clear-cut than any technical divorce. And because that is how I looked upon it, it will be wrong to blame me rather than society for that event—the marriage. I never considered it a marriage, nor accepted its responsibilities."[4] In 1957, when he was sixty-three, he acknowledged he had unknowingly ruined Ramdulari Devi's life, dedicating an ambitious and sweeping historical account of his father's village, *Kanaila ki Katha* (Stories of Kanaila), to "my first wife, whose whole life was sacrificed on the altar of my ambitions."[5]

Both Sankrityayan and Prasad refer to their childhood marriages as a farce—a *tamasha* (spectacle) and *khel* (game). The latter recalls the event as follows: "As a child, my sister (and I) used to enact the marriage of dolls. . . . This marriage was a little like that for me. I had no idea of the importance of the event or the responsibilities it entailed." In the single four-and-a-half-page chapter devoted to his marriage in his 660-page autobiography, he adds that he understood only that sometime soon his wife would come to live in their ancestral home in Jiradei, district Siwan, western Bihar, just as his older brother's wife had done.[6] His wife Rajvanshi Devi, younger than him, is unlikely to have been much better prepared.

When she came to Jiradei a year after their marriage, she faced the same restrictions as Prasad's sister-in-law, strictly confined in the inner women's quarters (*zenana*), with serious physical, not to say psychological, consequences. Writing his autobiography forty-five years into the marriage, Prasad noted, "It was only natural that the health of my brother's wife and my wife should deteriorate because of their confinement within the four walls of their room. Both of them suffered from rheumatism which left them a long time later only when they started moving about freely in the courtyard."[7]

Prasad estimated that he and his wife had spent less than forty-five months of those forty-five years together. Initially, he was away at school and college in the nearby town of Chhapra. Later, he went farther, to Calcutta, where he completed his MA in 1908, and then a bachelor's and master's degree in law. Returning to Bihar in 1916, twenty years after their wedding, he practiced law in the newly established provincial high court. Even in the early years, before the birth of their only child in 1907, husband and wife got little time together.

When he was home from school in Chhapra, Prasad slept in an outer room. At night, when others were sleeping, an older maidservant would wake him and escort him to his wife's room. "At daybreak, before others had arisen, I had to get up and come to lie down on my bed outside, so that no one would know that I was somewhere else at night!" He refers to his (and presumably his wife's) suppressed adolescent feelings. Once, when he was home for the holidays, his wife had an attack of cholera. He was understandably concerned. However, "it was considered bad form . . . to show much interest in one's wife. . . . I wanted to see her and get to know her, but could not ask anyone nor express the desire to do so. Perhaps it did not occur to my folks that I too was interested in her health [and her!]"[8]

In such tradition-bound circles, marriage and home were less about a couple's togetherness than the fulfillment of wider familial and ritual obligations. Marriage was a social responsibility, overseen by elders. It was required of both men and women, but hardly tied men down in the way it tied down women. Young brides, and children, remained in the care of elders in the bridegroom's family. As a practicing lawyer in Calcutta and in Patna, Prasad lived on his own, supported by servants, clients, dependent relatives, and other hangers-on. His wife and son joined him for a period in Patna. Once established in his profession and in full-time political work, Prasad had still less time for "my personal matters."[9] He returned to the village infrequently; sometimes it was to recuperate from exhaustion or illness. Even after restrictions in the home eased a little after the death of his mother, his wife, his sister-in-law, his widowed sister, and other women in the family came to visit only when he was ill in hospital, or jailed during anti-colonial campaigns. The women's desire for movement and diversion was satisfied only by visits to pilgrim sites and festivals: Gandhi's ashrams and meetings became part of this circuit once he was established as a Mahatma, saint and national leader of unparalleled stature.

Women's place and purpose in the home was given a new casing in the context of the powerful national movement for liberation.

Woman and Nation as Mother

In much of the modern world, both nation and woman have been imaged as mother—the first calling for sacrifice, the other sacrificing.[10] Modern nations supposedly command the respect, love, and loyalty of citizens by nurturing those citizens, providing food and shelter, comfort and community. At many points, however, this image of the mother is transferred from land and people, the abstract nation, to the real-life, physical, emotional being called woman.

Rajendra Prasad's reverential commentary on Gandhi's married life and his relationship with his wife—Kasturba Gandhi, née Kapadia (1869–1944), lovingly called Ba (Gujarati for mother)—articulates a widely shared view of the place of women in the nation among modern middle- and upper-middle-class groups in South Asia, reformist as well as traditional. Prasad first met Ba when she came to Bihar in 1917 to support Gandhi and his team in their very visible public inquiry into the conditions of the indigo-cultivating peasants of Champaran. On her arrival, Gandhi declared that Ba would relieve the Brahmin cook of the task of preparing food for the fourteen or fifteen lieutenants he had assembled for the inquiry. When Prasad and others expressed discomfort at the burden placed on this slender woman, Gandhi reassured them: she was used to such work, and more than capable of looking after them all.

The love with which Ba fed and looked after them, Prasad writes, was something he never forgot. His words are emblematic: "She was the very ideal of a Hindu woman, a symbol of Indian culture, and a bundle of love. She was truly 'Ba,' and 'Ba' she remained [to all of us]. On one occasion, Gandhiji said to me—'I too get great pleasure in calling her "Ba."' The two of them had of their own accord given up the relations that are commonly prevalent between husband and wife. She had in truth become 'Ba' [mother] to him too."[11]

A similar position emerges in Premchand's 1931 essay, "Nari-jati ke adhikar" (The rights of women), summing up the nationalist rebuttal of colonialist propositions about the fallen state of women and the oppressiveness of Indian homes: "The Indian woman has always been considered the goddess of the home," he wrote, "and she has a higher status than men in the society." Women lost this position on account of regrettable historical developments, which Premchand leaves unspecified. Men appropriated their rights. "But the wave of nationalism and enlightenment that has arrived now will obliterate all these [gender] distinctions, and our mothers [that is, all women] will be re-installed in the exalted place that is their right."[12]

The fact remained that half the population—and more, once we take the additional factors of caste and poverty into account—was denied even the semblance of equal access to jobs and education. Gandhi, always a forthright commentator on difficult issues, provides a succinct and clear exposition of the central quandary facing nationalists thinking about "the woman question." Thus, "I am uncompromising in the matter of women's rights. . . . So long as women in India remain ever so little suppressed or do not have the same rights [as men,] India will not make real progress." Further, "In the new order of my imagination, all will work according to their capacity for an adequate return for their labour. Women in the new order will be part-time workers, their primary function being to look after the home." And, directly to his countrywomen, "The future of India lies on your knees, for you will nurture the future generation."[13]

The phrase "on your knees" may mystify readers until they see the words that follow. Women's ordained task in the new India, as in the old, was to "look after the home," and to give birth and nourishment to the sons of India— and, since there is no escape from this, to daughters too. The underlying suggestion is that men belong to "the world," the domain of world history; women rule the home, the intimate space that they build and nurture through continuous and repetitive labor.

For men in South Asia, the distribution of gendered responsibilities and duties was rationalized through the representation of the ideal (modern, middle-class) woman as mother or mother-to-be. These ideal mothers were evidently asexual, immaculately conceiving sons and daughters for the continuation of community and nation, and caring for all those around them. They were imagined in contradistinction to the overly sexualized lower-caste (lower-class, laboring) woman, the fallen woman (prostitutes and adulterers), and the Western woman.[14] The implications for men's place in the domestic world were significant.

For many leading male thinkers and activists, the domestic became a space and time predominantly to rest and recuperate from illness, exhaustion, disappointment, or defeat, as well as to procreate, entertain, and establish and maintain status. They did not fully acknowledge their physical presence and responsibilities in the home, or their dependence on family, intimate relations, and extended kin. Instead, they often foregrounded an argument about the priority of their work in the "world," which necessitated their constant attendance outside the home.[15]

An Ideal Marriage

The charge of national work emerges powerfully in Premchand's marital history. His career is marked more insistently than Rajendra Prasad's by ideas of education and equality for girls and women. And in this instance, the matter of balancing public commitments against inherited traditions of caring for elders and the wider familial community adds fresh dimensions to domestic negotiations.

Schooled like Gandhi, Prasad, and likely Sankrityayan on the naturalness, responsibilities, and, perhaps, joys of wedlock, Premchand looked forward to the marriage his father and stepmother arranged for him when he was fifteen. He and his family were disappointed when they discovered that the bride, whom they saw for the first time after the wedding, was older, less "attractive," and less demure than they had expected.[16] His father died two years later, leaving Premchand as head of the household in Lamahi village, adjoining the ancient city of Banaras. He had a wife, a stepmother, a stepbrother, and sundry other relatives to look after. Struggling to make ends meet, he took on ill-paid tutoring jobs until he found a position in the government's education department in 1900.

When Premchand was posted some distance from Banaras, his wife often went to her parents' home in a neighboring district. The couple apparently shared little in the way of a physically or emotionally satisfying relationship. He might have endured the situation, Premchand told his second wife, Shivrani, had his first wife (unnamed in his writings and those of his biographers) and his stepmother not fought incessantly. Ultimately, in 1905, following a particularly bad clash between mother- and daughter-in-law and a possible suicide attempt by the latter, the young woman returned to her parents' home—permanently, as it turned out. Thus, some ten years into it, Premchand's first marriage ended. There was no thought of, and until the 1950s no need for, an official divorce.[17]

Egged on by his stepmother, Premchand married again within the year. This time, he arranged the match himself. Shivrani, his second wife, had been married as a child and widowed within months, at the age of eleven. The marriage accorded with the writer's idealistic leanings and his concern for the condition of Hindu widows—an issue about which he wrote continuously, from before this marriage until the end of his life.

When they married, Premchand was twenty-five, Shivrani seventeen—attractive, soft-spoken, polite, and reserved, yet strong-willed with a clear mind of her own, a dual personality clearly reflected in her *Premchand Ghar Mein*.[18] Premchand comes across in Shivrani's memoir, as well as in the recollections of other contemporaries and later scholars, as a delightful, modest, cheerful, hardworking, and responsible homemaker.[19] Her reconstruction of their life together is an account of blossoming understanding and affection, adventurous moments, playful exchanges and companionship, his desire to teach her languages she didn't know, and her willingness (and success) in learning—perhaps more than he anticipated. She recounts charming incidents of romantic interaction. For example, in 1933, resting under a tree by a canal near the students' hostel in Lucknow University, Premchand took a garland of flowers he'd just been presented at a literary meeting, put it around her neck, and declared, "There, we are now married out of our own desire!"[20]

The writer shared his fiction and nonfiction writing with Shivrani, and read her newspaper reports and stories in Urdu and English, languages she didn't know. He was pleased when she began to write and publish short stories, but hesitant about her making it her profession. "Why take on this headache?" he said to her, when critics responded to her stories saying Premchand must have written them.[21] It was enough, he seemed to suggest, that she looked after their home, their children, and him so wonderfully, with such efficiency and good cheer. Some competition developed between them in other arenas, including the dream of going to jail in the national cause—which she realized, and he to his regret never did.

Divergent priorities were evident in the home, whether flowing from the age gap between them or emerging out of their differing engagements in the wider literary and political world. Premchand was devoted to his family. He worked hard to make life comfortable for his wife and their three surviving children. At the same time, he considered it his responsibility to look after his stepmother, stepbrother, maternal uncles, and other relatives. In addition, twenty-four hours in the day seemed barely enough for Premchand's literary work—writing, editing, publishing—which overshadowed everything else in his life.

Premchand wrote little on his marital history. In the prelude, I quoted from the two paragraphs he wrote in a letter of 1935 on his and Shivrani's life together. Let me quote the statement more fully:

> My married life has nothing of romance. It is just the common type. My first wife died in 1904 [an "alternative fact," about which more below]. She was an unfortunate woman, not at all good looking, and although not satisfied with her I *pulled on uncomplainingly* just [as] all traditional husbands are [do?]. When she died I *married a 'Bal Vidhwa'* [child widow] and am fairly happy with her. She has picked up some literary taste and sometimes writes stories. She is a fearless, bold, uncompromising, *sincere lady, amenable to a fault and awfully impulsive.* She joined [Gandhi's] N[on] Co-op[eration] movement and went to jail. I am happy with her, *not claiming what she cannot give....*
>
> Well, life has been always to me work, work, work. Even when I was in government service I devoted my whole time to literary pursuits. I find pleasure in work.[22]

The words I have italicized speak of the national worker's sacrifice, even in the home; the acquiescence and emotionalism of "sincere ladies"; and a Gandhian acceptance of whatever deal life hands out to us. Here we have a cogent summary of the mainstream (male) nationalist ideal of the duties and responsibilities of men and women in domestic space. Shivrani Devi's reminiscences suggest she shared her husband's views to a large extent. Apparently, for her too, the ideal home was made by the elevated woman: a self-sacrificing, devoted wife and mother.

After their wedding, Premchand wanted Shivrani to take charge of their household, but refused to make this clear to his stepmother. Shivrani chose not to engage with the older woman and thereby invite conflict. The continuous bickering in the house made her long for the quiet of her parents' home, and she went back often. "I spent a month in his home," she writes, "and ten months in mine [her parents' home]."[23] It was many years into their marriage before tensions eased in this respect, with greater empathy between husband and wife and a somewhat reduced presence of in-laws. During the first heart-to-heart conversation she reports having with Premchand, regarding her status in his home and her mother-in-law's demands, he declares with tears in his eyes that he never had the good fortune of receiving a "real" mother's love. As she recounts it, the confession affected Shivrani deeply: "From that moment, I felt compassion for him.... I began to think of his home as mine."[24]

Shivrani wasn't aware when she and Premchand married that his first wife was still living. She believed the latter had died before this second marriage—as Premchand still suggested in the 1935 letter quoted above. In 1914, nine years into their marriage, she discovered, from a conversation she overheard with a visitor, the first wife's brother, that the woman was still living in her parents' village. Premchand's response to this discovery, "When someone no longer lives in one's heart and one's thoughts, she is for all practical purposes dead,"[25] was a lame cover-up. However, the point I wish to underscore is another.

Living out her ideal of the strong, and strongly rooted, middle-class Indian woman, Shivrani, on learning that his first spouse was alive, urged Premchand to bring her back. That was the Hindu custom, she declared. She would serve the childless older wife, along with the husband, their daughter, and any future children they had, as well as the mother-in-law and other relatives when they visited. She wrote to the first wife, inviting her to come and share their home. Correspondence between the two continued for some time. But the older woman refused to return unless Premchand went personally to fetch her, which he declined to do.

One last, poignant exchange, as reported by Shivrani, underlines my proposition about the couple's shared ideals of Indian womanhood. On his deathbed, in the pain of his final illness, when Shivrani Devi nursed him for weeks on end, Premchand made a closing confession. He told her then that he'd had a relationship with a third woman—begun when he was with his first wife and continued for some time even after he married Shivrani. "I know," she said, with tears in her eyes, urging him to rest and forget about this. As she tells it, he stared at her, then broke down, sobbing, "Oh God—if there is a God—make me well this one time, for the sake of this pure woman. . . . And if you cannot do that, then in my next life bring us together."[26]

Premchand wanted women in his new, renascent India to be educated, free, self-confident, enterprising, and creative. At the same time, they needed to be "Indian," preserving all that was good in Indian tradition. In 1933, when they were sitting on the Lucknow University lawns and he anointed Shivrani as his sweetheart, Premchand expressed his irritation with the university students walking together, talking and laughing openly. "Sensuous pleasure will never bring independence [national or individual]," he said. "Independence comes through asceticism, service and sacrifice. . . . Look at these people, acting like princes and princesses out on a stroll. The girls flighty as butterflies."[27] For him, the ideal woman was the self-effacing, self-sacrificing, loving, devoted mother: the opposite of the flashy, dressy, immodest, and shameless Western woman of anti-colonial (and postcolonial) mythology, suspicious traces of which appeared in the lightness and laughter of female students on the lawns of Lucknow University in 1933.

However, requirements of social and biological reproduction, and the treatment and recuperation of men during illness and old age, added other layers to the negotiation of roles and responsibilities in the domestic world. I have noted the consequences of aging and illness in the lives of both Prasad and Premchand. The issue emerges more acutely still in the tangled history of Sankrityayan's second and third marriages.

A Dreamer's Marriages

The young Kedarnath, renamed Rahul Sankrityayan when he embraced Buddhism in 1930, left his ancestral home decisively at the age of about twenty, a decade after his childhood marriage. Before that, he had already embarked on an unusual quest for spiritual and scholarly enlightenment. The quest lasted through his life: as a follower of the Arya Samaj and the Indian National Congress, a Buddhist, a communist and organizer of peasant resistance, and a scholar and teacher traveling far and wide, in search of ancient manuscripts and learned interlocutors. With his iconoclastic bent, Sankrityayan defied many social conventions, ordered beef (abjured by orthodox Hindus) loudly in busy restaurants, ate with people of all religions and castes, and married twice far outside his natal caste and community.

His second marriage occurred when he was in Russia. While teaching at the Oriental Institute in Leningrad for two months in 1937–38, he met and "became one with" Yelena (Lola) Narvertovna Kozerovskaya, an accomplished linguist and "scientific" assistant to Sankrityayan's host, the well-known Indologist and scholar of Buddhism Theodor Tzervatsky.[28] Barely a month later, in January 1938, Sankrityayan had to leave, because the Soviet regime had not yet processed the institute's application for a long-term position for him, and because the delay, and being in Russia, made it difficult for him to pursue his literary and political work on India.[29]

In March 1939, in jail for his part in organizing peasant resistance against extortionate landlords and officials in Bihar, north India, Sankrityayan learned of the birth six months earlier of a "beautiful, healthy" son, whom Lola named Igor Rahulovich Sankrityayan. Six years later—after several terms in jail, time spent mobilizing people for cultural and political struggle, gathering materials for his writing, and waiting for visas and permission to work in the Soviet Union—Sankrityayan returned to Leningrad in June 1945. He, Lola, and Igor were now together while he taught at the Oriental Institute. However, the experience was no honeymoon.

Sankrityayan was not the man he had been seven years earlier. Having gained wider recognition as an explorer and intellectual, and a more visible place in Indian political life, he was impatient with anything that took him away from his chosen tasks. His second marriage fell prey to his preoccupation with his literary, cultural, and political work. Between the alternatives of a relatively comfortable life in Russia—decent emoluments and the promise of spacious accommodation near the university—and his "real work" in India, he wrote, he knew where his obligations lay. After two years of an anguished if "sweet" life in Leningrad, he left. When he boarded ship, he tells us, "it was as if a weight had been lifted off my heart." For "the call of life's duty could not be bound by the chain of illusory love [attachment to home, wife, and child]."[30]

Leaving his wife and son in Russia, he returned to public work, protests, organization, and writing in India. A demonstration of workers greeted him with red flags when his ship docked in Bombay two days after Indian independence. Starting then, he was involved in continuous meetings, speeches, travels, and writing over the next decade—despite growing concerns about his health.

A little over three years later, in December 1950, Sankrityayan married again. His third wife, Kamala Pariyar, was twenty years of age to his fifty-seven. She came from a lower-caste family originally from Nepal, which had settled in Kalimpong, northeastern India. Sankrityayan was living there when she began working for him in June 1949. Kamala's father was dead. Her mother took in tailoring work, using a rented sewing machine until Sankrityayan bought her one. She and Kamala's brother, the oldest of five siblings, earned barely enough to meet the family's needs. Kamala weighed ninety-two pounds, Sankrityayan noted: "She wasn't constitutionally unhealthy. It was the family's extreme poverty that had made her weak."[31]

A matriculate with a good knowledge of Hindi and a little English, Kamala began transcribing and typing Sankrityayan's dictated work, and took increasing charge of his writing and his health. In August, three months after she became his assistant, he arranged for her to live in his house, to save the long walk to and from her home, often in wet weather, and to help with her further education, which he strongly encouraged. "Kamala and I had now become very close.... She gave me my [daily insulin] injections for diabetes and helped with my writing work. For some time now, I had wanted to find a stable set-up. This Kamala provided. In addition, I liked her disposition. She had a passion for reading and a sharp intellect, so it was natural we should grow close."[32] Soon, Kamala was accompanying Sankrityayan in his travels. "As an assistant in my writing and my doctor in these times, she is able to do a great deal for me. This thought forced me to keep her with me."[33]

Kamala knew nothing about Sankrityayan's Russian wife and son when she met him. She learned of their existence years later, again (as in Shivrani's case) from a third party. Possibly because of Soviet censorship, communications between Sankrityayan, Lola, and Igor dried up for five and a half years between 1948 and 1953. A letter from Lola arrived on September 3, 1953. By then Kamala and Sankrityayan had been married two years and nine months, and she was pregnant with their first child. September 5 was Igor's birthday: Sankrityayan telegraphed his greetings. On November 13, another letter arrived from Russia, with another photograph of Igor.

The resumption of correspondence caused Kamala distress. She wanted it ended. Sankrityayan ruminated in response: "What trust could one have in a father who disowns his son? When I got together with Kamala, I had no inkling that my relationship with Russia [i.e., Lola and Igor] could be restored. Now that this has happened, to break off relations with Igor would be inhuman." And, in a diary entry on November 14, 1953, "Since yesterday, I have fallen in my own estimation—forever. Kamala is right to think as she does. I took advantage of her helplessness. Justifying it all in the name of kindness, pity and what not. Why should she have any faith in me?"[34]

The Wanderer

On the question of intimate relations, and the importance of traditional family ties, Sankrityayan's views appear radically different from those of Prasad and Premchand. The scholar and seeker of enlightenment called for the realization of full human potential through unfettered exploration and pursuit of physical, emotional, intellectual, and spiritual yearnings among men and women alike. His relationship with Lola, especially in the early years, demonstrated this.

Nevertheless, notwithstanding the expressions of introspection and remorse cited above, Sankrityayan seems not to have acknowledged the burdens involved in sustaining a home and family. "Gods are greater than humans precisely because they do not have to worry about cooking/housework," he wrote.[35] The comment was made when he lived with his Russian wife and son in Leningrad between 1945 and 1947. The theme reemerges in his life with Kamala.

When Kamala became Rahul's assistant in 1949, one of the first texts she transcribed was his renowned *Ghumakkad Shastra* (The philosophy—or science—of a life of wandering). The book advocates a fluid idea of attachment and "home," as the seeker, the accomplished human, "wander[s] from one hearth to another."[36] "Wandering is the religion of humanity," Sankrityayan writes. "It is the only way to fulfil one's life, and make something of the individual and the society."[37] He refers to the Buddha, Guru Nanak, Dayanand Saraswati, and other sages as the great wanderers and makers of India, past and present.

The young man or woman who embraces the religion of wandering must follow his or her own desire, unmindful of "a mother's tears . . . a father's fears and sorrows . . . the wailing of a wife whom he has unthinkingly married, or the imagination [prognostications and fears] of an ill-fated husband."[38] Sankrityayan was aware of the challenges women faced in wandering alone. Many of his directives were addressed to men. Thus, "the wanderer who leaves his wife . . . is benefiting rather than harming" the nation, in that the act would help control a spiraling birthrate; and the woman who feels betrayed by such abandonment should take revenge on the society she lives in, for it is often the latter, not the immature young man caught in early marriage, who chained the two together.[39] That last comment, coming from a man who had abandoned not one but two wives already, seems bizarrely self-serving. As startling, perhaps, the person taking and typing his dictation was an impecunious young woman who became his secretary, nurse, and emotional and sexual partner, and moved into his home around this time.[40]

Kamala and Rahul married in December 1950 when they had shifted to Mussoorie, some two hundred miles northeast of Delhi. By then, Kamala was handling a forbidding array of tasks, managing household and servants as well as Sankrityayan's writing and correspondence, reading and singing to her husband (occasionally, lulling him to sleep), and more. Her work increased greatly after their two children were born in 1953 and 1955. She looked after the house, the children, her husband, and an endless stream of visitors, including her mother and siblings who came to help her, and to study, and stayed months or years. She also tried to keep up with studies for the higher education Rahul was determined she must have, to secure a good teaching job and thereby her and her children's future.

For his part, Rahul was impatient about the time Kamala spent on housework and looking after the children—even when the servants were absent or sick. He declared she was insufficiently committed to her studies, and blamed it on an "inferiority complex" stemming from her poor and disadvantaged background.[41] Increasingly concerned about the family's future as his health and strength declined, he pursued new projects and jobs in India and abroad, including a professorship in philosophy at a university in Sri Lanka from 1959 to 1961, to save money for their long-term security and a new home for them in Darjeeling, closer to Kamala's natal family.

The couple quarreled continually between 1956 and 1958 over his insistence that she accompany him on a still-unsanctioned trip he wanted to take to China and Tibet. Kamala could not imagine leaving the children alone: they were one and three in 1956. In the end, Rahul went by himself, in 1958. The family followed to bring him back after a stroke put him in hospital in Beijing.

In December 1961, another stroke left him mentally and physically incapacitated, unable to read, write, look after himself, or remember most things. From then until his death in April 1963, Kamala spent almost all her time caring for him, much of it alone with him in isolated and depressing hospital rooms—in Calcutta, Kalimpong, Delhi, and Moscow. It was after her husband's death that her life returned to anything resembling "normal," and she established herself as an educator and writer in Hindi and Nepali.[42]

Memories of the couple's last years together are detailed in volumes V and VI of Rahul's autobiography. Kamala compiled and published these, using the diary he kept until his stroke in December 1961, her own daily notes of his condition and behavior in the remaining two and a quarter years of his life, and the numerous letters he wrote to her between 1956 and 1961. In the course of her ruminations on her marriage and on the worldviews of men, Kamala refers to an admirer of Sankrityayan who proclaimed, in an extraordinary display of male privilege, that "Rahulji's third marriage, to Kamala, turned his life into hell. Otherwise, Rahulji would have continued fearlessly to roam the world like a lion." She comments tersely: "Yes, lions roam fearless . . . as long as they have strength in their bodies. And lions too need the company of lionesses. And lions too grow old and die one day. . . . Rahulji is no longer the 'daring Rahulji' of yesteryears. Now he needs an injection of insulin before every meal, and has many other bodily ailments."[43]

She could have said more. Writing long after his death, seeking to honor his memory and her love and reverence for him, she left it at that.

Father of a Community

My account of Indian public men's articulations of men's and women's place in the home and the world would be misleading if it portrayed these ideals as confined to a turn-of-the-twentieth-century generation of upper-caste Hindu households from a small part of northern India. In this section and the next, I set the example of the "clean caste" leaders alongside two from the depressed castes. The domestic life of Babasaheb (Bhim) Ambedkar, unquestioned leader of the Dalit movement, reproduces several of the motifs discussed above, not least regarding the exceptional self-sacrifice of both his first and second wife.

Bhim was the youngest of his parents' fourteen children, of whom five—three sons and two daughters—survived.[44] The family was among the more successful Dalit families of western India. Bhim's paternal and maternal grandfathers, and several granduncles, served in the colonial military. His father, a subedar-major and headmaster of various military schools established for the basic education of children and relatives of lower-ranking military personnel, read Marathi in both Devanagari and Modi scripts and knew English, the ancient Hindu epics, and the poetry of the great Bhakti *sants* of northern and western India with its anti-caste and anti-clerical leanings. When military recruitment of men from Dalit castes ended in 1893, he shifted to Dapoli, 220 kilometers south of Bombay; then to Satara, 150 kilometers east in the Deccan plateau, where he became a storekeeper in the public works department in 1894; and ten years later, when he retired from that position, to Bombay.

As a well-read man and a teacher, Bhim's father was committed to educating his sons. However, his pension was not enough to keep all of them in school in Bombay. An older brother took a job in a factory. Bhim, just entering his teenage years, stayed in school. He now developed an exceptional attachment to books and learning, isolating himself from other children in order to read. He was noticed by sympathetic teachers, social reformers, and philanthropists, who supported his quest for further education. Matriculating in 1907, still a rare accomplishment for someone of his background, he went on to obtain scholarships and an outstanding higher education overseas. In the United States and UK between 1913 and 1917, and 1920 and 1923, he received a doctorate from Columbia University, New York, as well as the London School of Economics, in addition to being admitted to the bar in London.

Long before that, in 1905, at age fourteen, Bhim was betrothed to the nine-year-old Ramabai, who came from a very poor family. Her mother had died early, leaving behind three daughters and a son. Her father, who worked as a porter and brought up the children, died in 1913 while at work transporting fish at a port near Dapoli. Married in 1908, Ramabai and Bhim lived with Bhim's father in Bombay, moving in 1912 to two rooms in a tenement, as I mentioned in chapter 2.

A son born in 1912 was their one child who lived. When Ambedkar left for New York in 1913, Ramabai was pregnant again; the child died in infancy. On his return from London in 1917, they had another son, who also died early. After his second sojourn in the West, they had a daughter and a son: neither survived. Ambedkar was broken by the death of a fourth child in July 1926. He wrote to a friend a month later: "There is no use pretending that my wife and I have recovered from the shock of my son's death . . . I do not think that we ever shall. We have in all buried four precious children, three sons and a daughter, all sprightly, auspicious and handsome.... My last boy was a wonderful child, the like of whom I had seldom seen. With his passing away life to me is a garden full of weeds."[45] Through the 1910s and 1920s, social and economic hardship dogged the family. Ambedkar's father died in 1913, followed by the older brother who was the principal breadwinner in 1914. While Ambedkar was in New York and London, his family relied on the money he could rake up. Two of Ramabai's siblings, her son, her widowed sister-in-law, and the latter's son lived together in the two rooms of their *chawl*, surviving on skimpy rations, of which Ramabai and her sister-in-law took a little after the children had eaten.

Between November 1918 and March 1920, Ambedkar was a temporary professor in Sydenham College, Bombay, with a salary many times what the family needed each month. He was focused, however, on returning to London to complete his studies. "Confident that he would raise the funds to complete his studies, he... rushed home every day from work and shut himself in one room of their tenement [to read]. Often,... [he] got so engrossed in reading that he forgot to have dinner, and Ramabai also stayed hungry."[46]

In 1920, after Ambedkar left for London, Ramabai's siblings took to manual labor to help make ends meet. When her eldest brother, who lived with them in the tenement, found no work, the women made cow dung cakes to earn what they could. Ramabai and her eight-year-old son often walked long distances to find cheap firewood for cooking—"after dark, so that the neighbors did not learn about [their] plight."[47]

From London, Ambedkar wrote to his wife of his own situation: "I get meagre food... have no money to send. Even so, I am making arrangements for you... If this takes time..., then sell the ornaments [she came with when they married] and feed yourselves. On my return I will make up for the loss of jewellery." He added he was sorry to hear about the illness of another child in the family, possibly another son of his sister-in-law, who passed away later: "That is fate. No point worrying about him."[48]

Through this time of hardship, books remained Ambedkar's primary indulgence. On one occasion, he spent five hundred rupees on a multivolume compendium on English law: "That's the kind of person I am," he told some followers. "My household keeps running only because of my wife and sister-in-law."[49] A July 1920 letter to his wife from London sums up his concerns: "Conduct yourself uprightly. Do not pick fights with anyone. Do not accept anything from anyone for safekeeping.... Do not let anyone touch my books."[50]

What saved the Dalit leader and his career, according to his biographers, was his wife's devotion. "Like Tilak, Gandhi and Savarkar, Ambedkar, too, was blessed with a great and good wife," writes Dhananjay Keer. "While Ambedkar was in America, this saintly woman lived in a state of extreme destitution ... without a whisper of grumbling, her eyes turned towards God for the safety and prosperity of her husband." When he was back, "she lived as sparingly as she could, kept herself from her husband's study, gave him no news of any illness in the family and saw that nobody disturbed him in his studies."[51] She even contributed funds from further sales of her bridal jewelry in 1930, when he had begun earning enough to begin building an independent house with a whole floor for his library.[52] However, Ramabai herself became weak and depressed from all the privation and the deaths of their children. Her husband sought medical intervention and sent her away for a change of air on more than one occasion. To no avail: she passed in 1935.

By then, Ambedkar was a top-rank public figure, representative of the Depressed Classes at the Round Table Conferences in London, someone Gandhi had to contend with directly. He went on to become the first law minister of independent India, and the chief architect of the Indian constitution. With his incessant work—his writings and his campaigns on behalf of the Dalits—his own health declined. In April 1948, anxious to pursue his goals to the fullest, he married Dr. Sharda Kabir, who was part of the team of doctors who treated him in Bombay. In a letter to a confidant, he spelled out what he needed in a spouse: "[She] must be educated, ... a medical practitioner and ... good at cooking. It would be impossible in our community to find a woman who would combine the three qualifications.... Fortunately, I have been able to find one ... from the Saraswat Brahmin community."[53]

When they married, Sharda was thirty-nine, Ambedkar fifty-six. They were drawn to each other, and she devoted the next decade to serving him and his causes. However, he warned her of the challenge she was taking on in a letter written two and a half months before their wedding: "I am no gay person—pleasures of life do not attract me. My companions have to bear the burden of my austerity and asceticism. My books have been my companions, they are dearer to me than wife and children."[54] At some level, Sharda—renamed Savitabai after the marriage, following local custom—agreed with him. Ambedkar was married to his books *and* to politics, she wrote to one of his lieutenants after his party's (and his individual) defeat in the 1952 general elections. Politics was his very being, she observed: "I dare say he will start running about if ... he were to be the Prime Minister of India. That is [his] desire ... and let us pray some day it will be fulfilled."[55]

His second wife's caste and class background made Ambedkar's second marriage more controversial than his first. Many of Ambedkar's Dalit followers had difficulty accepting her as his partner. In Dalit women's songs in Maharashtra, it is Ramabai who holds the position of Babasaheb's "beloved wife." One argument explaining his subsequent intercaste marriage is that the Baba (father) of the community could hardly marry someone from among his daughters: it is for this reason that he chose a Brahman woman.[56]

For all that, the motif of wifely devotion and sacrifice appears in the second marriage too. Many recent commentators—including Vijayrao Surwade, whose extraordinary personal archive has brought to light much new information on Ambedkar, and enabled Savitabai to add new documentation of her life with Ambedkar in later editions of her autobiography—underline her exceptional sacrifice and contribution as partner and champion in his political work, as well as his doctor and primary caretaker in the last eight years of his life.[57]

The argument about the exceptional needs of exceptional men surfaces in relation to political leaders of diverse communities. Gandhi and, to a lesser extent, Rajendra Prasad and Jinnah may be counted among them. It has been invoked for latter-day "Great Men" like Atal Behari Vajpayee and Narendra Modi too: people supposedly above the fray, servants and saviors of a larger community and country, unfettered by family in the way of ordinary mortals.[58]

Before I attempt to summarize the special circumstances and hence expectations of such luminaries, let me turn to my final example, Jagjivan Ram, once counted among the most important Dalit leaders of India and an important alternative voice to Ambedkar's.

A Successful Traditional/Modern Man

In a three-volume memoir, Jagjivan Ram's second wife, Indrani Devi (1911–2002), provides fascinating glimpses of her life with him.[59] Worshipful in its detailed recounting of her husband's career and achievements, the memoir is closer to Rajendra Prasad's autobiography centered on public life than to Shivrani Devi's account of her life with Premchand. Yet, told from Indrani's location, initially in Jagjivan's traditional, rural home and later in their various official homes in Patna and Delhi, it provides a telling commentary on another successful and idealistic public man's domestic world.

Jagjivan and Indrani's marriage in June 1935—his second, her first—was unusual in several respects. She was twenty-four years old, only three years younger than him, well-educated and a schoolteacher. The milieus of their birth and upbringing were very different.

Jagjivan was born in an Untouchable family in "backward" rural Bihar, best known in the colonial period for its supply of cheap labor to the expanding port cities of Calcutta and Bombay, and to distant plantations and colonies overseas.[60] He overcame the handicaps of his social and economic background to become one of India's best established and longest serving political leaders. Drawn into the activities of the Bihar Congress and Gandhi's campaign against Untouchability, he was elected to the Bihar legislature in 1937 and served as member of Parliament and central cabinet minister for nearly forty years from the 1940s, including a stint as deputy prime minister in the late 1970s.[61]

Jagjivan's grandfather was a landless laborer in Bihar. His father, Sobhi Ram (b. 1864), worked on a farm until age ten or twelve, when an uncle employed in the colonial army found him work in a military hospital in Punjab. He joined the Shiv Narayanis, a reformist Hindu sect influenced by the Bhakti *sants* and Sikh gurus that gained a considerable following among lower castes in northern India. Following marriage with a girl much younger than him, when his military contingent was posted to Bihar, Sobhi established himself in his home district as a farmer with some land of his own, and over time as a leader of the sect. Jagjivan was to benefit in his early educational and political career in Calcutta and Bihar from the family's relative economic security and his father's fame as a Shiv Narayani teacher.

Early marriage was a sign of respectability: Jagjivan was betrothed when he was somewhere between two and six (the reports vary). That marriage fell through; apparently, the girl's family was too poor to pay for a proper wedding. Jagjivan then married when he was eight or ten, around 1916–18. The bride, of similar age or younger, came from a "good," comparatively well-off family of their leatherworkers' caste, but did not move to her husband's family home until much later, possibly well into the 1920s.

The delay allowed Jagjivan to continue his schooling unhampered. He went to school in the district headquarters, Arrah, and at the old Hindu pilgrim site and renowned educational center of Banaras, 125 miles to the west in Uttar Pradesh. He finished high school in Calcutta, four hundred miles to the east, and attracted notice as a promising young social activist, buoyed by support from low-caste laboring migrants from northern India, many of who venerated his father as a Shiv Narayani teacher. Back in his village home, where Jagjivan was still based in the 1930s, his wife, mother, and other relations were sorrowful that he and his wife remained childless. Resisting pressure from elders, Jagjivan refused to marry again while his wife lived. However, she herself grew increasingly despondent, fell ill perhaps on that account, and passed away in 1933 or 1934.

Indrani, whom he married in 1935, was born and raised in the more "modern" surroundings of the industrial city of Kanpur. Her father was a "native doctor" in the British Indian Army until he retired, joined the progressive, anti-caste reformist movement of the Arya Samaj, and made a name as a medical practitioner, social reformer, promoter of education, and champion of the poor and needy in Kanpur. He and his wife sent their children to school (the two boys and three girls who survived from their ten), and all three daughters worked as schoolteachers for some time.

"In Kanpur," Indrani writes, "Father was greatly respected. Everyone knew our caste background, but no one looked down on us. Wherever we went, people honored us as the daughters of Doctor Sahib." However, she was denied admission to the solitary high school for girls in Kanpur, probably because of her caste background, and was sent to board at the Normal School in Lucknow, forty-five miles away. In the state capital, she suffered discrimination and exclusion at the hands of servants as well as Hindu students, though, she suggests, they accepted her in time on account of her abilities, cleanliness, goodwill, and determination.[62]

Back in Kanpur in 1931, she joined her older and younger sisters in schoolteaching. They followed stirring national events—such as Gandhi's march to the seashore in Gujarat to defy the colonial monopoly on the manufacture of salt, and the outbreak of a violent clash between Hindus and Muslims in Kanpur, both in 1931—while keeping up a busy schedule of work at home and at school. After their parents passed in 1930 and 1932, the older sister took on the responsibility of getting her younger sisters married. In 1934, the youngest was married into a very traditional, if rich, rural family—unhappily, as it turned out. A year later, Indrani married into Jagjivan's traditional but rather more forward-looking family. During the negotiations, Jagjivan stressed that he came from a family of working people, farmers, who did all their housework on their own. He also insisted that the wedding take place without any dowry or undue fanfare.

Indrani suggests she easily stepped into the role of traditional wife and daughter-in-law in her husband's rural home. She had married late, probably accepted marriage as the lot of women, and felt lucky in the generosity she found in his family. She writes of how her mother- and sister-in-law were unfailingly sympathetic, but also notes the reluctance of the men to allow the women too much independence. Her return to Kanpur for the one-year apprenticeship she needed to complete her teachers' training required her mother-in-law's intervention. The head of the household, Jagjivan's older brother, twenty-four years his senior, and Jagjivan himself were disinclined to let her teach, despite their progressive instincts. They acquiesced when their mother said, "There's no harm, she'll leave the job after working one more year."[63]

All the while, her husband and in-laws told her about village customs, and about Jagjivan's pranks and achievements when he was growing up. They praised his first wife, who was evidently much liked by the family and the village elders because of her good nature and untiring commitment to domestic work. Her husband and his mother spoke repeatedly of the cold winter night when his first wife sat up without eating until 4 a.m., waiting for her husband to return from election campaigning in a neighboring town. As Jagjivan put it in a 1978 interview, the act showed that "while she was unschooled, she was steeped in the traditions of Hindu womanhood . . . and just what a Hindu wife should be."[64] The newly married Indrani wondered if she could live up to her predecessor's high standard. "Then I'd say to myself, I'll definitely do it; I'll be like her."[65]

Indrani writes admiringly of her husband's large-heartedness, public commitment, and good cheer. She also records his long absences from home, even at critical times like the birth and death of children. She was with her natal family in Kanpur, and Jagjivan was out campaigning for the upcoming provincial assembly elections, when their first child was born in February 1936. On March 5, he wrote to her, "I received the happy news of the birth of our beloved daughter [literally, jewel-daughter] yesterday. I cannot describe the joy I felt. . . . Truly, her name Anandi [one who brings happiness, the name chosen by Indrani] is entirely fitting."[66] Five weeks later, when he attended the annual session of the Indian National Congress in Lucknow, forty-five miles from Kanpur by train, he asked Indrani to come there with her mother and their daughter. He was unable to receive them at the railway station but sent someone to escort them to where he was staying. For the next few days, she writes, "we attended Congress sessions, and heard the speeches of Gandhiji and Jawaharlal Nehru, before returning to Kanpur on the fourth day."[67]

In October, on an auspicious day at the end of the long, hot summer that followed her last year of teaching, Indrani returned to her marital home in the village with her daughter. In early January 1937, Anandi contracted pneumonia. On January 18, she died. Indrani "sobbed uncontrollably." The tragic news was conveyed to Jagjivan. He came as soon as he heard. Deeply saddened and guilty that he had not been there for his daughter, as his wife puts it in her laudatory memoir, "he reasoned with me, comforted me, and left" to resume his work.[68] This was to be the pattern of their life, even after Jagjivan moved to Patna, the capital of Bihar, and to Delhi, the capital of independent India.

Their son, Suresh, was born in Patna in 1938, bringing unrestrained joy to the couple and to family elders. A daughter, Meira, followed in 1945.[69] An exchange that occurred between those dates—at the time of the last great Congress-led mass campaign against the British, the Quit India movement of 1942—sums up the distribution of duties in the family. When Indrani said to Jagjivan, "This time I too will go to jail," he laughed. Then, seeing she was serious, he said, "If you go, who will look after mother, and Suresh? He is so young, how will he survive? Only one of us can go [to jail]." Her response, as she records it, was pithy: "OK... you serve Mother India by going to the public jail, I'll serve mother by staying in jail at home. Our duties are the same."[70]

That seems an appropriate place to conclude this chapter. I shall do so with a brief comment on the discrepant, if supposedly complementary, roles allotted to men and women in the anti-colonial struggle in India, and their implications for men's place in the home.

Men's Thinking, Women's Thinking

It is important to note that a powerful tradition of *tyag* (sacrifice of worldly desires and possessions), which in the past sometimes led to *sanyas* (total renunciation and withdrawal from society), was invoked by many male modern Indian leaders, even when they nominally continued to live with their families. Vivekananda, Aurobindo Ghosh, and not least Gandhi waxed eloquent on the ideal of the *karmayogi* (the seeker who seeks the higher life through service). Others fashioned themselves as *parivrajak* (*sanyasis* who spent their lives in wandering): they include Rahul Sankrityayan, discussed at length in this chapter; the militant nationalist leader Subhas Bose as he appears in his unfinished autobiography, *An Indian Pilgrim*; and Nirmal Bose, the anthropologist and Gandhian.[71] In all such cases—as *tyagi*, *karmayogi*, or *parivrajak*—distinguished men pleaded their inability to perform the duties that might be expected of men in the domestic space, even if some (like Gandhi) were deeply invested in the domestic and its workings.

Despite the variations in their personalities, inclinations, careers, and indeed social and cultural backgrounds, the men centered in this chapter, Rahul Sankrityayan, Rajendra Prasad, and Premchand, as well as Gandhi, Ambedkar, and Jagjivan Ram, often seem *most at home* away from home: outside, in the public domain, occupied in the task of intellectual, political, and national advancement. Premchand's characterization of his life as nothing but "work, work, work," and Rajendra Prasad, Ambedkar, and Jagjivan Ram's unflagging dedication to public service at the cost of time spent with family, were in line with Sankrityayan's advocacy of the imperative need for *ghumakkadi* (wandering) in the service of the young, emerging nation—a philosophy in which the evolved, enlightened human being, unburdened by worldly or familial constraints, roams freely as a lion, exploring, experimenting, learning, and preaching to build the good society.

This was a platform that neither Premchand's nor Sankrityayan's first wife could have shared—living alone to the end of their lives, following abandonment by their husbands when they were in their teens or early twenties, confined in the first case to her natal home and in the second to her father-in-law's. Nor, one suspects, would it be shared enthusiastically by Sankrityayan's more independent second and third wives, Yelena Kozerovskaya and Kamala Sankrityayan—or, for that matter, by Ambedkar's first wife, Ramabai, or Premchand's or Jagjivan Ram's second wives, Shivrani and Indrani Devi, for all their commitment to Hindu/"Indian" tradition.

The proposition that women managed the home, men the world, was complicated by men's dependence on family, home, women, servants, and other subordinates while they pursued their public work. The home and the family, and more specifically wives, daughters, daughters-in-law, and servants, served as caregivers, providers, sustainers, and nurses—for children, elders, husbands, and others who inhabited the domestic world. Women's lives and commentaries tell a more complex story than the autobiographical writings of these prominent, thinking, reformist men: of enduring tension and conflict over individual physical and emotional needs, anguish, pain, desire, and love, on the one hand, and social responsibility to those who made up the networks of intimate and wider community, on the other.

It is time to turn now to an examination of how this conflict played out in the lives of educated, forward-looking men and women of the succeeding generations.

4. Discipline

Love has nothing to do with it; love has everything to do with it.
— SAIDIYA HARTMAN

❀ ❀ ❀

In chapter 3, I underscored the new direction given by leading Indian public figures, in the early twentieth century and after, to *work* as *calling*: their emphasis on the respectability, indeed nobility, of working for a living, as against simply living on inherited wealth, and implicitly on the manliness of open dedication to work. I shift attention in this chapter to the professional middle classes—lawyers, doctors, teachers, bureaucrats—of a younger, Partition and Independence generation. I note their pride in their work for the nation's development, as well as the vulnerability they often betrayed in their public and domestic dealings. There are fewer writings on the lives and careers of the protagonists considered here, compared to the more prominent political and intellectual leaders featured in chapter 3. I rely more heavily, therefore, on the information provided in their autobiographies, and focus more sharply on the performance of memory: lives retold as the authors of the autobiographies imagined they were—or wished to be seen as being.

What I have called the Partition and Independence generation lived through the early and middle decades of the twentieth century. It was an era of militant anti-colonialism, hope, and optimism, demonstrated in extraordinary struggles on many fronts: Gandhian campaigns of civil disobedience, the Khilafat and later the Pakistan movement for the protection of Muslim rights, the emergence of women's organizations, assertive lower-caste and lower-class movements, peasants' and workers' risings, and left-wing associations of many kinds. Through the period, the numbers of people dreaming of middle-classness, modernity, and freedom rapidly grew. Across the subcontinent, educated men—and women in smaller numbers—sought new opportunities in education, business, law, medicine, journalism, and other modern professions. Out of this churning came a new breed of independent professionals who saw themselves as the makers of modern India, Pakistan, and later, after East Pakistan broke away in 1971, Bangladesh.

The parameters of the domestic world, seen by these professionals as a critical site for the advancement of selfhood and appropriate order in the world, also shifted. As people seeking modern education and middle-class careers streamed into the towns and adjusted to living in more confined urban spaces than they were used to in the countryside (cottages carved out of larger residential estates, or semidetached houses or apartment blocks in crowded business districts and streets), conceptions of family changed. The idea of the nuclear family gained importance in the context of urban and transferable jobs, even if three generations often lived together and the authority of the elders and ties with wider kin networks remained vital.[a] Talk of the need to break from arranged marriages and the restrictions of traditional community increased, middle-class men expressed their desire for female company and their commitment to wives and children more openly than before, and they more than occasionally took the initiative in choosing their own brides.

[a] The photograph on the cover of this book, taken in December 1935 to commemorate the wedding of Hameeda Omar and Akhtar Husain Raipuri, whose marital history I discuss at length in this chapter (especially in the next section, "Men Have Things to Do"), provides a succinct and unselfconscious comment on the persistence of these values. The bride and groom, whose wedding is being marked, are tucked away on the extreme right-hand side of the gathering, the bride sitting in the middle row, the groom standing behind her. The photo of the "Khandan" (or extended Omar family), taken in front of the bride's parents' home, built by her police-officer father, Zafar Omar, is dominated by the elders. The bride's mother and father are seated next to her in the middle row, on her right, and the oldest "elders," Zafar Omar's mother and father, are placed at the center of the assembly. The full list of family members in the photograph appears on page iv.

Yet, despite increasing opportunities for interaction with women who were their peers in educational, cultural, and occupational arenas, most men displayed signs of insecurity in the company of mature, independent women. It is notable that the women chosen as life partners tended to be far younger than the men, even in cases where prospective bridegrooms made the choice, let alone in marriages arranged by family elders. There was a decided preference for brides who had attended school but (hopefully!) remained innocent beings, in need of careful guidance. Indeed, the choice of the young and innocent appeared to be critical to many men's sense of manliness. Ironically, the choice was accompanied sometimes by the presentation of marriage as a constraint, if not a trap, by the more ambitious.

If chapter 3 focused on men preoccupied with public work, *looking in*, one might say, on their domestic worlds, this one takes a view that may seem to be the other way around—*looking out*, as it were, from domestic space. It is less concerned with an avowed sense of calling or sacrifice among men—though two of its male protagonists represent their obsession with their work as driven by an inner spirit beyond their control. I focus instead on mundane details of men's conjugal relationships, and on the discipline and duties imposed on their wives, who often gave up dreams of their own for the sake of their husbands.

In the sections that follow, I examine the marital lives of a police officer, Akbar Mirza (1909–1971), a member of the British colonial police service, who transferred to the Pakistan police in 1947; a radical intellectual, Akhtar Husain Raipuri (1912–1992), who became a prominent national and international educationist after his move to Pakistan in 1947; and the poet, teacher, and government officer Harivansh Rai Bachchan (1907–2003), already introduced in chapters 1 and 2.

Raipuri and Bachchan have left behind detailed autobiographies, which are rather different from one another. Raipuri's is a public commentary on the intellectual and political roads he traveled and the worldly challenges he faced and overcame, in greater or lesser measure. Bachchan's four-volume autobiography, cited earlier, is an unusually candid reconstruction of his inner life through adolescence and adulthood, his emotional entanglements, and his intimate relations. It is paralleled among the examples considered in this study perhaps only in the writings of Rahul Sankrityayan and M. K. Gandhi. Our third male protagonist, Akbar Mirza, left no written record of his life or career.

Alongside the two men's memoirs, however, we have incisive and delightful counterpoints in the autobiographies of two of the men's wives, Khurshid Mirza (1918–1989) and Hameeda Akhtar Husain Raipuri (1920–2009). As in the case of Shivrani Premchand and Kamala Sankrityayan's writings referenced in chapter 3, the autobiographies of these women, written after their husbands passed away, provide a testament to the love and loyalty evident in their marriages. At the same time, they point to men's and women's differing perspectives on the meanings of intimacy and home.

I begin by examining the domestic lives of the two Muslim protagonists, who moved with their immediate families in midcareer to spend the second half of their lives in Pakistan. I then turn to the marital history of my third example, a Hindu by birth, who never left his native land, living as he did farther east in the same province of Uttar Pradesh, with its "Hindu" majority.

Men Have Things to Do

The stories of the Muslim couples I center in this chapter, Akhtar and Hameeda Raipuri and Akbar and Khurshid Mirza, parallel one another in several respects but differ strikingly in others. Both are linked with Aligarh, the leading educational center of the north Indian Muslim elite. Both men married young teenaged brides from prominent Aligarh families, and both remained in one marriage throughout their lives. Multiple marriages were not the norm among Muslim professionals in twentieth-century India, notwithstanding the common belief that Muslim men typically marry several wives. Akhtar Raipuri, Akbar Mirza, and their families made difficult adjustments when they became citizens of a new homeland, Pakistan. Both cases are marked, finally, by the men's repeated expressions of frustration, especially in later life, and by their wives' emergence in independent careers after their husbands passed away.[1]

The differences begin with the primary sources we have for their marital histories. In the case of Akbar and Khurshid Mirza, only the latter writes of their life together. In the case of Akhtar and Hameeda Raipuri, we have two autobiographies. Akhtar was a prominent intellectual and writer, known in leftist literary circles from his student days. In his sixties, literary and publisher friends urged him to write about his life and career. After his death, they persuaded Hameeda to add her version of their years together. I begin with this single— yet double—life story.

In both Akhtar and Hameeda's autobiographies, Akhtar's intellectual and political world is central. The intensity of that focus reflects something of the tension they had to negotiate in the domestic arena. For their commentaries on what both regarded as a successful marriage are startlingly different—more divergent even than those of Premchand's and Shivrani Devi's cited in the prelude and in chapter 3.

Toward the end of her autobiography, *Humsafar* (Life companion), Hameeda quotes the sentence in which Akhtar summed up their marriage: "Hameeda is my life companion, and though all my life I tended to fly far away like a kite, she never let go of the kite string, or allowed anyone to cut it." That one sentence and the dedication of his autobiography to her, she says, was sufficient reward for all the love and sacrifice she had offered him.[2] At the same time, as she writes in the preface to her version of their marital history, "In the life I shared with Akhtar, I was always tongue-tied, I was overawed by him. . . . I was a different person in his presence, my real self in his absence. . . . Our life together passed happily because I never did anything he did not like."[3]

Akhtar's reflections on their togetherness are of another order. In his autobiography, *Gard-e-Rah* (Dust of the road)—a reference to the roads he traveled—he expands on his remark about his inclination to "fly away like a kite." "There is such self-sufficiency in my character that I . . . could never bring myself to ask anyone for anything, be it loved one or friend. . . . There was such restlessness in my disposition that as soon as I settled somewhere I felt the urge to move." He sums up his life's quest at the end of the book: "The search for Truth [literally, reality] I began when I was young continues in old age. . . . I have passed through the labyrinth of human friendship and disregard, and reached the goal of understanding human *being*."[4]

She muzzles herself, to become quite the opposite of the "new woman" she clearly wanted to be when they met. He becomes the "knowing man." How did these radically different positions color their domestic life?

When Akhtar and Hameeda first met in 1935, she was fifteen, getting close to matriculation from the renowned Aligarh Girls' School. He was twenty-three, finishing his master's degree at Aligarh University and already known as an up-and-coming writer and firebrand intellectual.[5]

Their upbringings differed. Akhtar was raised in his mother's household. Despite the strict purdah observed by women in her aristocratic Muslim household in Raipur, central India, she was proficient in Urdu, Hindi, and English, and published in leading women's journals—a woman of considerable literary talent and interests. Her husband, from Patna district in Bihar, employed as an engineer in a government department in Raipur, stayed some distance away from her family home where she lived with the children. The mother died young, when Akhtar was three years old, his older brother six. The father's interaction with his sons decreased further after that. He remarried and took on new commitments; his second wife lived in his family home in Bihar. The children stayed on in his wife's ancestral home. Akhtar grew up thus, as he puts it, "unfamiliar with the feel [*mahaul*, literally, ambience] of 'family life'.... We came to know life not inside, but outside, the home."[6]

Two boys from a relatively well-to-do family, spending time wandering, choosing for themselves from available alternatives outside the home, unfettered (even more than other boys from similar backgrounds) by parental control or discipline—who learned to be comfortable *outside* the home, perhaps less so *inside* it.

Hameeda grew up with five brothers and eight sisters, unconfined by purdah, as she says, in a large and relatively progressive family, also of landed, aristocratic background.[7] Her father, educated in Aligarh, was a larger-than-life figure, police officer and successful detective fiction writer. A house he built in Aligarh, named after his first novel, *Neeli Chhatri*, came to serve as an "overflow" boardinghouse for Muslim students too poor or too erratic to stay in the university's hostels. Through an activist son, the family also became involved with a circle of leftist students and intellectuals. Akhtar was part of that circle, living as a paying guest in a cottage near Hameeda's parents' home—an overflow from the overflow— when the two met and fell in love.

After completing his MA, Akhtar moved far south to the Deccan plateau to work with Maulvi Abdul Haq, *Baba-i-Urdu* (Father of Urdu), the renowned scholar, linguist, editor, and critic who was compiling a definitive Urdu dictionary at the time. From there, Akhtar wrote to Hameeda's father asking for her hand in marriage. Haq, who "adopted" Akhtar as his literary heir (and surrogate son), and Hameeda's leftist older brother, a friend of Akhtar's, were instrumental in persuading Hameeda's father to accept the proposal.[8] The marriage was solemnized in December 1935, a few months after Hameeda and Akhtar first met.

Hameeda details her parents' and elder sisters' concern about the speed of events and the challenges she would face in this marriage. She reports her mother telling her: "The boy is a writer ... every poet, every writer, every artist expects his wife to see the world as he does, to think as he does.... To negotiate the ups and downs of life with such a person is exceedingly hard. And then for a *simple girl* like you it would be impossible."[9] Hameeda's eldest sister—much older than her, widowed, and terminally ill with tuberculosis—is recorded as saying to Akhtar at the wedding, "Isn't it ironic that the *simplest* [least learned, literally, most foolish] of my sisters has fallen to the lot of such a scholar [literally, lover of learning] as you. Perhaps that is God's way of maintaining a balance [*sic*]."[10]

Hameeda's autobiography etches the constraints of her married life sharply. The tricks of memory, ego, and fantasy surely color her narrative, as they do her husband's. Yet, the self-absorption of intellectual men and the strictness of discipline for married women stand out in both accounts. Hameeda's quotations from contemporary letters, and passing references in Akhtar's autobiography, confirm the thrust of her story. More to the point, the particulars of their time together that the two emphasize tell us about their differing expectations of family and intimacy.

By Hameeda's account, Akhtar and his adoptive father, Abdul Haq, paid little attention to her after the wedding on the thirty-six-hour train journey from Orai, two hundred miles south of Aligarh, where her father was posted, to Haq's home in Hyderabad. They slept, woke, ordered meals, read the newspaper, discussed politics, and talked incessantly about the Urdu dictionary they were compiling. At one point, she picked up the paper, but put it down again to look out of the window. By her account, Akhtar commented, "You did the right thing, putting the newspaper away; it would hardly make sense to you. *Yes, do look at the green fields.*"[11] An incredible display of male arrogance, if that was in fact what he said; an astonishing indication of her recollection of their interactions, if it wasn't. A stunning performance of memory in either case.

Hameeda's discomfort continued in Hyderabad. After breakfast each day, the men read their newspapers. At 8:30 a.m. they went into their offices in the men's section of Haq's sprawling house, which she was forbidden to enter. They excluded her from "serious" conversations and their work on the Urdu dictionary. Haq asked her to instruct the cook on the meals to be prepared, and to pay the servants from the money he gave her to keep. She had no experience in these matters. Akhtar offered no help. Shortly after their arrival, the men left for a conference in Madras, leaving her with family friends. As she tells it, Akhtar did not come out of his office even to see her to the car that took her to them. His work was all that mattered to him, she writes: *"my existence is meaningless!"*[12] The phrase reappears several times in her account of the early days of their marriage.

The priority of her husband's work and vaunted independence was on display in later years in the manner of his decision-making at several critical junctures. When Akhtar began to work with Haq, they agreed he could leave as soon as preparation of the dictionary was finished. Haq also promised to help finance a newspaper the younger man hoped to start after that. Fifteen months after Hameeda arrived in Hyderabad, Akhtar decided it was time to move. He informed her, apparently without warning, that they were leaving for Delhi: "My work here is complete." In three days, they packed their belongings and left.[13]

In Delhi, Akhtar struggled for a few months to get a newspaper off the ground. He received some encouraging responses and contributions for the projected publication, but his hopes were dashed in the end by denial of official permission. At this point he decided, again unilaterally, to move: "It is imperative we leave Delhi as soon as possible. *I will need a few days to decide what we do next, and where.*"[14]

Deeply admiring of Akhtar's talents and commitment, Hameeda seems to have done everything she could to advance his intellectual and political ambitions. After the Delhi fiasco, she suggested he go overseas, as other privileged men (and women) had done, to pursue a course of higher studies and improve his prospects. As with permission to publish a newspaper, his application for a passport was initially denied: the Government of India was suspicious of the revolutionary views articulated in his writings. Hameeda seems to have used her father's connections, and other contacts she got from the distinguished Congress leader and poet Sarojini Naidu, whom she came to know in Hyderabad, to obtain passports for the two of them. She may also have helped generate funds for the trip and encouraged Akhtar to write journalistic pieces to cover costs during his doctoral studies in Paris; he chose France for its more intellectual ambience over England, where she had expected he would go, as many other Indian students and political activists had done.[15]

Their first child was born in Europe in 1939. Mother and child returned to India a few months later to allow Akhtar to work without interruption toward quick completion of his PhD. During their year apart, Hameeda claims to have found Akhtar a position in the Government of India's Information Office as officer in charge of translations from Urdu and Hindi for the radio—sending an application and appearing unannounced for an interview on his behalf! Akhtar accepted the position, she tells us, but not before venting his fury at her for thinking he would work for the British, and declaring that her policeman father must have come up with the idea: a reminder of the displeasure of other public figures like Gandhi, Ambedkar, and Sankrityayan, impatient with the world they lived in. "This is what happened throughout our life," writes Hameeda. "In my own imperfect [*ulti-seedhi*, right-or-wrong] way, I would do something for Akhtar, thinking it would please him. But Akhtar's habit of losing his temper never changed."[16]

"An Owl Trapped"

When Hameeda first met Akhtar in Aligarh, she asked him for a copy of his short story "*Zubaan-i-bezubaani*" (The tongue of speechlessness), which she had read in a journal lent by friends. She went on to ask for copies of other stories he was writing. Akhtar, bowled over by the "boldness" and interest of this petite, attractive teenager, rare among girls from respectable Muslim families, began smuggling love notes to her in stories he sent through trusted intermediaries.

And yet, as he began to woo her, his thoughts were interrupted by the self-image of a revolutionary.

"To win your hand," he said in an early (smuggled) letter, "I will not compromise my dignity or sell my conscience. *I am free and so I shall remain.*" They could be together, he wrote, only if she identified not with his person but with his ideals. She should not judge him by a yardstick applied to other men, for he was "indifferent to house and hearth, unconcerned with fame and power . . . wealth or self-interest."[17]

Akhtar's excitement on meeting Hameeda and finding in her a potential life companion seems to have been shadowed by a suspicion of marriage and domesticity. That was how his hero, employer, and adoptive father saw the matter.[18] Haq "accorded Urdu the deference due to one's mother," writes Akhtar. He treated the organization for the promotion of Urdu, of which he was secretary, "with the affection that is reserved for a daughter. Apart from his relationship with them [the organization and project of promotion of Urdu], he had no human bonds."[19] Forced into marriage by his parents, he apparently escaped on the night of the wedding. He never married again. Whenever they passed a wedding procession, Akhtar tells us, Haq would clap his hands and shout, "An owl trapped, an owl trapped."[20]

The "Father of Urdu" found in Akhtar the son and heir he needed to carry on his work. Perhaps that is why he supported his marriage. Akhtar reports overhearing him tell a visitor, "He [Akhtar] has such a [restless] nature that I am scared he may up and leave any day. But now, after his marriage, he can't go anywhere."[21] Domesticity is pushed to the margins, and yet, it is useful: the established way of freeing up space for the work of World History—also called men's work.

In Hameeda's reconstruction, however, Akhtar and Haq's prioritizing of their public, intellectual work was accompanied by a contrary desire. In Hyderabad, she was alone with "two children," as her eldest sister had predicted she would discover them to be—one young, one old.[22] Each sought to make her a confidant, sharing secrets and complaints about the other man/child. Her enterprise soon had them playing badminton and cards, and indulging in other pastimes they derided. They quickly came to cherish Hameeda's presence in the home. There was sheepish acknowledgment of this when they telegraphed from Madras to say they missed her. A few months later, when Hameeda went to see her eldest sister who lay dying in Aligarh, Haq sent Akhtar to fetch her after ten days, insisting she had been away long enough; as it happens, her sister had passed away before Hameeda reached Aligarh.

Akhtar's longing for family and home deepened after he and Hameeda returned from Europe. Back from Paris in the spring of 1940, he worked for the

Indian government's Information Office in Delhi; several other distinguished Urdu writers were working in the same radio broadcasting section. In 1942, he resigned to become vice-principal of the Mohamedan Anglo-Oriental College in Amritsar and editor of a leading Hindi journal, in place of a prominent Hindi writer and political activist he admired, who was jailed for his part in the Quit India uprising against the British. In July 1945, Akhtar moved to the government's Education Department, working from Shimla and Delhi. Hameeda believed he did this for the sake of the children—they had three sons by then, with two more to come—choosing "education" because it kept him in touch with reading and writing.[23]

He continued as an educationist in Pakistan, joining the Education Department after the family's harrowing escape in August 1947, then moving to UNESCO in Paris in 1956. In a notable career, he promoted schooling in lands far and wide, including Somalia, Iran, Pakistan, and several Southeast Asian countries, while still finding time for travel, hiking, and mountaineering. "What dangers did I not face in fulfilling my passion for mountaineering, and my wanderlust," he says in his autobiography, "and how numerous were the abodes I visited in order to satisfy my love for knowledge and art!"[24]

We have little information on what domestic work or physical care of the children Akhtar took on. It is unlikely to have been substantial, if we go by the evidence of other South Asian middle-class men. The reliance on servants for much of the physical exertion—part of domestic arrangements in most middle- and upper-class South Asian families—ensured that men could pretend their wives had little to do, and justified their reluctance to share in domestic tasks.[25] Among the less well-to-do, poorer relatives and other hangers-on took on much of the physical labor. Women were directly involved, if primarily in a supervisory position in upper-class households. The men of the family, especially heads of household and potential successors, rarely shared in the daily grind.

We know that Akhtar was away for most of his eldest son's first year, completing his PhD in Paris. When Hameeda and he lived overseas on UNESCO assignments during the 1950s and '60s, after their move to Pakistan, the older sons were working or in college. Close relatives, including Hameeda's brother, looked after the younger boys. Akhtar did arrange to work several months of the year from Karachi, and the boys spent their summer vacations with their parents, during which Akhtar tried to show them "every inch" of whichever country he was in.[26] For the restless, revolutionary intellectual was a doting father.

"His greatest weakness," Hameeda writes, "was his love for his children. They had only to ask for something, for their desire to be fulfilled." Her older sister put it more strongly: "Despite being so very sensible, Akhtar ... [will] try to snatch the stars from the sky if his children ask him to do so." The education of children, especially of sons, was now seen as an important part of men's domestic duties. Akhtar bought them books (and toys) non-stop, and began storytelling sessions when each child turned "two-and-a-half," lying side by side with the child. The precision seems to fit his character, although it may also reflect Hameeda's imagination at work. He never admonished his sons, she adds, even when he thought they had made serious mistakes and unwise choices.[27] Later in life, he lavished similar stories and affection on nieces and other girls in the domestic circle. Men like Premchand and Rahul Sankrityayan had done the same. But Akhtar's generation seems more involved in the raising of children, intervening in matters that fathers would earlier have left to the elders or to women.

In 1946, Akhtar stepped in to name his fourth son Navaid. Hameeda, in Aligarh for the delivery, had chosen the name Adnan (after Adnan Bey, the Turkish politician, writer, historian, and feminist) to rhyme with those of the first three boys, Kamran, Salman, and Irfan. But Akhtar was tired of names ending in *an*! Hameeda provides details of his "fascination" with the child. "He would have me put Navaid on his bed, take his little hands and feet in his own hands and look at them closely." He predicted that the boy would be a designer of buildings and a musician, and in later years sat listening to his son playing during sitar lessons, "his visage radiant with happiness."[28] In the event, Navaid became an architect and a fine musician. Akhtar would have been proud of his accurate predictions.

In his last years, when he lost his vision, Akhtar still maintained his routine at home. He woke early, strolled on the lawn with a son, had a cup of tea, shaved, bathed, and donned his trousers, shirt, socks, shoes, and watch; then, "punctually at eight o'clock," he sat on the veranda and called for his breakfast. The boys read to him from the English newspaper, *Dawn*, before leaving for work. After they left, Hameeda read from the Urdu paper, *Jang*. (To distract him, she also coaxed him into instructing the cook on the day's menu, pleading her exhaustion with the task. "Akhtar would tell him what went with what. He was particular about food," she writes. Men's interest in food, accompanied by regular advice and criticism, unaccompanied by any part in planning, preparation, or cleaning up, is commonly observed in South Asian homes.) After lunch at one o'clock, the elderly Akhtar retired to his room and fell asleep listening to the radio. At four, "having bathed and changed," he emerged for tea, then took another long walk.[29]

The evening was a time for conversation and laughter in largely homosocial gatherings over which Akhtar presided—in the manner of other successful male heads of household in the subcontinent. "All his life he enjoyed entertaining friends," Hameeda notes. "Whenever they came to our house, I personally cooked the food."[30] Chess, poetry recitations, and political discussions were the heart of these gatherings. In his later years, Akhtar could no longer play chess, but other aspects of this life continued. Most evenings, some acquaintances or his children's friends would join his court. Whoever came was asked to stay to dinner. Hameeda, "pieced together [after] my various operations," as she puts it, "would [sit] on a corner of my divan, listening to the interesting conversation and the . . . [conflicting] viewpoints. Akhtar would [be] like the centerpiece of [the] gathering."[31]

Irfan, their journalist son, read out his articles to his father before sending them to press—and Akhtar "invariably" had suggestions or questions, some of which vexed the young man. Later, when Akhtar had lost all hope of ever recovering his sight and became more depressed, Hameeda made greater efforts to meet his needs. She organized an "open house" for intellectuals and writers once or twice a month, occasions on which a dozen or score of Akhtar's friends, mostly male, would meet and revel in the company. "For many days after each such event, Akhtar would talk about it with pleasure."[32]

In the early 1970s, Akhtar began writing his autobiography. Seven monthly installments appeared in the journal *Afkar*, before a botched operation on the one eye he could still use rendered him blind. "But for the support of my wife [literally, life partner] and sons," he writes, "I would have long been dead." Throughout this time, the desire to complete his autobiography persisted. "For this, the cooperation of some lover of knowledge was needed." He found this in a young male writer, and then in a woman student who came to him for guidance in her doctoral work on Ghalib and "transcribed the rest of the [autobiography] with a great deal of patience and commitment."[33] He never asked his wife to help in the task.

One story, two conundrums. A wife committed to her husband yet far from satisfied with the confined domestic place allotted to her. A husband armed with unquestioned clarity about his right to make all major decisions, along with a wanderlust, a yearning for new adventures that would fulfill his inner soul and search for knowledge, living with his family, increasingly dependent on its support, but unable to fully acknowledge the fact.

Some of these themes reappear in the family history of the police officer Akbar Mirza and his wife Khurshid Mirza (née Jahan), although Akbar was far removed from intellectual or political work, and his wife's career as an actress was more obviously affected, indeed suspended for a quarter of a century, in large part because of her husband's discouragement.

"My Baby Darling"

We are handicapped in this instance by the absence of a first-person account from Akbar. But Khurshid's detailed, elegant, energetic, layered, and self-contradictory memoir gives us a fair sense of her own and her husband's ambitions, hopes, and frustrations. The two met in 1932. He was twenty-three and already a police officer, she a fourteen-year-old schoolgirl studying in the Aligarh Girls' School, founded by her parents. Three of Akbar's sisters studied in the same school: the youngest played a leading part in facilitating the match of her classmate Khurshid and her police-officer brother. Akbar and Khurshid married less than two years later, in 1934. They were together until his death in 1971, initially in different districts of the north Indian province of Uttar Pradesh, and then, after Partition, in various parts of West Pakistan, where he rose to the rank of assistant inspector-general of police in Quetta. They had three daughters, two within the first two years of their marriage and a third in 1939.

Khurshid was a loving spouse, fulfilling her duties as the wife of a respected police officer in far-flung districts of India and Pakistan with panache. Unusually, especially for a woman from a well-known elite Muslim family, she also gained success in her early twenties as an actor, singer, and dancer in the Bombay film world. She gave up her film career in 1944, at the height of her popularity, for reasons I address below. Later, long after she moved to Pakistan with her husband and children, she had a notable career as a leading radio and television artiste, gaining considerable prominence in the years after Akbar's death in 1971.

Akbar came from a business family that had moved to the north Indian plains from the northwest of undivided India (now Pakistan). The men—proud of their Central Asian roots and Pathan inheritance, tall, fair, independent, un-bending, "manly"—continued in business. Akbar, one of nine siblings, four brothers and five sisters, was the exception in choosing a career in government.

Khurshid was one of seven siblings, five sisters and two brothers. At a time when not many Muslim men were willing to let wives and daughters out of purdah, she tells us, her parents insisted that all the children be educated. They enforced strict purdah in their school and hostel to reassure parents hesitant about sending their girls to school, but were more flexible at home. Khurshid reports her mother saying to her father, "I am in purdah and shall observe it in front of your friends till the day I die. Maybe, the elder girls will have to wear a burqa in Aligarh but these two younger ones [Khurshid and her younger sister] never will."[34]

The three older sisters distinguished themselves in public life as intellectuals, activists, and educationists. Khurshid, the second youngest, was the anarchist:

creative, talented, "with too much energy and life in her," as a nephew of hers put it, to be quite like her "serious" elder sisters, with their intellectual and political commitments.[35]

Khurshid met Akbar in 1932, when she, her mother, and her younger sister visited her eldest sister, the famous writer and medical practitioner Rashid Jahan, then working in Lucknow. A whirlwind romance and marriage followed. Through the three months of that summer vacation, Akbar arranged outings and horse-riding trips for the girls. "When he saw me ready to jump from the saddle, he would invariably catch me before I hit the ground," Khurshid writes. "It made me feel quite fragile and feminine." "It was as if I was transformed from a boy into a girl in one fell swoop," she said in an interview in 1975.[36] For she was very much the tomboy at school, leader and organizer of many games, sports, and dramatic events.

The anglicized police officer—educated in a Methodist school in the foothills of the Himalayas, an inter-college athletics champion, keen sportsman and hunter—showed passionate interest in her. He smuggled notes into books he lent her to read, and on one occasion his photograph inscribed in English, "For my Baby Darling."[37] His parents sent her parents a marriage proposal soon after. The engagement was announced the day Khurshid finished her high school examination in 1933. Akbar now visited Aligarh frequently, sometimes with his mother, pushing for an early marriage. When he visited, Khurshid writes, "he was very unlike an ideal son-in-law. . . . He wished to be with me all the time which was not possible, so he sulked."[38] They married in February 1934, after Khurshid completed a one-year home sciences course in Delhi instead of the four-year college degree her parents preferred.

Akbar saw himself as a no-nonsense officer, self-sufficient and modern. He was stationed in remote districts in India, and later in Pakistan, in places where he had little in the way of a desired peer group. Khurshid's dynamism, energy, and sparkle enchanted him. "Worldly-wise" husband and dreamy teenaged wife began life together in the "backward" eastern Uttar Pradesh district of Azamgarh, where he was deputy superintendent of police, socializing regularly at the Officers' Club. She played tennis until the discomforts of pregnancy made her stop. Akbar continued with his days at work and evenings at the club, while Khurshid read books from the club's library and supervised the servants at home. She organized a "Fancy Dress" evening at the "purdah (women's only) club," in which many purdah-observing women enthusiastically participated, and the couple attended service at an Australian Mission Church "whenever we felt like an outing," after which the pastor and his wife "invariably invited us to a simple dinner."[39]

Khurshid reconstructs those early years as years of romance. In Gorakhpur, where the couple next moved, Akbar and Khurshid, led by a member of the elite Indian Civil Service and his wife, would drive to friends' houses "after everyone had gone to bed, honking and singing, persuading them to join them in a wild drive through the town," sometimes in convoys of three or four cars. In Saharanpur, his next posting, Akbar taught her to shoot with a .38 revolver, so she could protect herself and the children (they had two daughters by then) from dangerous animals including snakes that appeared in the vicinity. "Without telling him, I always carried that trusted little weapon in my purse when we went big game hunting, in case Akbar's rifle jammed."[40]

Their first child was born in 1935, the year following their marriage. They were still in Azamgarh, and the teenaged Khurshid was ready to have the baby in the Mission hospital. At Akbar's insistence, however, she returned three months before the delivery to her parents' home in the "advanced" town of Aligarh: they had electricity there! She stayed two months after the child's birth, partly because Akbar was looking for appropriate accommodation in the new district he had been posted to, Gorakhpur. During those months, she recalls, he missed her terribly: "A man who said he hated writing letters was now sending four to six page letters practically every day, pouring out his loneliness and heartbreak at this forced separation."[41]

Khurshid's memoir says little about what Akbar did at home in the normal course of domestic life. But we can guess the distribution of work. With government housing and perks, including servants' quarters, barns for livestock, and land for crops and fruit trees, much of the labor performed by servants, and Khurshid taking on all the supervision and planning, there was little he would have to do. Other stray bits of evidence fill out the picture.

Akbar was absent from the birth of their first child, having sent Khurshid to Aligarh for the delivery: out of a fear of hospitals, concern that his wife receive the best medical support she could get, or some combination of the two? The infant lived with them in Gorakhpur, a bigger administrative center on the Nepal border north of Azamgarh, with its large contingent of Indian officers. A second daughter was born there. Khurshid tells us that Akbar began staying out longer, playing poker and bridge late into the night. She attributes his changed behavior to the Indian officers whose circle he joined. Their lifestyle was "totally different from ours." These officers married early, she writes (suggesting perhaps that they were even younger than she was at the time of marriage), had little interest in women's education, and "accepted the joint family as a norm, where the male members were entitled to do as they pleased," as long the women were clothed and fed.[42] Fortunately, she adds, Akbar was soon allotted a house in another locality where they found "like-minded" friends.

Around this time, an older brother of Khurshid died in Aligarh, succumbing to kidney failure at the age of twenty-one. Khurshid and Akbar sent their second daughter, then six weeks old, to comfort Khurshid's devastated mother. They succeeded in lifting her spirits. Parting from the infant may have suited Akbar and Khurshid too. Regarding 1936 and 1937, Khurshid writes, "I had a responsible woman to look after Shabnam [the older daughter] and could safely leave her at home when I accompanied Akbar on hunting trips but, on longer tours, she came along." Or again, of 1939, when she entered the Bombay film world and their third daughter was born, "I was in excellent health *except for the occasional miscarriage* brought on by my hectic lifestyle, running off to accompany my husband on shikar [hunting expeditions], or playing strenuous tennis at the club."[43]

Khurshid's concealment of any pain or anguish in her miscarriages is at one with the society's naturalizing of women's suffering in childbirth and labor. Her reconstruction of her husband's reaction to her career in films is more contradictory. While Akbar openly expressed his love and concern for Khurshid, the dynamics of their relationship were complicated. He wanted her by his side all the time; and, as the *man*, he took the decisions—how late he stayed out at work or with friends, where she delivered their first child, whether she should pursue a career. The history of her connection with Bombay films illustrates the point well.

In 1939, an older brother and sister-in-law working in the film industry, who knew of Khurshid's interest in acting from her schooldays, introduced her to the manager of a major Bombay studio. The latter invited Khurshid and Akbar to visit: a paid holiday, with no strings attached. Akbar intercepted and read the letter addressed to her—something he did often—and refused outright. He relented when his boss, the police superintendent of the district where he was stationed, noted that Sir Richard Temple (a top-rank colonial official and the queen's cousin) was a managing director of the studio. Over the next five years, Khurshid appeared in several films and established herself as a presence in the industry. Her husband regularly laid down boundaries. In 1944, she retired, in part it seems because of an ultimatum from Akbar, in part because of questions her parents faced about a respectable (*sharif*) Muslim woman's involvement in films and her own sense of guilt that her daughters might feel neglected. "Akbar maintained a strange attitude towards my work," Khurshid writes in retrospect: "He enjoyed the benefits the money brought us.... He was supportive of my work in the cinema even in the face of opposition from his family and mine.... Yet he treated my work as a hobby, instead of giving it its due importance.... How does one explain the selfishness of a beloved husband who has to be reassured all the time that he has the priority in his wife's life, despite her professional commitments?"[44]

If someone has a *calling* here, it is Khurshid. Yet, she gives up her calling for the sake of her husband's career and his ego. The divergence in their outlook and temperaments led to somewhat different consequences in the Pakistani chapter of their lives.

Uprooted Lives

Romance and marriage involved periodic "uprootings" in Khurshid and Akbar's lives, in the form of official transfers.[45] A more obvious uprooting came with the family's migration from India to Pakistan in 1947. Like other Muslim civil and military officers, Akbar had to choose at this time between staying on in India or transferring to the Pakistani police. At the time, he was awaiting confirmation of his recommended promotion from the provincial Uttar Pradesh police to the national Indian Police Service. Unclear about the future, he took fourteen days' "casual leave" six weeks after the official Partition, and flew with Khurshid and their three daughters to Karachi. In the Pakistani capital, he received assurances of appointment at a senior rank with good prospects. He was allotted government housing, into which he shifted his and his elder brother's family before returning to India to resign.[46]

We do not know the extent of discussion between Akbar and Khurshid before he made the decision to move. Partition brought great uncertainty. No one knew what the relationship between the two new states—or indeed exactly where the national borders—would be. The violence, migrations, and chaotic attempt to divide the British Indian military and police into two, amid a crumbling colonial authority and the desperation of many British officials to get out, meant that little went according to plan. Perhaps Akbar and Khurshid believed, like many others, that the violence of the moment would pass, and people with family on both sides would be able to come and go as before.[47] Akbar's decision to migrate was bolstered by the fact that all his natal family—mother, grandmother, brothers and sisters, nieces and nephews—moved to Pakistan. Thirty-four of them were in a Victoria Road flat in Karachi when Akbar, Khurshid, and their children arrived on October 4, 1947. Khurshid accepted her husband's choice, although she was the only member of her natal family to move to Pakistan and clung to a sense of Aligarh as "home" throughout her life.[48]

Akbar's career was set back. He was unhappy with his first appointment in Hyderabad, Sindh, at a rank lower than he had held in India. His next posting brought little relief: he had worked chiefly in districts where civil servants lived and worked in their own little world and couldn't handle what he saw as the corruption and machinations of senior officials and political leaders in the Pakistani capital, Karachi. Downcast, "he started playing bridge with friends that gave him some measure of relief," writes Khurshid, "but, unfortunately, he got involved in poker and started losing big money." Ultimately, in 1953, fed up with the pressures he faced in the nation's capital, he asked for a transfer to the faraway city of Quetta, "where he could live in peace with his conscience."[49]

Their small family faced financial difficulties. They had lost the support of their wide social network in India. Akbar inherited a large sum at the death of his businessman father in 1946 while they were still in undivided India. He invested much of this along with earnings from Khurshid's films in shares, about which he knew little. He laughed off her advice to put a substantial amount in fixed deposits for each of their daughters. What remained from his ill-advised investments was "wiped out by the division of India," writes Khurshid. Overall, by her estimate, they lost over a hundred thousand rupees.[50] She sold pieces of her jewelry, wrote film reviews for a leading newspaper, and set up a one-woman advertising agency to promote Max Factor products licensed to a South African businessman who was their neighbor, to help pay bills.[51]

Khurshid had reinvented herself in their new country. She plunged into social and political service and volunteered for the National Guard, impelled by the violence against minority communities on both sides of the border, the suffering of refugees, and clashes between Indian and Pakistani forces in Kashmir. She was by Akbar's side at public functions, and commuted the long distance between Karachi and Quetta for a whole year after he moved there. Women were responding to "the challenge of nation-building," she writes. "We wanted to proclaim to the world that we were 'soldiers' of Pakistan."[52]

Through her work, she also kept her creative side alive. She built an archive of folk songs, collected from old women refugees from her home state of Uttar Pradesh in India; wrote talk shows and plays for Radio Pakistan and played parts in them (from 1951); and produced the first TV play in Pakistan (1956), using a TV unit installed by the United States Information Service at an international exhibition in Karachi. When Akbar retired in 1968, she resumed radio and TV work in Karachi. However, it was only after his death in 1971 that she returned full-time to TV performances, becoming "one of Pakistan's best-known television characters."[53]

Akbar, in turn, did everything he could for his wife and daughters. Aware how much Khurshid missed her father, siblings, and other relatives in India, he arranged for her to visit Aligarh regularly. A loving husband and father, he expressed his love more through gifts and outings than in everyday tasks like playing with the children, nursing, handling, comforting, or even tutoring them.[54] In Pakistan, the older girls were sent to boarding school and then to college, so they wouldn't suffer each time Akbar was transferred. Later, Khurshid took the lead in arranging their marriages. She was also the primary caregiver for the youngest daughter, born with Down syndrome, who passed away in December 1954, when Akbar was probably in faraway Quetta. After the child's death, Khurshid moved from Karachi to Quetta to be with him.

Akbar's paternalistic mode of caring for family, inherited from older generations, showed in diverse ways. In 1953, he took a government loan to build a house for his wife and daughters in Karachi, "Khurshid Villa," though the family had barely moved in when he left for Quetta. He built another home on a farm just outside Quetta in 1955, named "Sumbulistan" (the land/home of Sumbul, the daughter they lost the year before). In 1968, when his health took a turn for the worse, he worried that their Karachi home was too large for Khurshid to manage on her own, persuaded her to move to a smaller cottage near a shopping center, and invested the savings to provide her some financial security after his death.[55]

Akbar did not manage to reinvent himself in Pakistan to quite the same extent as Khurshid. While he withdrew into himself and brooded more, old patterns persisted. In 1964, when he took leave preparatory to retirement, he and Khurshid went to Europe on holiday. His health was declining, and he needed greater care, which Khurshid provided. In London, she wanted to visit the BBC to speak with Pakistani and Indian journalist acquaintances about a play she was writing. Akbar "refused to take me there or allow me to use the Tube [the underground railway]," she writes.[56] Khurshid was then forty-six, a grandmother, and a widely traveled and accomplished woman. To the end of his life, her husband seemed to believe that work was not for women, that *he* was the queen bee, and that he had to protect his innocent wife.

Who in this forward-looking generation of men and women was allowed a calling, and who made the sacrifices? The question surfaces again in the marital history of our third male protagonist, Harivansh Rai Bachchan. It is a particularly instructive example, since Bachchan's exhaustive reconstruction of his life and loves delineates the contradictions of men's domestic commitments even more sharply than the life stories of Akhtar and Akbar.

Dreams and Despondency

I have sketched Bachchan's family background in chapters 1 and 2. Born and raised in a materially less comfortable lower-middle-class milieu than the Mirzas and Raipuris, he rose to become a well-known poet, university teacher, special officer in the central government of independent India appointed at the behest of the country's first prime minister (whom he knew from their shared hometown of Allahabad), and later a nominated member of the upper house of Parliament from 1966 to 1972. From his teenage years, the halcyon days of anti-colonial campaigns led by Gandhi, he challenged many of the narrow religious and caste injunctions of his family and wider kin community. His poems "questioned the ritual and the authority of temple and mosque; they scorned the power of the wealthy and they rose above caste and religious difference," writes one commentator.[57] Both his marriages demonstrated his idealism.

The first occurred in 1926, when he was still living with his parents. He was eighteen, his bride, Shyama, fourteen. Despite his family's straitened circumstances, he insisted that the wedding be solemnized simply, with no demand for dowry from the girl's family. Unfortunately, as I have noted, the couple were together only a week after their marriage before Shyama went back to her natal home in another part of Allahabad to care for her tubercular mother and the rest of the family. As the oldest daughter, that was her duty. She returned occasionally, and briefly, to her husband's home after her mother died in 1929. Diagnosed with TB herself, and requiring medical attention, she lived mainly at her father's until her death in 1936.

Bachchan married again of his own choice when he was thirty-five, six years after Shyama's passing. His second bride, Teji Suri, a strikingly handsome woman from an aristocratic Sikh family who taught psychology in Fatehchand College, Lahore, was twenty-eight, and came from a different caste, religion, and province. One of his poems reads:

Tell them an inner flame has burned all those sacred books, my love
Should anyone ask the caste of lovers.[58]

It was a rewarding marriage. They were together for the next sixty years, until his death in 2003. Teji sacrificed her career, took care of every household responsibility, including the upbringing of their two sons, and gave Bachchan all the freedom and support he needed to realize his ambitions as an intellectual, a poet, and a man. I focus the following discussion of Bachchan's domestic being on what he tells us about his life with Teji. However, a few words about earlier romantic, emotional, and sexual entanglements are necessary for context.

Bachchan's autobiography reconstructs his inner life as one torn between a poet's need for solitude, indeed suffering, and a man's search for intimacy. "Already from my adolescence," he proclaims, "woman had become a part of my life, an indispensable need, irrespective of whether she caused joy or sorrow, made me agitated or gave me peace, became for me a problem—or a solution."[59] Apart from his marriages, he records several other life-changing encounters with women. I refer to three of these, alongside his two marriages.[60]

First is a brief but uncontainable involvement in his midteens with Champa, who was married for a tragically short time to Bachchan's non-kin "brother" and closest friend, Karkal, three and a half years older than him. When they married, Karkal told Champa about his beloved "twin," from whom he was inseparable. She welcomed their closeness, and from the start, Bachchan spent as much time with her as her husband. Each rushed to her side after schoolwork or other errands, sometimes to find the other had got there before him! Bachchan notes the "intensity and depth" of feelings they experienced, and the attraction, tension, and confusion they endured.[61]

Bachchan's romantic recollections of women transport him into a world of beauty and anguish. His first "real" vision of Champa, "in a blue saree, on the rooftop," leads not only to love and infatuation but to apperception of a kind of divinity. He compares her to John Keats's nightingale, the "light-winged Dryad of the trees," which disappears suddenly.[62] The teenagers' longings ended in a tragic sequence of events: his beloved brother's premature death, from a fever he developed after being caught in a rainstorm; Bachchan's spending all his time with Champa in the months of unbearable mourning that followed; her pregnancy resulting from their "involuntary coming together"; a pilgrimage to the hills organized by Champa's mother-in-law, in search of abortion and penance; and Champa's death from the physical exertions of the trip.[63]

Bachchan met Champa one last time when she returned from the two-month-long trip. His account of the meeting provides a disturbing example of the equation of "woman" with "mother" as well as object of desire. Champa looked aged, wasted, and blank, a bundle of skin and bones, with big, vacant eyes. While she was away, Bachchan had taken his high school exam and—predictably in his father's and perhaps his own view—failed. When the teenaged Bachchan told her, Champa, younger than him, offered solace: "The fault is mine. But I have been through the mill of repentance." She told him she had prayed for him in every shrine and every holy river or stream she entered. "You go now. Go back to school; study hard. . . . You will live long and achieve much." The autobiographer sums up the encounter as follows: "I felt as if Champa had become the age of my mother. She is speaking to me as a mother to her son. I bowed to her like a son and left for school."[64]

Within a couple of years, Bachchan's parents got him married, hoping that marriage would rescue their son from his melancholia. Bachchan saw his bride, Shyama, as a fourteen-year-old, guileless child, in contrast to himself—experienced and weary at eighteen. She brought to his mind Percy Bysshe Shelley's skylark: "an unbodied joy whose race is just begun."[65] The poem bears fuller quotation:

With thy keen joyance
Languor cannot be:
Shadow of annoyance
Never came to thee:
Thou lovest: but ne'er knew love's sad satiety.[66]

Through the years of marriage she spent in her parents' home, taking care of her mother and herself, he tells us, Shyama never dwelled on her suffering—or her desires. Bachchan named her Joy. She, in turn, called him Suffering, on account of all he told her about his sorrows.[67] Her death in 1936 was inevitably a tragic loss.

Three years later, some friends from Bachchan's poetry-reading sessions introduced the self-described lost and lonely poet to Iris, a woman of mixed, possibly Anglo-Indian background, whose father had converted from Hinduism to Islam and then to Christianity. Bachchan was fascinated by the tall, high-cheeked, blue-eyed, long-haired blonde woman, who was training in Allahabad to become a schoolteacher. They met periodically over the next two years. Mutual attraction seemed to grow, and Bachchan proposed to her. Iris turned him down, in his view because of fear of her parents' likely reaction.[68] There was another heartrending fallout for Bachchan. His father, apparently overcome by shock when Bachchan told him he'd decided to become a Christian to marry Iris, wilted overnight. He died a few days later, perhaps believing—more tragically still—that Bachchan had given up Iris on account of his, the father's, sadness.[69]

The painful Iris episode proved beneficial in the end, Bachchan writes. It saved him both from suicide and from falling into other temptations, among them, he suggests, the numerous young (as well as not-so-young) women swooning over his poetry recitations.[70] More to the point, perhaps, it led, on the rebound as it were, although he does not say this, to his second marriage, with the woman of his life—"Goddess! mother! companion! love! all in one."[71]

Less than two months after the death of his father, the friends who had introduced Bachchan to Iris invited him to spend New Year's Eve with them in Bareilly, 275 miles northwest of Allahabad. They also invited Teji Suri. Four years earlier, Teji had accepted engagement, on her widowed father's initiative, to an Oxford-educated man from another distinguished Sikh family of their native Lahore. The chemistry wasn't right, and after her father left Lahore to live nearer one of his older daughters, Teji ended the engagement. The wife among their host couple in Bareilly, who was principal of the college where Teji taught, hoped Teji and Bachchan might hit it off. They did, spectacularly!

Within twenty-four hours of their meeting, they were betrothed. The hosts asked Bachchan to ring in the New Year with a reading of his poems, especially one he had recited on his arrival that December 31, 1941, morning: *"kya karoon samvedna lekar tumhari . . . ?"* (What can I possibly do with your commiseration?) As he recited it again, and his voice faltered, tears welled up and fell from Teji's eyes; when the others quietly left the room late at night, Teji and Bachchan were weeping openly, in each other's arms.

The poet turns to the nineteenth-century Scottish novelist Robert Louis Stevenson to explain their union: "Love should run out to meet love with open arms . . . like a pair of children venturing together into a dark room. From the first moment when they see each other, with a pang of curiosity, through stage after stage of growing pleasure and embarrassment, they can read the expression of their own trouble in each other's eyes."[72] The next four days passed in a trance, writes Bachchan. He was with Teji all the time—sharing their pasts, arousing her compassion. She decided she would resign her Lectureship in Lahore and reach Allahabad by mid-January to marry him: standard practice in terms of who made the sacrifices. When they returned to their respective cities to prepare for the move, Bachchan was in disbelief, with nothing to assure him it wasn't a dream except the luggage she'd left for him to take to his home. Within a month, they married in a simple civil wedding ceremony in Allahabad, for which they paid from their savings. To live, as they say, "happily ever after."

It is time to examine some of the terms of that happiness.

A Poet's Dreams

In the months following their wedding in January 1942, the couple settled into new routines. Teji met Bachchan's family and wider community. With Bachchan and his nephew (the only other resident) often out of the house, she spent the days talking with her mother-in-law. She gave the older woman the gift of recorded music—through her father's "old-fashioned free-standing" Victorian gramophone, which she brought from Lahore. "As I came home from the university," writes Bachchan, "I would hear music drifting down the road," recordings of devotional recitations and *bhajans* sung by leading singers that not only inspired many of Bachchan's poems but "brought Mother a great inner peace [and] won Teji a place in Mother's heart."[73]

After their sons were born—Amitabh (who became the reigning idol of the Bombay screen in the 1970s) in October 1942, and Ajitabh (a successful executive and businessperson, who managed Amitabh's film career for a while) in May 1947—Teji was, in Bachchan's view, transformed by her maternal instinct.[74] The children now had top priority. She gave up the master's course she had started to qualify for a teaching job in Allahabad University, fearing it was leading to the neglect of her firstborn, even as she continued to manage a daunting array of tasks—housework, daily purchases, building their social circle, acting, teaching school for a while, organizing for the local branch of the All-India Women's Conference. It was symptomatic of her wide-ranging commitments that she rushed to the nearby district courts to provide first aid to injured students in a student-police standoff during the Quit India movement of 1942, when she was pregnant with their first child.

Through this blissful time, Bachchan devoted himself to his teaching and poetry. Yet, a peculiar restlessness persisted. In 1943, the year after their marriage and the birth of their first child, Bachchan joined the university's Officer Training Corps, established to aid in Britain's World War II campaign. That summer and the next, he took university student cadets to two-month-long summer camps. In the summer of 1945, not long after the deaths of Teji's father and his own mother, he went away for an eight-week training course for volunteer officers like himself. In 1952, when their second child was about to turn five, a series of lucky breaks enabled him to go to Cambridge. He spent the next two and a quarter years there, completing his PhD, while Teji looked after their home and the children.

Having chosen the genre of candid autobiography, Bachchan asks himself why he needed such escape. For the first time in his life, he notes, he was in a happy and stable marriage. He had a comfortable home with an accomplished, handsome, loving wife and two little boys, who had no one to support them in Allahabad but himself. In addition, the family was now financially comfortable. "What craziness then possessed me that made military training imperative?"[75] His ruminations are noteworthy.

Throughout his autobiography, Bachchan emphasizes the "feminine" side of his personality. The feminine aspect and the poetic instinct are central to his views of himself as a man: at bottom, he may have seen them as one and the same. His first wife, Shyama, had bestowed on him the name "Suffering." He embraced the name. It fit well with his self-image as a brooding, pensive poet: "a poet is suffering incarnate."[76]

Bachchan pleads helplessness in the face of his "inner desires [literally, character]." The struggles of the preceding eighteen years had made him incapable of resting, or appreciating comfort and softness. He felt an unseen urge to find "something I could fight with, be hurt by, overcome . . . something I could wrestle with, even without victory or defeat." He wonders whether all of this flowed from a fear that he was not man enough. He describes Teji as the "man" in his life, perhaps too conveniently. She took charge of everything, dominated him fully, he writes—even as she did all the housework, took care of the children, and handled every attendant responsibility. "From a psychological point of view, it would be only natural for me, faced by the 'inner man' in Teji, to become more conscious of the 'inner woman' in myself, and to seek to negate it.... Perhaps my subconscious sought to awaken the man in me by leading me into military dress."[77]

The memoirist does not mention the idea of the runaway father, or the resistance to being tied down by the daily round of domestic work and care, very much in evidence in the attitude of men in South Asia and elsewhere. We may add another persistent desire: the need to be free, independent. Rarely is this desire connected with an idea that boys and men imbibe from childhood, the sense that homes take care of themselves—or at least, that women, homemakers, will take care of them—and the resulting belief that the domestic, like other arenas of emotional engagement, requires no more than partial commitment from men.

Domesticity and the "Man" Question

Many "old" beliefs regarding the natural inheritances of men and women, their innate qualities, roles, and responsibilities, followed the Indian middle classes of the Independence generation into their new professional, political, and social locations. The primacy of men's careers continued to be seen as necessary and natural. The nitty-gritty and daily grind of domesticity remained the charge of women: this was *their* domain, tied to their natural inclination and talent as homemakers, caregivers, mothers. The men had different obligations. Husbands, and heads of households, were to provide for the family—wives, children, aging parents, servants, and other relatives, whoever was included—and to guide, care for, and make all important decisions for their wives and dependents.

Some of these inheritances had to be preserved, it was claimed, for the preservation of the rich society and culture of South Asia. The new man—or the aspirational new man—was the middle-class professional; the new woman was his educated companion, still bound by domesticity. The relationships of Akbar with Khurshid and Bachchan with Teji appear at first sight to buck the trend. Yet, the convenience of living with a woman who needed little guidance or protection did not affect the equation, or our male protagonists' deep-seated beliefs about men's and women's fundamental nature and needs. Underlying all this was the paradoxical conceit that men were, at heart, radically independent—people who could do without domestic ties, whatever the evidence to the contrary.[78]

What surfaces once more is the modern (middle-class) male fantasy of a categorical division between the "home" and the "world," the "private" realm of the family and the "public" realm of world history. The latter—the time and space of the society of the future—loomed large in the lives of the professional men centered in this chapter, determined to change themselves and their worlds. What this commitment did not affect significantly was their engagement in the everyday—the time and space of the domestic—except to the extent that, in that spatio-temporal domain too, men's concern with rewriting the "world" often had priority.

Nevertheless, as this chapter should have shown, the contradictory pulls of freedom and discipline, and the imbalance between the demand of unfettered freedom for men and disciplined freedom for others, generated new kinds of tension in the modern family. I return to a fuller discussion of these issues in Part III of this book. Before that, I need to say something about the majority of the Indian people, working men and women, for whom the character of the home and the world, the new man and the new woman, was rather differently ordered.

5. Dignity

Ours is a battle for reclamation of human personality which
has been suppressed and mutilated by the Hindu Social System.
— B. R. AMBEDKAR

❊ ❊ ❊

The history of domestic structures and relationships takes on a very different aspect when we move from the world of privileged and relatively comfortable elites to that of the subordinated and stigmatized, that is to say, the majority of the laboring poor in South Asia. What we find here is an alternative perspective on the supposedly discrete spaces called the home and the world, the allegedly separate universes and responsibilities of men and women, and underlying discourses of lineage, culture, tradition, honor—terms that in India always imply cleaving to the existing order.

The preceding chapters have indicated the fluidity of boundaries between the domestic and the wider public world in modern South Asia. Even for those counted among the middle and upper classes, playgrounds, parks, bazaars, schools, places of worship, and celebrations of festivals and marriages were spaces into which domestic concerns extended in important ways. Women, men, boys, and girls from different households and social groups interacted across walls and partitions, on the ground and on rooftops, sharing intimate information, gossip, food, friendship, and dreams. "Respectable" individuals and families sought to discipline the morals and manners of lower-caste and lower-class inhabitants in their neighborhoods.

For the laboring poor, the boundaries were far less clearly marked, far more permeable. For them, the neighborhood was, and is, in a tangible sense, the home. The local community, *basti, mohalla*, is "family."[1] Domestic activities overflow the confines of their cramped huts and tenements and continue in town and village streets and squares. Men and boys sleep, and to a large extent live, outside traditionally recognized domestic space. At the same time, the four corners of working people's improvised dwellings mark a place not only of retreat but also of paid as well as unpaid labor—though the payment might be no more than a pittance.

Through the later nineteenth and the twentieth centuries, growing numbers of upper-caste and upper-class nationalists, reformers, and thinkers spoke of a divide between private and public, inner and outer, the personal and the political. They equated these domains, consciously or unconsciously, with the future time and space of World History—as against the gritty time/space of the present. In the same breath, many of them declared the rules of the domestic, of everyday space and time, to be an invaluable inheritance—one that had to be preserved, albeit admitting of some reform. The Dalit struggle, with that of other sections of the working classes, was, by contrast, emphatically future-oriented. Their call for an overhaul of the existing order could not be compromised by casual assertions of the satisfactory state of life in the existing domestic world. Let me spell out the context.

Working people's struggles for radical change acquired significant new dimensions in the colonial and postcolonial period. Individuals and communities belonging to the lower castes and classes had long employed a host of methods to combat the humiliating material, social, and cultural circumstances of their existence. When they could, they voted with their feet to escape famine, war, and other conditions of intensified oppression; moved to other regions where missionaries or rulers had opened up new avenues of employment or settlement; sought shelter in new religious environments. Many gathered around protestant and anti-caste movements in the Indic pantheon: Bhakti *sants* (preaching the idea of direct access of every true worshipper to a divinity that knew no distinctions of caste), the *warkari sampradaya* (tradition of wandering mendicants or pilgrims), and the Sikh *panth* (or pathway), among them. Others embraced more unfamiliar names and identities in religions such as Christianity and Islam, deemed "foreign" by Hindu spokespersons even though they were part of the tapestry of India since the early centuries after Christ and the Prophet Muhammad. Colonial and postcolonial dislocations and developments greatly magnified these exertions among the subordinated classes, giving them not only added momentum but also a new scale and intensity.[2]

In the transformed setting, as D. R. Nagaraj puts it in a discussion of the Dalit movement, "the idea of an exodus . . . [of] escape from persecution and a journey towards a Promised Land" took on new meanings.[3] This included significant efforts on the part of subaltern groups to opt out *en masse* from religious traditions that upheld the caste order. The massive conversion of Dalits who followed Ambedkar's lead in embracing Buddhism in 1956, numbers that have multiplied manifold in the decades since then, is perhaps the best-known example. But there were many others.[4] The move to "convert" was accompanied by other novel kinds of lower-caste and -class assertion. Among these were attempts at Sanskritization (drawing up new, illustrious caste histories and adopting upper-caste practices and rituals) and Westernization (adopting English ways, language, and education) as means of upward social mobility. All of this was accompanied by determined efforts to move out of the "backward" countryside into the more anonymous towns and cities, and to obtain a formal education that could open up access to new jobs and lifestyles.[5]

Nagaraj sums up the historical tendency evocatively: "The Promised Land is now the modern city."[6] The city—the Promised Land—had diverse implications. Recall the careers of members of the lowest castes and classes who found avenues of employment and upward mobility through recruitment in the colonial army and its ancillary institutions: Ambedkar's and Jagjivan Ram's forebears, discussed in chapter 3, provide good examples. The erosion of some opportunities in the later nineteenth century with the colonial embrace of notions of martial, agricultural, and criminal castes (communities whose character and occupations were supposedly predetermined by birth, as the most reactionary supporters of the caste system, and now the colonial regime, declared) was a blow to many among the downtrodden. Leaders of Ambedkar's Mahar community were particularly disturbed by the disbandment of the Mahar regiment in the army. Yet, other possibilities emerged. Increased mobility, and industrial and urban expansion, meant new job opportunities and new horizons. And an unexpected new vision appeared—the idea of education as a magic wand, a guaranteed route to freedom, self-respect, and dignity.

In the pages that follow, I examine the implications of these radically altered conditions and possibilities, and of the new political awareness among the working classes, for the domestic lives of individuals and families from disprivileged backgrounds. For this purpose, I turn to the rich archive of Dalit reminiscences, autobiographies, and autobiographical fiction that appeared in the late twentieth century, part of the literary and political renaissance spawned by the Ambedkarite movement. As in the case of the memoirs from higher-status Hindus and Muslims that I have used in earlier chapters, this evidence too comes from the pens of educated and broadly middle-class individuals: professionals, writers, bureaucrats, and "housewives." It is worth noting, however, that the educated Dalits' concern with the future leads to an unusual engagement with the past. The new breed of Dalit intellectuals focus attention on the lives of their forebears, reconstruct the places in which they and their parents grew up, and write (often programmatically) about the conditions of their depressed castes and communities. In the process, they underline their view of the changes that must be made, and have already in some measure begun to be made, in the wretchedness inherited from earlier times.

Several of the writings I work with, and the individuals and families centered in them, have been introduced already: among them, the autobiographies of Kausalya Baisantri (b. 1926), Baby Kamble (b. 1929), Omprakash Valmiki (b. 1950), and Narendra Jadhav (b. 1953).[7] Along with these writings, I introduce another remarkable memoir not discussed so far: the autobiography of Vasant Moon (1932–2002), born and raised in a working-class slum in the industrial city of Nagpur, central India, who became a midlevel bureaucrat and the distinguished editor of the multivolume collected works of Dr. B. R. Ambedkar, commissioned by the government of Maharashtra.[8] I supplement these sources with contemporary reports and scholarly commentaries on diverse aspects of the new Dalit struggles and aspirations, as these affected the lives of men, women, and children in familial space—and beyond.

The individual sections of this chapter focus on different autobiographical accounts in order to highlight discrete aspects of the struggle for "human personality" or dignity. As in earlier chapters, this is a rough-and-ready heuristic move. The diverse aspects of this struggle are present in all the life stories I consider. However, their separation into different kinds of dreams, sacrifices, and assertions foregrounded by the male and female writers may help to clarify the new strains and contests that emerged in the Dalit domestic world.

Dreaming of Modernity

It is appropriate to begin with Ambedkar's views on education and modernity, since his inspirational life story is at the heart of most of the Dalit accounts discussed below, and we have seen (in chapter 3) his own determination to acquire higher degrees and other accoutrements of successful citizens, even at great cost to himself and his family.

The young Ambedkar's extraordinary education and rise to stardom in the 1920s, and reports of others who succeeded in acquiring education and a place in public life without reaching the same heights, became a lodestar for large numbers of men and women among the lowest ranks of India's laboring population. It is necessary to stress that the equation of education with liberation was not given from the start—always there, "natural," and to be expected. It took the example of exceptional and unexpectedly successful individuals, along with their vision and commitment, to generate the belief in education as the key to social advancement, and to produce a movement charged with immediacy and excitement. This is what the Dalit story in the twentieth century was centrally about, and it was accompanied by apparently trifling concerns with things like clean clothes, shoes and socks, and "English" ways. Ambedkar spelled out the platform in his speeches and writings through the 1920s, '30s, and '40s.

Ambedkar's career focused the importance of intellectual and personal "improvement." He articulated his famous slogan—"educate, agitate and organize"— in 1924, in the vow unanimously adopted as the goal of the membership on the foundation of the Bahishkrit Hitkarni Sabha (Association for the Uplift of the Excluded/Outcastes).[9] Education was at the heart of that quest. But the matter of self-help, self-improvement, and self-respect was never removed from the call for education.

The emphasis, I suggest, is less on the prestige, honor, and name of the family, community, or nation, as on the dignity, humanity, and self-respect of individuals who must hold up their heads wherever they may be, whatever the circumstances. For Ambedkar, the individual striver matters as much as the community she or he would uplift.[10] There is an echo here of Gandhi's *satyagrahi*, that is to say, the vanguard—Du Bois's "Talented Tenth." However, in the case of the Dalit leader, the aim was emphatically the making of the modern, one might say bourgeois, citizen—a fully-formed individual, complete in him- or herself, depending little on props like inherited community or family.

Thus, in a surprising speech in the Bombay Legislative Council in March 1927, Ambedkar criticized the government's scheme of scholarships for Depressed Class students. The chronic poverty of these communities often led parents to use the money for domestic expenses, he noted. His solution was to divert the scholarship amount toward the building of hostels where promising students would be protected from social demands and "wean[ed] . . . from evil surroundings."[11] His own political initiatives reinforced the proposition. In 1928, he established the Depressed Classes Education Society, a large part of whose work was to build hostels for high school students from depressed classes in Bombay, Pune, Nasik, and other districts of Maharashtra. In the 1940s, he went on to found the People's Education Society, which established critically important pioneering institutions such as Siddharth College and Milind College, along with ancillary high schools, night schools, vocational centers, and hostels.[12]

From the 1930s until his death in 1956, the Dalit leader underlined the importance of education, rational thought, and entry into the bureaucracy. But his stress on clean clothes and refined, "standard" language as signs of progress and modernity was no less insistent. In an address to the annual Depressed Class Conference in 1942, he congratulated his mainly Dalit audience on their growing political awareness, progress in education, and entry into the army, police, and legislatures, and added: "The greatest progress that we have made is to be found among our women folk. Here you see in this conference these 20,000 to 25,000 women present. See their dress, observe their manners, mark their speech. Can any one say that they are Untouchable women?"[13]

In the fragmentary autobiographical memoir he wrote in the late 1930s or 1940s, likewise, he recalled the first train journey that he and three other children of his extended family took to Goregaon, where his father was stationed as a cashier in the army. "We were well-dressed children," he wrote. "From our dress or talk no one could make out that we were children of . . . untouchables."[14] In the same vein, Ambedkar expressed his admiration for the modernity of the West, for education overseas, for the learning that an English education allowed, and for "outsize fountain pens," even as he condemned the importance attached to marriage in India and, especially, the detrimental consequences of early marriage.[15] It is important to put this in the wider context of colonial/imperial dominance and its effects.

The desire to be "modern," like a sahib, a professional or genteel member of the bourgeoisie, with signs of "advanced" Western learning and culture, has been widely observed among aspirant middle classes across the modern world.[16] In nineteenth- and twentieth-century India, many ambitious men insisted their children speak, dress, and eat like the English. "The canker has so eaten into the society," Gandhi wrote in 1921, that "in many cases, the only meaning of education is a knowledge of English." Indian boys and young men were learning English as a means of obtaining government jobs, girls "as a passport to marriage." He knew "families in which English is being made the mother tongue" and men who were sorry "their wives could not talk to them and their friends in English."[17] By the mid-twentieth century, many among the laboring poor also saw education, preferably with a large dose of English, as a primary path to liberation.

Among the Dalits, there was a decided quest for formal schooling that could lead the younger generation out of the gutters of indignity and humiliation.[18] For Ambedkar, however, this was never a quest for education or westernization alone. "Ours is a battle for reclamation of human personality which has been suppressed and mutilated by the Hindu Social System," he declared in the 1942 statement I cited in the epigraph. The statement goes on: that human personality "will continue to be suppressed and mutilated if in the political struggle the Hindus win and we lose." Hence his "final words of advice" to his Dalit audience: "educate, agitate and organize, have faith in yourselves and never lose hope."[19]

Firing the Dalit Imagination

Dalit accounts of changing domestic aspirations in the twentieth century highlight the desire for education, economic opportunities, and human dignity, often more than the need for love, companionship, marriage, and progeny. Notwithstanding the immiseration and back-breaking labor they describe among their communities, many of these memoirs offer an uplifting history of anticipation and hope.[20] Baby Kamble succinctly delineates the grounds of hopefulness: the "three jewels" Ambedkar gave to the Dalits, "humanity, education and the religion of the Buddha." With these in hand, she declares, "We began to walk and talk. We became conscious that we too are human beings."[21]

The Dalit struggle for change found in the figure of Babasaheb Ambedkar, a cherished symbol, and in his call to "educate, agitate, organize," a practical political program. Dalit memoirs are replete with accounts of the excitement that news of Ambedkar's doings produced among large numbers of the downtrodden in town and country. Kamble captures the mood in her account of how her grandparents, and hundreds of other villagers, responded to their first sight of the Dalit leader at a meeting in western India in the 1930s.

The crowd was overcome with joy, she writes, when Dr. Ambedkar, someone from "their own Mahar community," arrived in a car, dressed in European clothes, speaking the white sahib's tongue. The words she puts into her grandparents' mouths are notable: "My, my, that Bhimrao Ambedkar, that tender young boy! He has returned after getting educated with the sahibs beyond the seven seas. . . . So tall, so strong, so fair, with such a high forehead. He dresses like a white sahib and looks like one too. When he got out of his car, it was as if a governor had stepped out. And what a speech that was! As if it was the court of Indra [the king of the Hindu gods]!"[22]

Dalits far and wide wanted to follow in Ambedkar's footsteps, even if they could not aspire to his stature and greatness. Thus, the figure of the far-seeing and indomitable man makes repeated appearance in Dalit writings. Kamble herself writes of how her father and brother inaugurated the Ambedkarite movement in the districts of western India where she grew up. Her father, she says, gave up his work as a labor contractor, bringing financial hardship on the family, because of his devotion to the struggle. Let me provide two other striking illustrations of the same kind of commitment, one from western, the other from northern India.

In Narendra Jadhav's rags-to-riches story, describing his family's transition from hard labor in the fields and factories of Maharashtra in his parents' generation (the 1920s and on), to high bureaucratic and intellectual office in his own (1950s onward), to a cosmopolitan, global citizenship in his children's (1970s on), the father appears very much in the image of Ambedkar, leading his children out of slavery.[23] The author attributes the family's success to the exceptional drive and determination of his father, shaped in Narendra's telling by the example and speeches of Ambedkar. As a commentator on the memoir puts it, "The Father from the little hamlet of Ozer, involved with the nitty-gritty of everyday struggle for existence, is according to the author eternal because he is not an individual but a striving force."[24]

Narendra's description of his father's physical appearance places him squarely in Ambedkar's time: "Medium height. Dark, asymmetrical face. Stern manner.... *Dhoti* [loincloth], white shirt, khaki coat and black hat.... A staff in his hand: only, the staff was used less for support than to intimidate [others].... Dada's self-confidence was extraordinary [*khupats daandga*]. 'Get me a long enough stick, I'll flatten this circular earth and show you,' so he would announce like an Archimedes."[25] The Archimedean parallel, Narendra's nod to scientific modernity, is in line with Ambedkar's call on his followers to educate and modernize themselves and their communities.

The memoirist recalls the impact of Ambedkar's speeches in progressive Dalit homes in western India. The army of local leaders and activists who emerged in Bombay in the 1940s and '50s, inspired by Ambedkar, had two things in common, he writes: "immaculately clean attire and impressive oratory." They laid stress on the importance of books and formal education, but no less on refined speech (*sadhu bhasha*) and manners, clean clothes, and shoes. In huge processions on Ambedkar's birthday, the women activists were all "dressed in white." His own working-class parents, while thrifty about clothes, "insisted that we always wear shoes." They "brooked no compromise in this regard. . . . Their idea of being 'up-to-date' was firmly linked to wearing shoes."[26]

The quest for education for freedom began even before Ambedkar's call to "educate, agitate, organize" had gained a countrywide following. Omprakash Valmiki, noted Hindi writer and government officer, who grew up in the 1950s and '60s in the outcaste quarter of a north Indian village some distance northeast of Delhi, documents his father's dogged efforts in this regard.

At a time when Dalit children were rarely accepted in the village schools, and when children's labor was required early in most poor people's homes, Om was the only child in his family who went to school. He started with informal lessons that a Dalit Christian provided on his visits to the village: "I alone was sent to Sevak Ram Masihi. My [five] brothers worked. There was no question of sending my sister to school."[27] The oldest brother's death in his twenties brought harder times for the family. As an annually reemployed servant in the house of a well-to-do Taga (or Tyagi) landowner, he had brought in a large part of the family income.

Om's father's entreaties succeeded in getting his youngest son admitted to the local Government Basic Primary School. The child, aged five, was taunted and bullied by the higher, landowning-caste Tyagi students. The situation became worse when the Tyagi principal of the school ordered him to sweep and clean its classrooms, verandas, and spacious grounds, as his caste was meant to do. The father, passing by, saw his son sweeping the grounds. He couldn't contain his rage. Valmiki comments on "the courage and determination with which Father confronted the headmaster that day."[28] His father's angry, and sorrowful, appeal to the village headman, and the latter's intervention, led to Om being treated a little bit more like other pupils—although the slights and taunts hardly disappeared.[29]

The father was enormously proud of his son's achievements. He called the boy *Munshi ji* from the time he enrolled in primary school; this title is usually reserved for official scribes and learned men, including distinguished intellectuals and writers like Munshi Premchand, discussed in chapter 3.[30] His child would be respected. He would give up demeaning work, be a *babu*, a clerk or a bureaucrat, and uplift his caste. The father's admiration grew as Om advanced through school and college. He listened attentively when the teenager expressed frustration at the community's continued practice, on the occasion of weddings, of going around the homes of the upper castes begging for blessings and food. From the day he heard Om say this, the head of household decided to end the practice in his own family.[31]

However, despite his determination to secure formal schooling for Om, his father sometimes had to compel the boy to fulfill some part of the family and caste's traditional work. Om reports an incident when, unable to handle all the work that day, his father sent him on a task he had never undertaken before—killing and cleaning a piglet sold to a higher-caste customer for sacrifice at an annual ritual in the village's mother-goddess temple. Om's mother was furious when she saw her son return distraught and bloodied from the job, and the parents fought angrily over what they could not help.[32]

The family faced a crisis when Om finished fifth grade, hard-pressed to find the fees for his admission into middle school. His young sister-in-law—still grieving over the death of her husband, his oldest brother—came to the rescue. Against Om's father's distressed plea, urging her not to do it, she pawned her silver anklet, the only piece of jewelry left from her wedding, to pay the fee.[33] There were other times too, as Om reconstructs the story, when his mother and sister-in-law sought to shield him from the demeaning work his community was forced to do, and thus safeguard his education and the chance to escape from the wretchedness of low-caste life in the village. Here is one more example that the writer details.

One day, when Om was in high school, a landowner's bullock collapsed and died while being led back from the fields. The landowner informed Om's family that clearing away the carcass was their caste duty. Om's father and older brother were away; only his mother, sister, and sister-in-law were at home. His mother asked her husband's brother to help. The latter agreed but wanted an assistant for the task. At a loss, Om's mother had Om fetched from school. "Mother didn't want me to do this work. I'd never done it before. However, she wasn't in a position to forego the ten or fifteen rupees we'd get from the sale of the hide," he observes.[34]

At the place where the bull had fallen, Om's uncle began skinning the animal. In a while, he asked his nephew to take over, so that they could get the job done before nightfall. He instructed the boy on how to use the knife, taking care not to pierce or damage the hide. Om's hands shook as he touched the handle. "That day," he writes, "something inside me broke. I was being sucked deep into the very swamp from which I had to extricate myself. The circumstances conspired to drag me down."

It took hours to skin the bull, cleaning and drying the hide as they worked. Then, tying the hide in a sheet, Om's uncle took up the load and started for his home two miles away. He walked fast, trying to forget the weight on his head. Near the village bus terminal, he put the sheet down: his nephew had to take it from there. Om pleaded with him to carry the bundle a little farther. It was near school-closing time, his school was a mile or so from the bus stand, albeit in a different direction, and he was fearful of fellow pupils seeing him with a blood-stained load on his head. His uncle refused.

"Only my soul knows how I negotiated the crowded bus-stand that day," says Valmiki. He staggered home, clothes soiled from top to bottom, blood stains all over. "Mother let out a wail when she saw me.... Sister-in-law said, 'Don't make him do this.... We can stay without food.... Don't drag him into this dirt...' Those words live with me to this day, a beacon light shining in the dark."

In this fight for liberation, women were as involved as men—working, like the men, often more incessantly than the men, simultaneously on many fronts. Indeed, as Valmiki indicates in his account of his family's history, mothers, daughters, sisters, and sisters-in-law were sometimes at the forefront of the struggle for a new Dalit dignity. Indeed, the sacrifices of women, mired in the domestic sphere but insistent on transforming the public one for their children and grandchildren if not for themselves, are a notable feature of the Dalit renaissance.

Sacrificing for the Future

There is no dearth of evidence that scores of fathers like Valmiki's and Jadhav's, and as many or more mothers, dedicated their lives to fighting for a different, less inhuman life for their children. A particularly poetic example is found in Vasant Moon's autobiography, *Vasti*—a celebration of the *vasti* (Marathi for neighborhood or community, *basti* in Hindi/Urdu) in which he was born and grew up, and at the same time a celebration of his mother and of the Ambedkarite movement.

Moon dedicates the work to his mother, Purnabai, with these words:

During our infancy Purnabai's father removed her permanently from the harassment of her drunkard husband. But then [soon afterward] she lost the shelter of her father and mother. Her lot became one of wandering barefoot and feeding her two small children through... daily labor. The cracks in her heels vanished only when she died.

At a time when all the children in the neighborhood... called their mothers "Ma," she taught us to call her "Mother," like the children of the elite. She took care of us, raised us, and taught us the new alphabet: the A of "aspiration," the B of "Babasaheb" [Ambedkar], and the C of "confidence."[35]

Moon's family belonged to the same Mahar caste as Ambedkar. The *vasti* where Purnabai (or Purna, without the honorific *bai*) and her children grew up consisted of four to five thousand people in a two-hundred-by-two-hundred-yard area, framed by four roads. The eastern end of the *vasti* was marked by a long apartment building; beyond that was a mixed colony of "Brahmans, Marwaris, Bengalis, and Madrasis." The Dalits "never built their huts or tried to carry on their daily affairs beyond [their area]. If the family grew, if space became insufficient, they would rent a room in a neighbor's house, but never leave the community." The houses were mainly old mud structures with flat roofs. There were several single-storied brick houses, and a few Mahar merchants had double-storied houses with the upper stories made of wood. From the windows, "women could lean out to chat with the women of the house beside them."[36]

Unpaved alleys and lanes crisscrossed the settlement, with two three-foot drains to carry away wastewater. The main road in front of the drains served as common space where people gathered in the evenings: the houses were too small and crowded together for verandas or compounds in the front or back. To the northeast of the settlement was an old temple dedicated to the deities Vitthal and Rukmini, and beyond that a public toilet. The facility was divided into eight compartments, for women on one side, for men on the other, back-to-back. They were "toilets that told stories. . . . Women found it a convenient place to voice their domestic complaints. Men from the other side [occasionally including a husband] could listen to [overhear] their laments."[37]

His mother's family was among the better-off Dalit inhabitants. Her father had done reasonably well for himself, working as a tailor and a cinema manager in places near Nagpur: he befriended European and Parsi entrepreneurs, and returned to the city owning a house and some other property. He gained the reputation of being a sahib from the way he dressed and comported himself. Purna's maternal grandparents were also well placed, with significant property and a big house in the countryside.

Life changed for his mother, Moon tells us, when she was married off to a widower who had four daughters and a son from his first wife: the oldest daughter was older than Purna. Purna's father went forward with the marriage, fearing that at sixteen, his daughter was getting too old to find another groom. The bridegroom was financially comfortable. As a driver for a Parsi family, he earned over twenty rupees a month, not a small sum for a worker in those days. Unfortunately, he was given to drink. By Moon's account, he sometimes lost all his wages to drinking, or to robbery when drunk. Neighbors often picked him up from the gutter. And he regularly beat his young wife, Purna.

In the end, Purna's father took his daughter back, along with her two children, then aged three or four and one. Her father's death a little later increased her hardship. A half brother of Purna's, unseen until then—born not of the first wife, but of another relationship before her father's first marriage—arrived with his family, asserted his rights, and took control of the house. Purna's mother was still alive, working in the mills, but ill; she was soon bedridden for the remaining year or so of her life.

Before the death of her father, Purna "had never put a foot outside the house to work," her son writes.[38] Now she was out daily, foraging for work, leaving early, returning late, with bits of food or other meager earnings. For some time, she and her children lived on the veranda of her father's house. Later, acquaintances helped them rent small, decrepit rooms in crumbling huts in fetid lanes. In one—a tiny, "two-roomed" space, a six-by-six-foot room with a four-by-four-foot veranda that they used as a kitchen—Vasant slept on the veranda, "with my feet beside the hearth and my head in a different corner."[39]

His mother moved from one job to another, cooking and washing dishes for various families, until a short-tempered but kindhearted Parsi employer found her a job in the Model Mill in 1946. Her son was now fourteen, her daughter two or three years younger, and both were going to school. Purna was paid three rupees and given a dearness allowance, or supplement for the high cost of living in the city, of three rupees. However, Moon recalls her saying, "We can live happily for the whole month on those six rupees."[40] A regular income seemed like a lifeline, and *a home*—at last.

The family's sense of self-respect, and determination to change their world, was evident already in Purna's father's time. Moon recalls the care with which his grandfather dressed him for school: a shirt, tucked into his shorts, with the straps of the shorts taken over the shoulders and buttoned in front, over his chest; socks and canvas shoes; and a small handkerchief in his pocket. With the dream of sahibdom for his grandson, he sent Vasant to the nearby Normal School run by the government, where the medium of instruction was English. Other relatives supported the dream. When Vasant passed his grade IV exam, Purna was afraid he might have to stop school, for she couldn't afford the monthly fee of six annas (a third of a rupee) required for the middle school. An uncle took the boy to a prestigious high school in the town, got him admitted, and paid the fee.

By this time, the Ambedkarite movement had begun to affect religious beliefs and social interactions among Dalits in Nagpur, and to erode their long acceptance of a submissive relationship with higher-caste communities. At one stage when Vasant, now recognized as a promising student, and his mother and sister were finding it hard to get one square meal a day, he recalls, local activists of the Dalit Samata Sainik Dal (a volunteer youth corps founded by Ambedkar to promote education and the fight for equality) accompanied the boy to other activists' homes to collect food every night. "Many people gave me food.... They also helped in providing books and notebooks for my education."[41]

With this support from his community, his mother, and his little sister, Moon outdid himself. He found employment in the Post and Telegraphs Department after his BA, went on to complete an MA, was appointed to the important civil service position of deputy county commissioner in 1955, and later was handpicked to be the chief editor of the multivolume edition of Ambedkar's writings and speeches in English, sponsored by the Maharashtra government. When he moved to his Post and Telegraphs office, his mother was still laboring in the mills. She earned nothing compared to her son's 110 rupees a month, but refused to quit.[42] Several months after he was appointed deputy county commissioner, she finally gave up her job, acceding to his entreaties that she should take it easy now.

In her old age, retired and living with her son, by then a respected bureaucrat, Purna would watch over his books carefully, refusing to let any visitor touch them if they came before he got back from his office. If a postman asked her to put a thumb impression on a receipt for some delivery, she'd quietly ask him for a pen and sign her name, Purnabai. She had studied up to third grade, a substantial education for a girl in her generation. Signing her name and reading the newspaper—later fancies—were practices she continued until she lost her eyesight in her eighties.[43]

Baby Kamble's account of her elders,' as well as her own, investment in education is comparable to Purnabai's as recounted by her son. The woman writer in Kamble, however, also underlines the obstacles she faced in her home as she struggled to fulfill her dreams for her children—and herself. She describes the aspirations and arrangements in Mahar families in the villages and small rurban towns of Pune and Satara districts, southeast of Bombay, where her natal and marital families came from.

I have noted that Kamble's father was a labor contractor, employed by the British in canal building projects; later he worked on the Mumbadevi Temple in Bombay and a government-sponsored dairy in Pune. He had "a bungalow with a large courtyard" when he worked in Pune city, she writes, and "no shortage of servants."[44] Since he traveled a fair bit, Baby Kamble and her mother lived in her maternal grandparents' home in Veergaon, Pune district, until she was eight or nine.

This side of the family had benefited from opportunities that came with British rule and colonial capitalism. Her grandfather and granduncles worked as butlers for various British officials and "spoke excellent English." Their house was "a storehouse of food," the only Mahar household in the locality that had and served tea! The dozen or more Mahar households in the Maharwada (Mahar *basti*) of Veergaon were like an extended family for her, she writes. As a child from a relatively prosperous household, several members of which had gone to work in distant places, she received special treatment and respect from the community. The move to her father's house in Phaltan, Satara district, occasioned by the onset of puberty, and her marriage at the age of thirteen, brought dramatic changes in her life.

She moved into her husband's crowded home in Phaltan, with fifteen or sixteen people living in it. Her husband, who had studied a few grades more than her and participated a little in the Ambedkarite movement, was suspicious and narrow-minded. He demanded she stay strictly within the confines of the home, just as her Ambedkarite father had expected her mother to do. Economic advancement and upward mobility, accompanied as they were by middle- and upper-class codes of respectability, often led successful men to demand that the women of the household stay strictly within the four walls of the dwelling.

Baby Kamble worked from morning to night to meet the demands made of a young wife and daughter-in-law. Over the years, fulfilling the standard expectation of a married woman, she gave birth to children. Of her ten, three died early. She sent the surviving three sons and four daughters to school and records their education and advancement with pride. They became bank officials, schoolteachers, lower-level government functionaries; the two youngest daughters, who did not take up paid employment, were housewives, married to a rich farmer and a doctor, respectively.

With her imagination and enterprise, Kamble contributed to the family's welfare in other ways as well, both inside and outside the house. She rescued her husband from his prolonged joblessness, coming up with the suggestion that they start a small trade in groceries, procuring grapes and other products purchased loose in the surrounding countryside to sell in their village. With the grocery store set up in a small front room of their house facing the central courtyard of the Mahar neighborhood, she and her husband gained an independent, if small, source of income. She and her siblings seem to have used their reading skills and the shop for the advancement of the Dalit movement too.

In the long hours she spent sitting at the shop, waiting for customers, Kamble also began jotting notes on her life and her community. She showed her jottings to her brother, and later to a visiting American researcher whose enthusiasm and mediation led to their publication. It was only when her memoir was serialized in a well-known Marathi journal in 1982 that her family found out she was writing.[45] Later, she followed the autobiography with a collection of poems, established a government-approved residential school for socially disprivileged students in a small village near Phaltan, and received awards for her literary and social work.[46]

Kamble's act of writing, rare among the Dalit working classes and practically unprecedented for a Dalit woman, let alone one who had studied only to grade IV, is one of the most striking dimensions of her quest for freedom: a freedom she sought for herself and those around her. Yet, she kept her writing hidden from her husband and other elders in her household for two decades. She had to, for reasons I spell out in the next two sections.

The Dignity of Men

Dalit writings, I have suggested, establish the Dalit search for home in twentieth-century India as a vital political and economic struggle as well as a wrenching emotional, cultural, and physical one. The Dalit home is—like the promise of a just society and nation of equal citizens—categorically in the future. Yet, no such aspiration for freedom and equality is ever unmixed or straightforward. There are signs of the (re)entrenchment of a modern patriarchy in the course of the remarkable Dalit struggle for liberation from class and caste oppression. The ways in which the needs of men and boys continued to be privileged, and those of girls and women dismissed, perhaps marks the boundary where the Dalit counterpoint—the Dalit challenge to the standard nationalist and reformist notions of the good society—stopped short, as has been the case in many other radical political movements.

There has been an important scholarly debate on whether there is a Dalit patriarchy as distinct from, say, a Brahmanical patriarchy.[47] Several scholars have made the point that patriarchal structures in India are laden with assumptions that are classist, casteist, colorist (women must be fair, or at least not too dark; men can be anything), and let us add colonialist (men who have access to formal schooling and English are somehow, axiomatically, modern). Yet, patriarchal norms differ between middle- and upper-caste elites, on the one hand, and working-class and lower-caste communities, on the other. Note the incidence of strict purdah and the prohibition of widow remarriage among the "respectable," or—among the less privileged lower castes and classes—the greater vulnerability of women on account of their work and presence outside the home and the predatory sexual and physical demands of upper-caste and upper-class employers and officials.

Variations in patriarchal arrangements and practices flowed from well-known differences in the economic and social circumstances of the "big people" (*bade log, bhadralok, ashraf*), as against the laboring poor ("small people," *chote log, ajlaf,* "vulgar" and "base"). Consider the matter of inherited wealth and property. Given the practical absence of both in the lives of the poor, the question of what husbands and wives, brothers and sisters, sons and daughters might claim or inherit was largely irrelevant among the subordinated castes and classes.[48] In part for that reason, in part because of the need for all available labor, there is little disapproval of girls and women marrying again if they are widowed or if marriages fail for other reasons. The need to use all the labor at hand in the family underlines another radical divergence. Young men and women, and younger boys and girls, must fend for themselves as soon as they can—even if marriage is seen as the primary requirement for fulfillment of a girl's or woman's life, as compared to a steady job in addition to marriage and householdership in the case of men.

Nevertheless, the quest for upward mobility and higher status—and the fact that the middle and upper classes, upper-caste Hindus and Muslims, established the ideal of a modern domestic order in the context of India's anti-colonial struggle—exacerbated many regressive patriarchal practices among the subordinated castes and classes. Ideas of female modesty, invisibility, and self-sacrifice, the careful monitoring of girls' and women's movements and activities, and the naturalization of childbirth were reinforced. And Dalit progressives, like those among more privileged communities, often fell back on ideas of the natural qualities, talents, rights, and responsibilities of boys and girls, men and women.

I have noted that among the working and unemployed poor, the men's position was similar to that of women and servants in many respects. Like many of the women, they were employed and paid—if only minimally—for work outside the home. Working-class women contributed to the household income and were sometimes the primary breadwinners. They could assert their independence more than women in middle- and upper-middle-class circles. They had, and sometimes showed they had, the financial and mental strength to walk out on their husbands, if it came to that, and marrying again, if they were widowed or alone, was not taboo. Even so, societal pressures, a single woman's vulnerability, and the arrogance, entitlement, and self-confidence of the male meant that men commonly became "men," "little kings" or rajas, once they entered the domestic space.

A great deal of ethnographic, journalistic, and anecdotal evidence points to a replication of the upper-caste allocation of men's and women's duties—even in the matter of cleaning and washing children's bodies and clothes. Kausalya Baisantri's description of her parents' daily routine in 1930s and '40s Nagpur captures something of the rhythm. Her father worked in a bakery for eighteen years, including Sundays and other holidays, leaving early, returning late—"so tired, he slept as soon as he'd eaten. . . . He was home so little that we thought of him as a guest."

Later, once he found a job in the mill where her mother worked, the parents began going to the mill together and returning together, earlier in the day. It took them an hour to walk back, buying vegetables on the way. The father was now at home more; the family sometimes ate together. But the mother did the cooking and washed the clothes—theirs and the children's, and no doubt other family members' and visitors' when required. She woke early to fill water from the public tap. Her husband cut the vegetables and got the woodfire going, then bathed. The wife (or one of the daughters) would have ground spices the evening before. She would now cook rice and a vegetable, before washing her husband's and her own clothes, if she could. "Mother and Father would eat a little, if there was time, and take some food with them."[49]

Through the daily grind, Kausalya's parents put all their children through high school or beyond, except for the eldest, Janabai, who was born before they had steady jobs. Janabai ended up in a punishing "traditional" role as older sister, wife, and mother: looking after Kausalya when their parents went to work; marrying when she was thirteen, perhaps in the early 1930s; giving birth to eleven children, of whom five lived. Kausalya comments on her sister's condition: "Sister would have a child every two years. The first was a girl, then three boys. All three fell ill and passed away. [Indeed] all of sister's eleven children were ill much of the time.... Her husband too fell sick repeatedly, and the cost of doctor's fees and medicines ate up much of what they earned. Her financial situation was ... terrible." Janabai learned tailoring and earned something by stitching clothes for stray customers; later she supplied clothes for the inmates of an insane asylum. Often, says Kausalya, her arms ached from overwork.[50]

It was the same in Vasant Moon's home when he and his sister were growing up in Nagpur around the same time, although in this case there was no man in the house. Moon describes his mother Purnabai's routine once she had obtained a stable factory job. She had to be at work before 7:30 a.m., and it took forty-five minutes to reach the mill. She was up at 4:30 to bring in the water and start the cooking of vegetables and grains she had bought or collected the previous day. By six o'clock, she was entrusting the children to neighbors and asking elders to look out for them: "'Look [child], don't wander around uselessly;' 'Now ... go to your aunt and do your homework;' '[Neighbor, please] keep an eye on my house.'"[51]

Because of the mother's work schedule, the children woke before dawn. They would finish the cooking their mother left half done. "Of course," writes Moon, "I would only light the stove; [my sister] Malti did the rest of the work." Before Purna returned from the mill late in the evening, "Malti would bring water and do other tasks. When she came Mother would do the cooking ... while chatting with her neighbors." Purnabai rested a little, chewing her *supari* (betelnut) before she slept. When she could, she also scrubbed and washed her children, who like all the boys and girls in the *vasti* bathed in the open. She washed their clothes at the same time.[52]

The Jadhav family provides another predictable example. The head of the household, Damodar Jadhav, took the critical decisions: who would go to school, and for how long; or, earlier, the decision to leave the demeaning and destructive conditions of Mahar life in the village, and head to Bombay to find whatever jobs he could. The women worked more in the home, at first in the village, and then in Bombay. In the 1950s, when the family of nine (father, mother, grandmother, and six children) lived in a small one-roomed apartment in Wadala, the distribution of work was telling. Narendra's father was employed in the Bombay Port Trust railway. The children were at school. Narendra's mother fetched the water, bought groceries, cooked, cleaned, and washed vegetables, clothes, dishes, and bodies, helped no doubt by the children, especially the girls, as they grew up—all of them supervised by a nearly blind grandmother.

The pattern recurred in Omprakash Valmiki's north Indian village in the 1950s, '60s, and after. Valmiki describes the work the family engaged in: removing animal carcasses; killing animals, skinning them, and cutting meat for customers as well as for family and kin; working the farms. The men—along with growing boys—did more of the farmwork and took primary responsibility for clearing animal carcasses, curing the skins, and carving the meat. Om's oldest brother worked as the bonded servant of a landowning family until his early death, which left the family in dire financial straits. The second oldest left to seek his fortunes in Bengal, returning after years of unsuccessful effort to work in the fields, where Om and another older brother also worked regularly. His mother, sister, and sister-in-law participated in working the fields and cleaning landowners' houses and courtyards. But they took exclusive charge of cleaning, cutting, and cooking food, fetching water, and washing clothes.

It may be well to reiterate the point that the gendered division of labor was not based on physically observed sexual assignment alone. Younger males in the house often served heads of household much as women did. Indeed, some tasks—massaging an older man's feet or arms or back, dealing with customers or alms-giving benefactors, fetching coal—might be seen as more appropriate for younger males than for girls or women. Omprakash Valmiki writes of how he had to serve when he was living with his maternal uncle in the city of Dehradun, while studying in the Intermediate grade, preparatory to college.

Om's uncle took him into his one-roomed house, in a lower-caste neighborhood of the city, to enable him to continue his studies, which the caste-ridden teachers in his parental village had begun to obstruct even more after he graduated from high school. An older brother of Om's, working in the Survey of India office, already lived with the uncle. But the uncle got affronted by Om's growing political interests and his participation in nonacademic activities such as student demonstrations for a more expansive and scientific (less "Hindu" and less "traditional") education—especially since these often kept Om out late. Fearful that the uncle would throw him out, and thus disrupt his studies again, Om redoubled his efforts to keep him happy. For all that, he writes, "keeping his *hookah* filled with tobacco, massaging his feet, putting oil in his hair, all I did for him, still failed to please him."[53]

Yet, those marked as females by birth were especially disadvantaged. The subordinated status of girls and women emerged clearly in the matter of schooling. We have seen how the dream of modernity, and of the self-respect and pride that came with Western education and manners, led Vasant Moon's grandfather to send his grandson to an English-medium government school in Nagpur. The proud elder reportedly said, "Vasant should not even get dust on his feet. He will be a saheb." In the same vein, Vasant's mother zealously guarded his books when she lived with her son after quitting her job in the mills: "These are used for work. Please look at them [only] after Saheb comes."[54] Nonetheless, such ambition was reserved for the male. The opportunities for education provided to Vasant and his sister were completely divergent. Vasant obtained a higher education and considerable acclaim as a government officer, writer, and editor. Malti studied only up to grade III, the same as their mother.

Vasant tells us that Malti "came of age" when he was in college. She would have been thirteen, he fifteen or sixteen at the time. In line with expectations among Indian families across class and community, the goal now was to get Malti married. Purnabai soon found an appropriate groom, who worked as a clerk in the post office. The wedding took place when Vasant was taking part of his BA examination. "I failed the B.A. exam," he writes. "But the seven-hundred-rupee scholarship I . . . [got] that year from the Indian government helped to pay for my little sister Malti's marriage in the courtyard in front of the [neighborhood] temple."[55]

Omprakash Valmiki's simple statement of the inconceivability of any formal education for his sister—"There was no question of sending my sister to school"—was in line with this thinking. The outlook was shared, in different ways, to different degrees, by women as well as men, town-dwellers as well as villagers. Traces of it come through in the economist and educationist Narendra Jadhav's account of his family's "triumphant escape from India's caste system."[56]

In Narendra's natal family, male and female siblings did not have access to the same education and opportunities. He and his brothers received postgraduate education and went on to distinguished careers. The eldest joined the prestigious Indian Administrative Service, successor to the colonial Indian Civil Service; the second worked for Gulf Air as a ground engineer; the third was deputy commissioner in the Bombay Municipal Corporation at the time of retirement; the youngest, Narendra, shone as an economist, writer, bureaucrat, public figure, and member of Parliament. Their sisters, Leela and Trusha, received far less schooling, and while they were married comfortably, they never went on to formal careers or public positions of their own.[57]

"He Was My Husband, After All"

I will use Baby Kamble's experience as my final example. For, with all her enterprise and drive, this remarkable Dalit activist and writer hardly escaped the damaging consequences of the patriarchal order. Kamble's father, a follower of Ambedkar, sent his daughter to school along with her brother. She studied to standard IV before she was married off for fear that she was getting past marriageable age. Boys in the family studied further. One of her uncles was the first Mahar of Phaltan to complete high school. Her older brother and "around forty other boys" followed his lead, and, as she reports, her brother joined other Dalit youth in organizing the local Mahar community in the fight for a better future.

Baby Tai (Aunt Baby), as Kamble was known in later life, says that her father's and brother's example drew her into the struggle for Dalit rights against upper-caste oppression. After her marriage, her initiative allowed her and her husband to open a grocery store in the front part of their home. In the hours of minding the store, as I've noted, she began writing her autobiography. Yet, no one in her extended family except a brother knew about her writing until her memoir was published in the 1980s. Asked by Maya Pandit, the translator of her autobiography into English, why she hid her work, she said: "First, because of my husband. He was a good man but like all the men of his time and generation, he considered a woman an inferior being. He would not have tolerated the idea that I had taken to writing."[58]

Her husband and family elders were, like other men (and older women) in the community, hostile to any sign of independence among younger women. Kamble's eye-opening interview lays this out elaborately. She recalls how deeply suspicious her husband was of her littlest moves, and how he beat her repeatedly on flimsy grounds. She comes back to the point several times. "All my life I had to face this violence.... [T]his was the life most women led.... Women used to be afraid of even looking up at their husbands. . . . My husband always called me an ignorant woman. . . . A wife's place was near her husband's feet. Fathers used to teach their sons to treat their wives as footwear!"[59]

Baby Tai's father, a relatively prosperous and respected member of the community, treated her mother the same way. He kept her confined in his house "like a bird in a cage," and thrashed her "almost . . . daily" for any disagreement or supposed insolence, Kamble wrote in her autobiography. Family honor was judged "in proportion to the restrictions imposed on the women of the house. . . . People would tell each other how . . . [Pandharinath Mistry, her father] kept his wife completely hidden in the house so that even the rays of the sun did not know her." "Not sending [letting?] the women out was considered to be a mark of real manhood," she added in her later interview.[60]

Pressed by Maya Pandit on why she never felt the need to write about the physical and psychological violence she suffered, she responded simply: "Well, he was my husband after all! . . . Besides, I had my community to consider, our lack of education, progress. It would be so demeaning [to suggest that they were backward or hidebound]."[61]

Kamble's matter-of-fact statement exemplifies where the Dalit attempt to radically overhaul the social and cultural status quo reached its limit. She acknowledges her own acceptance of the existing hierarchy and oppression, and to some extent of the outlook that undergirded it. "My son had started going to school when I started to write. So for me he was a knowledgeable, learned man. I used to be scared of both my son and my husband, scared of their reaction. . . . I never retaliated."[62] Simply because that was how things were; because that was the asserted nature of men; because she could not let down her community, which—like other subordinated minorities, Muslims, Christians, Anglo-Indians, and more—was at the receiving end of a new, modernizing, upper-caste-Hindu-dominated nationalist regime.

In the same interview with the translator of her memoir into English, Baby Tai came up with her critical, and to my mind powerful, conceptualization of the "nature" of men—which, along with men's far more commonly expressed views about the "nature" of women, provides a central thread for my reflections in the two concluding chapters.

Part III

History in a Visceral Register

6. The Things Men Touched

From afar, one may imagine that one perceives the pattern. But . . .
one is not challenged—or, more precisely, menaced—by the details.
—JAMES BALDWIN

❋ ❋ ❋

I will return now to an issue with which I began this book: the question of epistemology, *how we know what we know*, attended at the same time by an anti-epistemology, *how do enlightened thinkers and citizens not see what is plain for all to see*—the extent of caste, class, and gender discrimination, patriarchal privilege, and everyday violence that runs through modern South Asian society and history. The answer, it seems to me, lies in a failure to touch the visceral register of history, which is apprehended in some measure in an archive of prejudice, and hence of elitism and stigmatization, privilege and hauteur, indignity and humiliation: in "the spat-out, half-suppressed . . . gesture of disdain . . ., the pause and the recoil, the refusal to touch, what in India is called Untouchability."[1]

I center the matter of the visceral register and its intangible, evanescent archive in these two concluding chapters by returning to diverse indications of men's privilege in the domestic arena revealed in the time and space men occupied in the home: the place given to them for their physical occupation, business and pleasure, the areas they frequented, the company they kept, their ability to work or play—cards or chess or "philosophizing"—undisturbed, as well as the clothes they wore and the food they were given (better and, traditionally, before the women in the household). In making this move, I organize my argument around the things men touched and did in the home, literally and metaphorically.

The present chapter focuses on three dimensions of men's doings in the home: *permissible things*, the objects, bodies, and work men touch in domestic space; *permissible languages*, used by men and women in conjugal interactions; and *permissible moods*, sometimes suppressed, sometimes openly expressed. "Permissible" of course in terms of the patriarchal order: indeed, not simply permissible but even required. We might think of these three dimensions as three registers of male hauteur, arrogance, and entitlement, or alternatively insecurity, expressed in different kinds of behavior and interaction.

I begin with a rough-and-ready attempt to summarize the doings or activities of men in the domestic arena through listing the objects they touched in their daily routines. I go on to explore what men touched, and did not touch, through two other kinds of evidence: the words or forms of address employed by husbands and wives in daily interaction; and moods or comportment, as reflected in the many kinds of male restlessness and impatience I describe in the third section.

In the process, I hope at least to "touch" the visceral register, and capture something of the *feel* of familial interaction among diverse inhabitants of the domestic world in modern South Asia. How does men's ambiguous presence and lordly comportment affect the lives of men and women sharing a home? How does it condition men's and women's lived experience in this intimate, inner world?

Doings: A Preliminary Inventory
of Things Men Touched

An impossible task. How does one draw up a list of the things that anyone touches in private space—or, for that matter, in public? Nevertheless, even where we have no option but to resort to what the concerned men and those around them say about what they do in the home, or imagine they do, or wish to do, this seems to me to be a useful way of tying together various aspects of the history of domestic life I have sought to trace in the preceding pages.

Let me begin with the commonplace, a few generalizations that for a time applied over much of the world. Men touched food—to eat, though not to cook or prepare it. They touched beds, or sheets or makeshift mattresses on the floor—to sleep, but not to tidy or clean them. They touched women—but women as bodies more than as thinking, emotional beings.

What men touched depended on class, status, and self-esteem. Those who thought of themselves as belonging to the "better classes" turned away from anything they considered low-brow or mundane. They handled only the more "important" tasks in the domestic sphere, tasks in which mistakes were deemed to be risky. They kept control of property and wealth, including bank accounts, checkbooks, and hidden treasuries in the home, even when they handed keys or papers to women and other trusted family members for specific errands. They decided on the purchase of the grander, more expensive items: electronic goods, refrigerators, cars, and houses in recent times; perhaps elephants, carriages, cattle, and land earlier. Men participated in, even conducted, major rituals in the home—on the most important days of the religious calendar, at significant festivals, at marriages, and so on. The "minor" occasions and practices, including daily prayers and the maintenance of a prayer room or shrine on a shelf, and much of the preparation for larger rituals, were typically left to women and underlings.

Men of upper- and middle-class background in South Asia avoided physical labor, contact with body waste and other polluting substances, work that soiled them in any way. They steered clear of routine domestic work: looking after children and elders, cutting vegetables and cooking food, cleaning floors and furniture, dirty clothes and dirty bodies (except their own). The clothes and shoes they needed for work, or after a bath, were ready for them; in aristocratic households and those aspiring to aristocratic status, servants, wives, or children might help men put them on. The cleaning and washing of infants and little children was largely left to the women, including older daughters and nieces, sometimes still children themselves, and to servants. This applied even to fathers who wanted to see their children, admired the little fingers and toes and expressions of infants, or watched the progress of older children in schoolwork and extracurricular activities, as Akhtar Husain Raipuri did.

There were variations, of course, depending on individual personalities, inclinations, and contexts. Gandhi cleaned his own toilet and forced his wife, Kasturba, to do the same, despite her considerable discomfort. Premchand lent a hand in cutting vegetables, feeding and dressing the children, and caring for the sick, when need arose. Ambedkar "occasionally, on a holiday, . . . cooked for himself," recalls Devi Dayal, employed as a young man to look after Ambedkar's library; whenever he did so, "he invited others to share the meal." Dayal records one instance from 1944, in the period between Ambedkar's first and second marriages, when he "prepared seven dishes, which took him three hours."[2] As regular routine, however, women and servants did the cooking. The dirtier work of clearing human excreta, bloodstained clothes, and garbage was handled by Untouchables.

In a comment on the domestic needs and cares of her father, Kasim Beg Chughtai (1861–1936), who was a judge in the princely courts of western India in the early twentieth century, trailblazing feminist writer and critic Ismat Chughtai (1911–1991) sums up the prevailing conditions of domestic order in many elite households. One day, perhaps in the early 1930s, her father was appointed as a judge in a small principality in Rajputana (today's Rajasthan.) At the news, "everything turned upside down" in their Aligarh home. "Father could not manage a moment without Mother." The parents left for Rajasthan, taking along one of their children—an older brother of Ismat's who battled severe illness for years before his death in 1941 at the age of forty-two. The four younger boys were left in the care of the eldest son and his wife in Aligarh. Of the four daughters, the older ones were already married, the younger ones, including Ismat, in boarding school. "Father simply sent . . . the money to cover their costs."[3]

For Ismat's mother, Nusrat Khanum, who was born probably in the 1870s and died in 1967, the experience of domesticity and childcare was very different. Her writer daughter points to a critical part of it as follows: "We were so many children [four sisters and six brothers] that my mother was nauseated by the very sight of us. We had tumbled out one after another, pummeling and battering her womb. Suffering continually from nausea and labor pains, she saw us as nothing more than a punishment. Her body had spread out like a front porch when she was still young. By the age of 35, she had also become a grandmother—subject to all kinds of new demands."[4] The "punishment" of looking after ten children, and an eleventh in her husband, in addition to the servants and other domestic requirements.

The next generation, that of Ismat and her husband, did not have as many children as their parents and grandparents, though contraception continued to be frowned on and progeny was still seen as a gift of God.[5] Yet in other respects, as we have seen, men's—and, albeit far more circumspectly, women's—assessment of the rights and responsibilities of men and women remained largely unchanged.

Recall the daily life of Bachchan's grandfather Bholanath, a lower-level official of respectable inheritance, caste, and social standing. In his youth and again in his mature years, that is, before and after his tenure as a jailer in the post-1857

British colonial administration when his leisure time would have been some-what reduced, he lived the life of a gentleman of leisure in his hometown of Allahabad.[6] His room in the men's section of the house contained his bed, hand-written manuscripts of texts he had copied, and his spectacles, pen and ink, spit-toon, and hookah. Often a chessboard took center stage and consumed his and his fellow chess players' day. They interrupted the game only when forced to do so: by the call of nature, as they might have said, or to eat, following repeated en-treaties from denizens of the inner quarters—including the women, who could not eat until the men had eaten.

The latter rule was observed through Bachchan's father's time as well. Pratap, employed as a clerk in a press in Allahabad, woke at 3 a.m., took a ritual bath in the river Ganga several miles away, and left for work at nine after his morn-ing meal. If the meal was not ready and he left without eating, a servant, family member, or neighbor brought it to him and waited to see him eat, so the women at home could also eat. Pratap often spent twelve hours at the press, especially when he was still low in rank. At the time, he regularly got home well after dark. The younger children were often in bed, and all he himself could do was eat and fall asleep.

I will round off this rehearsal of "respectable" men's routines and what they touched in the home with two examples from the next generation, living through the high tide of anti-colonial struggle and Independence—the poet and university teacher Bachchan, and the writer and educationist Akhtar Hu-sain Raipuri. For most of their careers, Raipuri and Bachchan lived with their immediate, nuclear families in small, modern houses, without the strict division of men's and women's spaces that was observed in their parents' and grandpar-ents' homes. In neither case would the spouses in the two families fit popular ideas of a run-of-the-mill middle-class South Asian housewife or husband: that is to say, until they did!

As Akhtar's wife, Hameeda, recalled it, her husband's work routine varied little from the day they married in 1935 to the end of his life in 1992.[7] His wak-ing hours were organized fixatedly around pen, paper, and office, even when the office was a room at home, or a table and chair on one side of a room, as it was at some points. During his last years, when he was virtually blind, he still woke early, walked a little, shaved, bathed, dressed as if for the office, and sat down to breakfast "punctually at eight." His sons and wife read to him through part of the morning. Presumably, he rested, listened to the radio, and drank something cold or warm between times, before his lunch at 1 p.m. After that, he withdrew to his room, listened to the radio and slept, woke at four, bathed, and dressed for tea, before another walk and an evening spent, ideally, with visitors (mostly men, but now sometimes including women and curious children) and animated conversation in his "court"—what Bengalis call "*adda*."[8] The round of activities matched earlier decades when he was a busy educationist and bureaucrat, if on a reduced and slower scale.

Compare Bachchan, the poet, who writes of the continuous quest for companionship and love in his personal life, a search fulfilled very substantially in his second marriage, with Teji. Throughout this highly educated, accomplished, and famous couple's time together, Bachchan kept away from touching any housework, childcare, shopping, or planning for the household. Teji shouldered the burden, even the buying of cars and refrigerators, to leave her husband free, as he puts it, for his intellectual and creative work.

What men touched depended on class and social aspiration. Among the laboring poor, there was—and is—no separation of home from work, and no escape from grinding labor, day and night. Women contribute in wages to the household income; they are sometimes the primary breadwinners. For all that, there is more than an echo of middle- and upper-class distribution of domestic work between male and female, including cooking, caring for children, and washing clothes. Recall a few examples I have cited.

First, Kausalya Baisantri's father, who found regular factory employment in the industrial city of Nagpur in the 1940s sometime after his wife, and earned less than her. The two bought vegetables from the market on their way back from work, and he cut the vegetables. But she did the cooking and washing of clothes—her own, her husband's, and the children's, as well as those of other family members and visitors, if necessary.[9]

It was the same in Vasant Moon's home. His mother had left her drunken husband. She did everything in the home and at "work," which was in a factory in her later years. Her school-going children completed some of the work at home after she left for the day. Yet the older child, Vasant, "only [lit] the stove." His younger sister did "the rest of the work," fetching water, cooking, cleaning, the lot. Their mother finished what was left undone when she returned in the evening, bathing the children and washing the clothes before she slept.

Indrani Jagjivan Ram encountered a parallel division of labor between men and women in her husband's village in rural north India. On the day she arrived as a new bride, an unending stream of visitors came to her husband's home. The women of her husband's immediate family and wider network of kinsfolk conversed endlessly, sometimes addressing her, as they went in and out of the room where she was sequestered. All through the hours, they were washing, cleaning, cutting, and preparing mountains of food, even as they stole glimpses of the long folk drama being performed outside from the late evening onward. Meanwhile, the men of the family and the village, and male guests from farther afield (many of them laboring and farm-working members of their Dalit community), engaged in boisterous conversation and laughter, as they sat feasting and watching as much of the play as they wanted.[10]

In another illustration of the severity of the accepted order, women and men of Omprakash Valmiki's lowly caste community continued these practices even while they sheltered one year from a terrible rainstorm in their village, six hundred miles northwest of Jagjivan Ram's. The rainy season, with its overflowing drains and filth, and the hidden animals and insects it brought out, always compounded the distress of the local poor. That of 1962 was especially bad. Days of continuous rainfall were followed by a night of such heavy downpour that many of the villagers' makeshift clay huts collapsed. Om's parents' house lost part of its roof, and the family was up all night, shivering and huddling together. At dawn, as people shouted and asked after neighbors while the rain continued relentlessly, Om's father managed to persuade someone in a nearby landowner's family to let them take shelter in his dilapidated outhouse, which lay locked and unused. Before Om's natal family could move their possessions into the shelter, another thirty or forty people had joined them there.

Valmiki describes the succeeding scene. Borrowing cow dung cakes, used as fuel, from different landowners' houses and placing them in "stoves" formed by a triangle of three bricks, or simply stones if bricks weren't found, eight or ten poor families lit separate cooking fires. "The smoke from the fires made it hard to breathe. The men's company [sic] had gathered in the verandah of the outhouse, smoking their hookahs. The women were struggling with the stoves. The children's screaming was such that it drowned all other sounds."[11]

One last example must suffice to conclude this summary of men's and women's domestic duties in working people's homes. In the English rendition of Narendra Jadhav's memoir—a book that reads a bit like a romantic epic about three generations of one family—the author includes a caustic exchange between his mother and his father on the question of the upbringing of their children. The words he puts in the mouth of his mother speak to a widely observed pattern of the distribution of work, and privilege, in the household, and capture what were likely common tensions too. "Your children? Your children? . . . Is it not I who bore and raised the kids, bathed their mud-caked bodies, and washed their bums? Who got up at five o'clock in the morning to pat fresh bhakris for them? Who stayed up all night through the children's teething and . . . illnesses? I labored while he snored under his blanket. . . . And he says they are *his* children!"[12]

I will refer, finally, to one other area of conjugal interaction, which I mentioned at the start of this section on things men touched: men's physical and emotional contact with women. Men repeatedly, insistently, touched their wives for sexual release and pleasure, as well as for procreation. This was their "right."[13] Across class and caste, marriage gave men license for this privilege, or perhaps more accurately, enhanced it.

Rashid Jahan, Ismat Chughtai, and other political and social activists writing in the mid-twentieth century condemned the historical construction of women as little more than "baby-producing machines."[14] In her commentary, Chughtai summoned up the history she learned from a south Indian Christian teacher in her missionary high school in north India. Men and women worked together and shared a great deal in the relatively egalitarian tribal societies of early times—including the care of the children of the community. As settled agricultural societies, landowning, and the matter of property inheritance developed, however, "Man became the provider . . . woman's spiritual god, [and] it became a woman's duty to serve the man." A woman could live peacefully, in relative comfort and security, so long as she "pleased her man and produced multiple children": "soldiers" is how Chughtai describes them in the context. After that the woman could easily be discarded, like an "old, worthless [cow]," for she lived at the mercy of her husband and sons.[15]

I have cited Chughtai's comment on how her respectable, "aristocratic," middle-class mother had spread out—"like a front porch"—at a young age, from the strain of non-stop labor and childbirth, and how she could barely cope with the sight of her children: a common physical and psychological consequence of sexual relations in marriage even among the more comfortable classes in South Asia well into the middle of the twentieth century. Women from working-class backgrounds describe the same kind of punishment rather more starkly.

The birth of children was an unremarkable, ordinary ("*saamanya*") event in her parents' working-class neighborhood, Kausalya Baisantri observes. Her parents had eleven children. Five daughters and a son survived. Kausalya's eldest sister, married at age thirteen, also had eleven children, of whom five lived. Kausalya notes that her mother and sister were delivering children around the same time, and that the latter had a child every two years. The sexual exploitation of wives continued into Kausalya's own relatively more comfortable middle-class life in the years after India's independence: importunate husbands like her own, she says, needed a wife "only to cook [their] food and satisfy [their] sexual hunger."[16]

Baby Kamble described the situation in her rural community in the middle decades of the twentieth century as follows: "A woman had babies continually until she reached menopause. Perhaps this was possible because of our natural [inner] strength. . . . Of these [infants] one or two might survive; still they contributed to the labor of the community. Afterwards, the cycle of births continued."[17] In spite of her own political awareness, education, and Ambedkarite activism in her own overcrowded household, she herself had ten offspring, of whom three died.

If marriage provided a license for men to use women's bodies at will, so did class privilege. Recall the servant girl Nandi's sharp retort in Attia Hosain's *Sunlight on a Broken Column*, when the aristocratic family elder Uncle Mohsin accuses her of being a female of loose morals: "A slut? A wanton? And who are you to say it who would have made me one had I let you?"[18]

Class power counts, and often expresses itself precisely in the sexual predation of lower-class women and servants. So does patriarchal privilege more generally: the so-called "needs" of men, especially after the tiring labor of a day at the office, or supervising laborers and artisans, or working hard in fields and factories. Part of the natural order of things: men must be men. The younger daughter-in-law and central female protagonist of the classic 1962 film *Sahib, Bibi aur Ghulam* symbolizes the condition. Her husband—the *sahib* (master) of the title, who humiliates himself as a *ghulam* (slave) constantly seeking pleasure and solace in the company of his intensely desired courtesan while lording it over his homebound, duty-bound, loyal wife (*bibi*)—tells her that the sexual appetite of men in his family can hardly be satisfied by their wives alone. Such latitude is never available to women, including the wife in this film, pining away for the love of her husband and the fulfillment of her own sexual desire.[19]

Conditions of patriarchal privilege, and men's right to sex, did not commonly allow a touching of emotions, a communion of souls, the companionship and deeper personal connection that women often longed for. I address this issue in the next two sections through an analysis of other patterns of domestic behavior that are seen, and yet not seen.

The Language of Hierarchy

Speech acts have their own visceral implications. Rules of interaction in the home —the words and ways men, women, and children are required to adopt—are reminders of the weight of socially ordained hierarchies. Among middle- and upper-class families in colonial and early postcolonial India, except perhaps the most Westernized, wives rarely addressed or referred to their husbands by name. They spoke of them instead in the respectful, venerable form as *thou/vous* (*aap*), or in a third person plural register as *they/them* (*unka, ve, unhen*), used in Hindi, Urdu, and other Indian languages for people of higher status, ranging from elders to this-worldly lords and masters to other-worldly gods. Wives would speak accordingly of what *they*, the husbands, like, say, or do, where *they* have gone, when *they* will return. In interactions with children, the husband would be *your father* as well as *they*.

Women also referred to their husbands as the father of so-and-so in conversations with outsiders. They might invoke them with a caste title followed by the honorific *ji* or *sahib*—Pandit ji, Thakur sahib, Syed sahib, Khan sahib, Singh sahib, and so on—or use their surnames, with the addition of the same sort of honorific. By contrast, husbands commonly called their wives by their first names, frequently a name given to the woman by the husband's family after marriage. In "respectable" circles they may also have added an honorific: thus, Indrani or Shivrani Devi, or Hameeda Begum. In interactions with outsiders, men regularly referred to their wives as so-and-so's mother, and with children obviously as "your mother."

Forms of spousal address loosened in the decades following Partition and Independence. For one thing, the vocabulary expanded with the increasing infiltration of English, the latter stimulated by greatly increased educational opportunities and growing urbanism. Some middle-class men and women came to speak of their spouses in English as Mr. or Mrs. Singh, Khan, Tandon, Ram, and so on. In conversations with third parties, these men and women might also refer to their spouses as "my wife," "my husband," or "my Mister," the first word commonly enunciated in an Indian language (*meri, mere, hamare, maazhe*), the second in English, with the English serving as euphemism and cover. Among upwardly mobile families that moved successfully into the ranks of the established middle classes, husbands or sons might also be referred to as "Sahib," as in "we must wait until Sahib comes"—sometimes a direct reference to professional or bureaucratic positions the men occupied. We saw an early example of this in the case of Purnabai, speaking of her bureaucrat son, Vasant Moon.[20]

The appearance and pace of change in conjugal interactions has been more dramatic in the later twentieth and early twenty-first centuries, especially among the diverse professional, entrepreneurial, and service-sector employees crowding into India's more cosmopolitan cities, many of whom aspire to corporatist lifestyles and the American Dream as portrayed in cinema and social media. Many men and women coming of age during this period, from lower- as well as upper-caste and class backgrounds, routinely address and speak of their spouses by given or first name. The most "advanced" among them in the bigger cities sometimes live together openly, if discreetly, without marrying. For most of the population, however, in town and country, the structure and reverberations of older forms of address and older hierarchies live on. It behooves us, therefore, to attend closely to examples of practices in these earlier generations.

Throughout their autobiographical accounts, Shivrani Devi, Kamala Sank- rityayan, Hameeda Raipuri, and Indrani Jagjivan Ram write of their husbands in the third person plural. This seems fitting, since they write in memory of these men, and celebrate their successful lives and careers. Exceptionally, Ha- meeda uses her husband Akhtar's first name in many of her comments, indicat- ing something of a greater independence in both her upbringing and her choice of a husband. Khurshid Mirza, who wrote in English, does the same—for the same reason.

Shivrani Devi uses her husband's pen name, Premchand—the name by which he was best known—only once, in the first sentence of her memoir. For the rest, like other women of earlier, pre-Independence generations speaking about their husbands, she uses the venerable *thou/they* form and leaves out the subject of many sentences altogether: the reader already knows who the speaker, actor, doer is. In her three-volume memoir, Indrani Jagjivan Ram refers to her husband in the same way.

Both Indrani Jagjivan Ram and Kamala Sankrityayan refer to their husbands as *swami* (lord), a metaphorical usage that has literal, real-life implications. With the thirty-seven-year age gap between her and her husband and her much hum- bler background, Kamala indexes the male/female hierarchy and its expectations more sharply than many other women who have written about their marital lives and families. In the final two volumes of his autobiography which she compiled, as well as in other writings after his death, she writes of her husband as Rahulji, Panditji, Mahapanditji, and Guruji. The last three terms translate as "respected" learned one, most learned one, and teacher, respectively: forms of address that amplify the terms *swami* (lord) and *bhagavan* (god). "Rahulji," she says in the last volume of his autobiography, "*you* [*vous*] were more than my husband; *you* were my god." Elsewhere, "I respected *him* blindly because I venerated/wor- shipped *him*."[21] There is deep reverence for her husband here, in what is at the same time a performance of the self—for herself and for his followers.

The husbands' manner of addressing their wives follows a different trajectory. In his letters to Indrani, Jagjivan initially uses the formal *vous* form (*aap*), as in an early letter of September 1935, written to her when she had returned to teach in Kanpur after her first short time in his village.[22] Within a few weeks, how- ever, his sense of intimacy and husbandly authority has grown enough to let him switch to a more egalitarian and familiar mode (*tum*).[23] Rahul Sankrityayan, in his turn, regularly referred to Kamala in the formal *aap/thou/vous* form, in his autobiography and in communications with friends. This could be reflective of an inner anguish, a sign of distance as well as respect for this woman, his wife, his nurse, and the mother of his children, who was so much younger than him:

someone whose talents and courage he admired, who was dependent on him, and yet needed to be self-assured and independent. Are they the words of an aging man in poor health, who believed he did not have long to live, was deeply concerned about the future of his wife and two little children, and felt guilty about how he might have taken advantage of a girl of humble background less than half his age, as he suggests in a diary entry?[24]

Like Jagjivan, but more demonstratively so, Rahul was a devoted, caring, and loving husband and father. This was in keeping with his self-image as a noncon-formist intellectual, rebel, and wanderer seeking knowledge, the higher life, and the good society, disdainful of society's petty regulations and rituals. His letters to Kamala suggest his unconventionality in their intimacy and open declarations of love. His love and expressions of desire were especially marked when he was on the road, fulfilling public commitments, chasing after rare ancient texts, or teaching overseas, as when he accepted a professorship in Sri Lanka from 1959 to 1961. He wrote from Sri Lanka, soon after he reached there in 1959, that at his age (sixty-six at the time), his young wife and little children were all that he lived for. He had accepted the job and separation from them only to secure their financial future. Then, and in earlier correspondence when he was away, he addressed Kamala as his love, his lover, the love of his life, his very life (*pyari, priye, priytame, pranapriye, pranasame*)—his all. He invariably signed off with the intimate, egalitarian term *tumhara* ("yours"), and letter after letter carried kisses to her and the children and embraces to her (*aalingan*, a term that, because of its rare use in Hindi, implies more than embraces, "the coming together of two bodies").[25]

For much of their time together, however, Rahul's behavior was marked by a more confusing and contradictory pattern: restlessness and irritability when he was at home, greater restlessness and sentimental attachment when he was away. There seem to be two different desired selves in contention here, although, in this as in other instances, the author may not always be conscious of the self he performs. Ambedkar was more self-aware and courageous than most in articulating a sense of his divided self.

In chapter 3, I quoted a letter Ambedkar wrote to his fiancée two and a half months before his second marriage, in which he frankly asserted one aspect of his self-perception: "I am no gay person—pleasures of life do not attract me. My companions have to bear the burden of my austerity and asceticism. My books have been my companions, they are dearer to me than wife and children." He went on: "Morally I am intractable and I do not tolerate any lapses from strict rules of morals. I have recounted these facts about myself to give you some idea of what a difficult customer you have to deal with."[26]

Two and a half weeks later, he was writing very differently, of the liberated, modern, romantic man in him—of love at first sight, emotional and sexual desire, and his opposition to the joint family that prevented fuller expression of these. Let me cite two letters in which he uses the affectionate diminutives, Sharu and Raja, that he and Savita had chosen for each other.

February 19, 1948: "I said that you were [the] first to be a casualty. But you were quite right in saying that I had concealed my feelings.... For I too was a casualty from the very beginning. I wonder if there is a similar case [anywhere else?] of love at first sight from both sides." February 21: "Sharu says that Raja is her divinity; but it is equally true that Sharu is Raja's divinity too.... Raja's Sharu and Sharu's Raja firmly believe that there is a single soul that resides in them.... One soul saw the other soul, both recognized a common identity and embraced each other.... Raja is certain that nothing except death can break this embrace."

Weeks later, addressing a concern he sensed in an April 6 letter from Savita, a fear that he might claim "husbandly" rights over her body, he reassures her: "This is [your] imagination and nothing else. In marriage at a young age, the sexual desire is strong and man takes forcible possession of his wife's body. My marriage is the marriage of old age. The desire for company is much stronger than the desire for sex. Therefore you have no reason for nursing fears in this regard."

Thus, men in diverse locations, privileged and not so privileged, understood conjugal relationships in a noticeably paradoxical manner, combining concern, care, and perhaps tenderness with pedagogic disciplining, admonition, and indulgence. The contradictory stance of teacher and elder, as well as spouse, showed in men's comportment in the domestic world in a multitude of ways, including a range of tempers that I will bundle under the rubric of restlessness.

The Mood of Restlessness

As the preceding pages have indicated, men regularly fell short of becoming the "accomplished" human beings they believed they were—or could be, if given full freedom to express their inner selves. In the event, men's ambiguous commitment to the domestic often surfaced in expressions of boredom, impatience, irritability, anger, and suspicion, tempers that are readily noticeable in the case of ambitious, creative, and sometimes very successful men. I will begin with boredom, which appears to be the most benign among these, returning for this purpose to the meditations of the poet, teacher, and romantic Harivansh Rai Bachchan.

Bachchan's intimate four-volume autobiography bares his soul, his innermost thoughts as it were. The narrative is striking, as readers will know by now, for its statement of the author's needs, inclinations, and perspectives as a man, and for his admission of some of the resulting incongruities. Bachchan's self-image as a poet sets the tone for his reconstruction of his life, his social and cultural inheritance, and the stirring political times in which he lived. His celebratory, yet confounding, account of his satisfying marriage with his second wife, Teji, provides an uncommon demonstration of the restlessness of men in domestic space.

In this second marriage, Bachchan felt an unprecedented sense of well-being and happiness.[27] A comfortable home, a handsome, accomplished wife, and soon two little boys: a small, loving family that depended on his income, which his university lectureship and earnings from his poetry readings and publications provided adequately. Nevertheless, as we have seen, a curious restiveness persisted. Bachchan was quickly bored by his routine in this uplifting time. He had to branch out. In 1943, 1944, and 1945, he went away with volunteer cadets and colleagues from the university for eight weeks of military training each summer. In 1952, when their sons were five and nine, respectively, he went to Cambridge, where he spent over two years completing a PhD while his wife and sons stayed in India. What led to these repeated attempts to get away? he asks himself.

The answer would appear to lie in the lyrical selfhood he wished to inhabit. Bachchan was tickled by the name "Suffering" that his first wife, Shyama, used for him. It encapsulated everything contained in his notion of a poet. His bearing in his second as in his first marriage was that of an obsessive, introverted dreamer, thinker, and revolutionary. In 1946, when he, Teji, and their infant firstborn stayed with a family in Pune who knew Teji from Lahore and treated her like a daughter, her friends were puzzled by Bachchan's somberness. "Does he never laugh?" they asked. The poet in Bachchan apparently approved: "Solemnity defines my being, though I know it is tiring and unhealthy." Indeed, he says, "I have suppressed the desire for sleep.... It seems a sheer waste of time."[28]

Yet, his "manhood" was at stake in other ways—troubled by what he describes as a strong "feminine" aspect in his being. "From a psychological point of view, it would be only natural for me, faced by the 'inner man' in Teji," to seek to negate "the 'inner woman' in myself." This, he thinks, might explain his escape into military training—and to Cambridge. Bachchan does not ruminate on other possible contributing factors I mentioned in chapter 4: the runaway father unwilling to be burdened with the daily grind of domestic work and care, or the notion that homes are simply there when needed, somehow nurtured by the natural homemakers, women—leaving men free for the larger tasks of the public world. The ambiguous commitment to the domestic that this implied was reflected in men's moody behavior in that space.

Boredom was one manifestation of men's discontent amid the everyday routine of domestic life. Restlessness frequently appeared in more openly conflictual forms. Clashes arose from the unresolved contradiction between the position of husbands, heads of household, and elders in general, as teachers and "lords" as well as providers of love and support: in this respect, husbands were in the position of a parent.[29] Conflicts flowed too from some men's belief that the women who were their life partners wasted too much time on routine, and unimportant, domestic tasks. Or, alternatively, from the belief that the women did not do enough—or were not good enough—to fulfill their domestic duties, straying too much, perhaps, from the straight and narrow path that was their inheritance.

An account of one exchange between Ambedkar and his first wife, Ramabai, captures the tension and frustration powerfully. In 1926, when both husband and wife were overcome by the death of a fourth child, their youngest, Ambedkar moved out of their shared domestic space. He started living in the office he had found three years earlier in a nearby auditorium established for workers by a local philanthropist, and returned to their tenement home infrequently. On days when he did not eat the food Ramabai sent for him, she remained hungry as well. Ambedkar then tried to ensure the lunchbox was returned empty, however he disposed of the food. Like Ramabai, who was now sickly and weak, Ambedkar too became weaker. He contracted malaria, yet did not go home. Ramabai went to his office, massaged his feet, and pleaded with him to come and rest. "Shouting, he told her to go away. She left sobbing."[30]

In earlier years, Ambedkar had pressed on his wife the need to educate herself. Friction followed. Ramabai told a close associate that "when Ambedkar pushed her to learn to read and write," she sometimes retorted, "I am illiterate. If that bothers you, get an educated woman as your second wife. But I am not going to study at this age." At this, Ramabai went on, Ambedkar "[would fly] into a rage and shut himself in a room." Ramabai, we are told, took it in her stride, telling her woman friend that "she was used to seeing him behave like 'a small child.'"[31]

Rahul Sankrityayan, who shared Ambedkar's position on the relatively unimportant character of household work, lays out his reactions to his wives' domestic commitments more fully. His autobiography reveals his obvious impatience with the domestic preoccupations of both his second and third wives. The impatience is expressed directly in the record of his interactions with the latter. Love and concern for young Kamala and their two children was clearly mixed with what he saw as the responsibilities of an elder. Through the 1950s, early in their marriage, Rahul insisted that Kamala devote less time to housework and more to her PhD. He pressed her too to accompany him on various planned or projected research trips in India and overseas. His openly expressed affection for her and the children was accompanied by aloofness, irritability, and a hypercritical stance, behavior that led her to remark that it was impossible to understand his "*vichitra*" (strange, weird) attitude toward women.

Kamala's response to his admonitions was like the response of many others in her position: "Reading and writing was not the only work there was. The household and children [still toddlers] ... needed care"—as did her aging and ailing husband. "How could a *grahini* [housewife, but more precisely, 'the woman of the home'] turn her back on the home?"[32] She knew she had to develop her abilities and stand on her own legs, she wrote in a long letter that she left for him on his desk in their Mussoorie home in January 1955, and that she would have to take care of herself, of their daughter, and of the child they were expecting—a son born three weeks later. But her husband's constant carping only weighed her down. "Swami [Lord], *you are making me a cripple*, instead of readying me for this struggle. *Your repeated hammer blows are driving me to madness.*"[33]

A forlorn note enters Kamala's reflections on this period. "What has happened to him?" she asks. "Why does he act so aloof? What have I done to spoil his life?" Why the irritability, constant criticism, stormy moods—nastiness? Concern for the future of his wife and children did not make the behavior acceptable. For Kamala, the criticisms became unbearable. "Finding fault all the time. A human being can only bear so much. Yet, I never fought with him, I quietly shed tears." "I had never ever expected such common behavior from such a great scholar as Panditji.... To mentally torment a helpless woman in this way did not show a [noble] soul like Panditji in good light: that much I said to him even at the time."[34]

The situation worsened after a stroke in December 1961 left Rahul mentally and physically incapacitated. In the last fifteen months of his life, until his death in April 1963, Kamala was his primary and often sole caretaker for long periods of the day and night, as he was moved from one hospital to another in Calcutta, Darjeeling, Delhi, and finally Moscow. The small, five-foot woman occasionally had to lift the body of this six-foot-tall, raging, wailing man-child, entirely on her own. She was at times too scared even to enter his room: "But if I don't, he searches for me.... My spirit is very low. I spend my days crying."[35]

Sankrityayan's temper—and tears—surfaced only when he had largely lost control of his body and mind. In other cases, tempers flared earlier. Hameeda Raipuri records her husband Akhtar's responses to several of her initiatives. One outburst occurred when she lined up a position for him in the Government of India's Information Office while he was in Paris in 1939–40, completing his doctorate. Akhtar accepted the position, she observes, but his first response was outrage at her for thinking he would work for the colonial regime—an assertion of the man's exclusive right to decide what he, and his loved ones, needed to do. He magnified the contemptuous note by adding that her father, an officer in the colonial police, must have dreamed up the plot.

She writes again of his rage when she had a government house allotted to the family after they moved to Karachi in 1947. "Did we come to Pakistan to grab people's property," she reports him screaming, as he tore up the allotment certificate. "He . . . took his bath and left the house, bristling with anger," returning at midnight. "It was the first time he had done this," she writes, and "I trembled." Another summary comment in the autobiography she wrote in his honor after his death puts it differently: "In my own, innocent, unpracticed way, I would do things thinking they might please Akhtar. But Akhtar's habit of losing his temper (*bigadne ki aadat*) never changed."[36]

There is little sign here of men touching women's emotion or sensitivity—let alone their reason, if that was ever acknowledged. What men touched, or responded to, repeatedly appears to have been their own ego. Among the working classes, the opportunity for men to prosper in their careers, or to pursue dreams of intellectual or political achievement, was far more constricted. Yet, the impulse to keep their charges in order is not altogether absent. Male ego, and insecurity, led to general suspicion of women's interest in anything outside the strictly prescribed—a suspicion that frequently led to physical violence against wives and other young female members of male-dominated families.

Baby Kamble writes about this kind of behavior in the small towns and villages of western India, even among newly educated, politically conscious, and upwardly mobile families. Here, as in other parts of the country, downtrodden men treated their own daughters-in-law and wives as "slaves."[37] The upholders of a jealous patriarchal order defended their honor by mutilating the bodies of "wayward" women and girls in their households. Many of the latter, dependent and vulnerable minors, were punished for the smallest offenses or signs of independence, including suspected exchange of glances with male strangers. "Dalit men did not hesitate," one distinguished Dalit scholar comments, "in chopping off the nose[s] of those Dalit women who according to the former failed to abide by the patriarchal norms."[38]

Kamble's father, a politically and economically "advanced" member of his community, kept her mother confined in his house and "beat her daily" for expressions of dissent. Kamble's husband, far less enterprising than her, treated her with suspicion, beating her repeatedly for imagined transgressions. "All my life," she says, "I had to face this violence."[39]

Sonubai Jadhav's position of rebelliousness mixed with resigned acceptance provides a concise summary of the overall tenor of relations in her working-class home; I cite the words from her son's somewhat romanticized account of her exchanges with her husband, Damu. First, Sonu: "It's always you, you, and you, Damodar Runjaji Jadhav. What about me? I am the insignificant Sonu, always nodding her head to whatever you say and walking behind you like your shadow?" Damu: "I am going to get converted [to Buddhism, as Ambedkar had suggested they should] and so will my children. . . . And so will you. . . . You will do as I say."[40] "It was an unwritten rule in our house," Sonu adds, "that my man's word is law."[41]

Sonubai's reply to a Bombay journalist's question about what she admired most in her husband—that he "never drank, never abused me. Best of all, he never raised his hand [on] me"[42]—provides striking testimony to a widespread, yet clearly stoic, acquiescence in husbandly authority and its attendant ills. So does Kamala Sankrityayan's remark that though her revered husband and teacher, Rahulji, "never raised a hand on anyone, not even on me," his sharp criticisms of her in his diary and letters to friends were "veritable slaps on my face."[43]

The language of restlessness—absence/presence, boredom, aloofness, irritability, rage, suspicion—was part of the regular repertoire of disciplining employed by men in South Asian homes, "aristocratic" and "plebian," upper caste and lower. Much of this flowed from underlying beliefs, shared by men across the social spectrum, about the nature and aptitude of men and women, to which I turn more directly in my final chapter.

7. The Nature of Men

Man marries today to obtain an anchorage in immanence,
but not to be himself confined therein; he wants to have hearth and
home while being free to escape therefrom; he settles down but
often remains a vagabond at heart.
— SIMONE DE BEAUVOIR

❋ ❋ ❋

I will focus in this final chapter on three dimensions of men's and women's thinking. First, men's views of the nature, inclinations, and responsibilities of women,
which make for the latter's place in the domestic world, seen as *their* domain.
Second, men's interpretation of their own responsibilities, which are seen as lying outside the home in the public sphere, the realm of World History, *their*
domain. Third, *women's thinking* on *men's thinking* and on *the nature of men* —
a move on my part to examine a commentary that might be seen as mimicking
the essentializing quality of men's remarks on women.

Two themes, elaborated early in this study, figure here centrally. The first pro-
pounds man's need to sally forth in search of knowledge, a nobler form of being,
and the good society of the future. The second posits woman's involvement in
the world as quintessential mother. In my concluding reflection on these motifs,

I will juxtapose these with a third proposition, Baby Kamble's concept of *navra-pana* (husbandness), which is what in her view gave men their sense of identity and self-worth: "I am a man, I am superior to women, I am somebody."[1]

Kamble's articulation counters patriarchal society's sweeping claims about the proper roles and responsibilities of men and women with a declaration on the nature of men. The declaration pares the matter of domestic hierarchy and male privilege down to its rudiments: an assumption, and assertion, of the innate talent, capacity, and potential of men, and more broadly, that of elders—that is, men plus older women who have graduated to adopting the position of men.

The arrogation of husbandly authority and manly entitlement derives from the concomitant sense of women's and society's dependence on men. The edifice of the South Asian world-in-the-home (*ghar-sansar*) was built on this ground. I shall begin therefore with the theme of women's essential nature as posited by men, on which men's ability to do what they do or want to do in the home, and indeed the entire organization of domestic life, depends.

"Little Mother"

In Tagore's classic novel *Ghare Baire* (*The Home and the World*), the protagonist Sandip's aged spiritual guru greets his pupil's young wife at their first meeting with the words, "May God protect you always, my little mother."[2] In Bengal, the view of girl/woman as mother extends far beyond an aristocratic Hindu elite. Daughters and young girls are routinely called *ma* (mother), not only by family members but even by strangers. The term is commonly used for young girls in Muslim families as well, in both West Bengal and Bangladesh.[3] Other Indian languages and idioms reflect a similar belief regarding the essential qualities of the female.

Leading thinkers from different provinces saw nation and woman as homologous in their roles as eternally protective, caring, self-sacrificing mother. I have quoted Premchand's 1931 essay, "Nari-jati ke adhikar" (The rights of women), on how the new wave of nationalism would "obliterate all [gender] distinctions" and somehow at the same time restore "our mothers" (girls and women) to their "exalted place" in the society. For Rajendra Prasad, Gandhi's wife Kasturba was "mother" to all—"the very ideal of a Hindu woman, a symbol of Indian culture, and a bundle of love." For Gandhi, women were "the future of India . . . nurtur[ing] the future generation."[4]

Bachchan's extended reflections on women and womankind provide an even more striking exposition of this belief, and of its implications for men's pursuit of their prescribed—or chosen—paths. I will restrict myself to his comments on three women with whom he had intimate relationships. I will argue that his thinking was shared to some extent by the women—although the rather different character of their choices and acceptance needs to be borne in mind—and refer to some of the physical and emotional consequences they suffered.

Let me return to his first love, Champa, his non-kin but closest brother Karkal's wife, who became pregnant when she and Bachchan "came together," almost unconsciously as he says, in the months of mourning that followed Karkal's premature death. Champa's mother-in-law took her away to Badrinath in the Himalayas (the northernmost of four major pilgrimage destinations that devout Hindus are urged to visit at least once in their lifetime), pursuing in this instance abortion as well as penance. Bachchan's recollection of his meeting with Champa when the women returned from their two-month-long journey is an unnerving illustration of the common equation of woman and mother.

Before her death, Bachchan declares in the first volume of his autobiography, written over four decades later, Champa revealed to him the "mother-form ... inherent in every woman." In the second volume, published the following year, he goes on to say, "Woman is in essence, precisely, a Mother. Compassion, tenderness, affection [*daya, karuna, mamta*] are the fount of her love." "Woman's love is but an aspect of her parental feelings [*vatsalya*]." Thence, to what he learned from Champa's sacrifice: "From the day of her return from Badrinath, when Champa addressed me as if I were her son, took all my sins into herself, blessed me and sent me off, and then a few hours later departed this world, I have used the benediction '*O Ma!*' [Oh Mother!] to remember her and all other women/mothers [*maa jati ki sari nariyan*]—alive or dead—who came into my life in any form."[5]

The self-sacrificing mother-figure appears again in Shyama, to whom Bachchan was married shortly afterward. At the time of their marriage, Shyama was fourteen, Bachchan eighteen. He had hoped, he says, for a bride who would understand him, lighten his soul, and share his burdens. The person he saw, in the formal daytime exchanges and secret nightly meetings of their first week together, was altogether different: "simple, little, innocent, unworldly, cheerful."[6]

During the years that followed, when Shyama was at her parents', nursing her tubercular mother and then herself, having contracted the disease, Bachchan corresponded with her. He visited her when he could escape from school and the tutoring jobs he'd taken on to earn money for his studies, stealing a few moments of privacy and companionship with her. When he mentioned his hesitation about entering university because of the fees, she sent him the hundred rupees she'd been given at her wedding for a necklace. "Your higher studies are more important than a gold chain," she wrote. "How much she had grown in one year," he ruminates in his autobiography; "I realized for the first time that she was no ordinary being."[7]

From the moment they first met, Bachchan writes, "she struck me as the embodiment of innocence. Somewhat removed from this crooked world, somewhat afraid, as if she was eager to merge herself completely in another. It was perhaps my [good] fortune that I appeared before her, and she had no choice but to merge herself in me."[8]

There was something "divine" or "spiritual" (*daivi*) in Shyama, he adds. She always knew what Bachchan wanted and did everything for him without being asked. When she discovered she had TB, she tried to keep the seriousness of her illness hidden from him. She did not want anyone—neither Bachchan nor his parents, nor her father and siblings—to be anxious about her. Therefore, "she drew on all her strength to ensure that no one knew of her disease or pain . . . her body's internal decay for years."[9]

Women's pain is normalized by Bachchan—and by his society—through the elevation of the physical, worn-out body of an earthly being to the status of disembodied, eternal, ethereal Mother and goddess. Sadly, this historical inheritance has led to their physical pains and burdens being minimized by women themselves. Recall Khurshid Mirza's reference to her "excellent health except for the occasional miscarriage." Or the examples I have cited of middle- and upper-class as well as working-class women birthing babies continuously, often until they reached menopause, and nurturing them till adulthood, whatever the costs.[10] The normalizing of women's pain reappears, unexpectedly, in the life of Teji Bachchan, so different in age, upbringing, education, experience, and self-confidence from Shyama and Champa, who were still in their early teens at the time of their weddings.

When Teji and Bachchan married, she was twenty-nine, he thirty-six. Bachchan describes Teji as a pillar of strength in every sense of the term. By his account, she was the dominant partner in their marriage. And yet, it is the "motherness" in Teji that stands out in his recollections. He notes that Teji grew up without a mother. "She has made up for the absence of a mother's love, and the pain that flowed from it, by developing an especially tender mother's heart." It was with a mother's compassion that she engaged the world—and her husband and family. She gave up much, including her career, to "take full charge of our house and the care of three males": that is, Bachchan and their two sons, all of whom—including himself, "an incapable, limited, unconventional, impractical" poet—he describes as artistic, idealistic, and ambitious.[11]

Teji's love for him was rooted in compassion and tenderness, Bachchan writes (the twin English meanings are encapsulated in the Hindi *karuna*): more specifically, in "a mother's tenderness" (*maatra-karuna*). His love for her, on the other hand, was rooted in gratitude (*kritagyata*). Further, "Compassion is nobler than love; for love is tinged with selfishness." Teji's maternal instinct and mother's love only deepened with the birth of their children. "From the moment woman becomes a mother, her children become—literally—first-among-all, primary, incomparable." For Teji, "the children have always come first," writes Bachchan, "and I have joyfully encouraged her."

Bachchan's characterization of Teji as an all-powerful, all-seeing mother allowed him to leave her with the housework, the care of the children, and all attendant responsibilities, and justified his absence from the home for long periods: military training in the three summers following the birth of their first child in 1942, and doctoral work in Cambridge for twenty-seven months a few years after the birth of their second in 1947.

During his time in England, Bachchan appears to have been unaware of the fears, difficulties, and dangers that confronted his courageous wife, living on her own with two little boys, supported only by a young male relative and a maidservant, in the conservative society that India was, and is. While he was overseas, Teji had to bear not only the gossip of idle neighbors and wags but also advances and threats from wanton admirers, while managing a middle-class home and two growing children on quite limited resources. She contributed to Bachchan's costs in Cambridge into the bargain. Yet she kept the financial and emotional costs from him until his return, for fear that worry might interrupt his work for his PhD. It was on the day of his homecoming, at night when the children were safely in bed, that her strength broke down—and Bachchan learned what she'd been through.

Bachchan describes his first sight of the family from his compartment when his train steamed into the Allahabad railway station. The boys looked well, and of course bigger. But Teji's appearance was alarming. "What had she done to herself? The fresh flowers she wore could not hide her withered look." At night, once the lights were turned off and the children asleep, she fell, crying, into his arms: "like a broken shoot," in his words, "without support, helpless. Her breath came as if from an exhausted, broken body."[12] It was a long time before she was able to speak, and then she let it all out. "That [she] had sold her last pieces of jewelry. / That there was no money left in their account. / That there was no food left in the house. / And that the ration for the next day had been bought with the five pounds he exchanged on the ship for seventy-five rupees."

To deal with a "gentleman" admirer and supposed family friend, who had hounded her and threatened in anonymous letters to abduct her children, Teji had begun to sleep a little during the day, and stay awake—reading—at night.

Months of this topsy-turvy and nerve-racking routine had left her wasted in body and spirit; her physical appearance showed it. As she finished her story of this admirer's importunities, including a coerced evening trip to the riverbank where he drew out a pistol, Teji said to Bachchan, "Never leave me alone again."[13]

Like labor—and the millions of working people, including women of all classes, who enabled societies to sustain, build, and reproduce themselves—the domestic was invisible, yet always, already there. Already accounted for in the form of "woman," its unshakable foundation as mother, homemaker, and domestic, a natural condition that made it possible for leading men to go forth in the noble venture of making the new man (and new woman), the nation, and the society of the future.

The Accomplished (Hu)Man

The slogan of life as "work, work, work," articulated by leading public figures of the early twentieth century, required total dedication to the task of regenerating self, community, and nation.[14] Out of this idea emerged new notions of the accomplished (hu)man, "higher" ways of being, and the "good" society—and, attendant on these noble aspirations, the likelihood of failure.

I referred in chapter 3 to the powerful tradition of *tyag* (sacrifice of worldly desires and possessions), and the ideals of the *karmayogi* (the seeker who seeks the higher life through service) and *parivrajak* (literally, recluse, ascetic, or sannyasi, one who has withdrawn from the world, now interpreted as a new kind of reformer, centrally engaged in making the world), invoked by many leaders of modern India. Gandhi is probably the most prominent example of such sacrifice and service. But there were many others, such as Dayanand Sarasvati, Vivekananda, and Subhas Bose, among luminaries I have mentioned, and Ambedkar and Rahul Sankrityayan, central figures in my discussion in the preceding pages. Indeed, Sankrityayan's elaboration of the philosophy of wandering in his extensive oeuvre provides a particularly arresting instance of the contradictions at the heart of men's thinking about their role in the world, and the implications of such thinking for domestic life in South Asia.

In a series of writings beginning with *Ghumakkad Shastra* (Treatise on wandering), published in 1949, Sankrityayan presented a robust exposition of the idea of wandering as a necessary path to individual and social enlightenment. *Ghumakkad Shastra* spelled out his views on the qualities of a consummate human life: "Wandering is the religion of humanity. Whoever gives it up is unworthy of being called a human being." "Wanderers are the most accomplished (*shreshth*) human beings": witness, the Buddha, Guru Nanak, Dayanand Saraswati, and other makers of India.[15] He might have added the Prophet Muhammad, Jesus Christ, Martin Luther, had he cast his net farther afield.

Following criticism from women readers that he had said little about women in the 1949 text, Sankrityayan added a new chapter in a second 1956 edition. In this chapter, entitled "How Can Young Women Take Up the Path," he mentioned female "wanderers" he had seen in his travels in Ladakh, Tibet, and Korea in the 1920s and '30s, women who were traveling on their own in search of knowledge and enlightenment. The examples include two young women from France and the United States, and women from the Himalayan region on India's northern border, as well as women ascetics and worshippers traveling alone to pilgrimage sites in India: for "another name for pilgrimage is *ghumakkadi* [wandering]."[16]

As an idealist and strong advocate of women's rights ("Women are not born simply to produce babies"), Sankrityayan stressed men's and women's equal access to *ghumakkadi* as a nobler way of life. His advice to parents who wished to restrain daughters, as they earlier restrained sons, was: "Let them become wanderers, and travel to different lands through wild and difficult paths." Elders could not be their armed guards; "they will be protected only when they can protect themselves."[17] And to women: "The *dharma* [duty, religion] of wandering is not a narrow dharma like that of the Brahmins.... Women have as much access to it as men. If they wish to fulfil themselves and make something of the individual and society, they too should unambiguously embrace this dharma."[18]

Yet, the author's argument about women's ability to take on a life of wandering was far from persuasive. He recognized the difficulties women faced in choosing such a life. Knowing the attraction that men and women feel for each other, he advocated the Buddhist ideal of "non-desire," "turning away," to deal with the problem. "Young women wanderers should know that if a man becomes the cause of bringing a child into this world, he is not tied down by it. If he is very liberal and kind [*sic*], he can make some arrangement and resume his unrestrained journey. But the woman wanderer who makes one such mistake is crippled for life."[19]

With all that, the thrust of his argument was that giving in to sexual and emotional desires—and even more so, to marriage and domesticity—tied men (and women) down. Where does this leave his radical construction of the new man and new woman, the matter of sexual and emotional fulfillment he advocated, the production and reproduction of the species, to say nothing of the domestic dependence of men as well as women? Sankrityayan addresses the question in other writings, including his 1958 biography of Swami Harishanand, whom he christened *Ghumakkad Swami* (The wandering religious mendicant).[20]

Named Harishchandra when he was born in 1889, three or four years before Sankrityayan, Harishanand came from a poor household. He lost his mother at birth, his father a few years later; in his teens, he left home to become a *sadhu*, a wandering ascetic in search of spiritual truth. He then became a successful practitioner and leading expert in Ayurveda, an ancient Indian medical system based on knowledge of rare roots and plants; a nationalist organizer and activist jailed for his participation in the anti-colonial campaign in the 1930s; and finally at the age of fifty-two a householder. As a householder, he continued his scientific and medical work, putting his considerable income from his medical practice and sale of medicines into the service of the poor and needy, and supporting laboratories and publications for research on and dissemination of the knowledge of Ayurveda.

Harishanand's life paralleled Sankrityayan's in many ways—including *ghumakkadi*, a commitment to scientific, demonstrable knowledge, political activism, and a late marriage with a woman over thirty years younger than the men. An unambiguous admirer of the Swami's life and career, Sankrityayan found in him an older brother. His biography of Harishanand reiterates the arguments of *Ghumakkad Shastra*, with added emphasis on a scientific temper leading to experimentation, observation, and analysis, as against blind faith in received wisdom and texts. "[The Swami] had chosen his path with the highest goals in mind. From the start, his emphasis was not on texts, but on experiment." He studied the literature of "Greek, Egyptian, allopathy, homeopathy, bio-chemistry, chromopathy, naturopathy, and other medical traditions," along with Ayurveda. He refused to be bound by any dogma; even Ayurveda was not infallible. "Practical results [*upyogita*, literally, usefulness]" were the test.[21]

Suddenly, in 1941, at the age of fifty-two, in the midst of this search for scientific truth and social and political justice, the Swami became a householder. Sankrityayan spells out the reasoning, uncannily similar to his own when he married Kamala in 1950. Harishanand was aware of the problems he faced with advancing age and declining health. Despite a large circle of friends and hangers-on, "there was no one who would support him fully in his . . . declining years . . . no one whom he could call his own, and who could call him hers/his. . . . He thought only a woman could fulfil that role. Nature has made man and woman dependent on one another. *The service and support a woman can provide, no one else can.*"[22]

The Swami advertised in the newspapers, specifying the kind of woman he wanted, indicating that the civil marriage would involve no expense, and promising to look after his wife well. He interviewed fifteen applicants and selected Janaki Devi, a young Brahmin woman from a small town five hundred miles to the southeast of his abode in Amritsar, and two hundred miles beyond Delhi. She was twenty to his fifty-two. At a very early age, she had been married to an old man, who passed away in less than six months, before she had moved to his house. Because of her father, a small-time medical practitioner, she had some schooling. The Swami and she met and agreed to marry.

Janaki was, by Sankrityayan's account, everything Harishanand needed. She was an extraordinary cook, fed guests magnificently, and looked after her husband with great care. In 1949, her husband fell prey to a digestive disorder that seemed untreatable. He stopped eating, became emaciated, unable to stand or walk easily, and occasionally fainted. But for his wife's constant nursing, he would not have recovered. "Seeing the [miracle-making] care she gave him during his incurable [sic] illness," writes Sankrityayan, "the Swami would have congratulated himself on his choice [of a wife]."[23] Yet, despite her gentleness and calmness, the strain of looking after her husband showed in Janaki. She was often stern and sometimes lost her temper.

Sankrityayan's autobiography records his reactions to one of her outbursts. "On September 9 [1955], there was a clash between *Bhaiya* and *Bhabhiji* [that is, the Swami and his wife, whom Sankrityayan looked upon as an older brother and sister-in-law]. *Bhabhiji* should be appointed head of the enemy forces. She was spitting out poison against [all] men. I became nothing but a mute on-looker." Sankrityayan goes on, however, to elaborate his thinking in a five-point manifesto:

1. An older man should never marry a young woman. 2. He who has not taken on the responsibilities of a householder to the age of 50 should be doubly careful: "Never ever! Never ever!" [This phrase, which appears in Sanskrit, translates literally, "That's not it! Not it!"] 3. That he has not taken on the responsibilities of a householder all that time means that he was fired by some ideals. Such a person should be even more wary of shackling himself. 4. Anyone who has spent a long life wandering the world should keep far away from marriage. 5. If in addition he is addicted to a quest for knowledge, the prohibition is absolute.[24]

Thus, the philosopher denounces anything that goes against the realization of an ambitious man's full potential. In the cause of "man," and of "mankind," he sacrifices the cause of ordinary living men and women. The positions of householder and homemaker are best avoided, he says: a bizarre proposition, given his own marital history and dependence on women and their domestic worlds.

Other men considered in the preceding chapters had a similarly ambiguous approach to marriage and domesticity—enhanced by old age and declining health but not restricted to that stage in life. Recall how Ambedkar described himself as married to his books and declared that any companion or spouse of his must live with the fact. Compare Abdul Haq, who, in the words of his lieutenant Akhtar Husain Raipuri, "accorded Urdu the deference due to one's mother" and treated the organization for the promotion of Urdu "with the affection that is reserved for a daughter." And Raipuri's assessment of himself as a person whose literary and political commitment left him "indifferent to house and hearth, unconcerned with fame and power . . . wealth or self-interest. . . . There was such restlessness in my disposition that as soon as I settled somewhere I felt the urge to move. . . . All my life I tended to fly far away like a kite, [my wife] never let go of the kite string, or allowed anyone to cut it."[25]

The Domain of World History: Men Educating Women

And yet, wherever thinking and progressive men entered into marriages—as most of them did—they saw it as their task to educate the women, "minors," who came into their lives. This was a vital part of their thinking about the nature and commitments of men. Thus Gandhi, who reflected seriously on men's responsibilities in the home, embraced what he learned from the examples around him and from the cheap pulp literature that was widely sold in his adolescence and youth. He saw it as the duty of husbands to educate, coach, and discipline their wives. The position of teacher and guide was more easily assumed, given that women and girls were commonly "outsiders" when they came into their husbands' homes, usually younger (though this was not true in Gandhi's case), financially dependent, and often without ready access to formal education and outside contacts.[26]

The Mahatma writes of how quickly he claimed husbandly authority when he married. He and his bride, Kasturba, were the same age, thirteen. This did nothing to reduce his possessiveness, jealousy, or bullying, nor his attempt to educate her. Kasturba was illiterate when they married, he tells us, and could only "with difficulty write simple letters and understand simple Gujarati" in later life. He counts this as his failure: "she was educated neither by her parents nor by me at the time when I ought to have done it."[27]

When Gandhi wrote his autobiography, the couple had been married for forty-five years. They had worked together for decades in his campaigns for radical social and political change. Nevertheless, Gandhi acknowledged, he and his wife were not in agreement on every issue, and she did not approve of all he preached and did. However, he wrote, he saw no point in discussing the differences with her, given her lack of learning. Perhaps, he went on, "Kasturba herself does not . . . know whether she has any ideals independently of me [*sic*]. . . . But she is blessed with ... a quality which most Hindu wives possess in some measure.... [W]illingly or unwillingly, consciously or unconsciously, she has considered herself blessed in following in my footsteps."[28]

Other men, less "tormented" than Gandhi, articulated the same kind of position regarding husbandly authority and responsibility far more simply. Take Thakur Amar Singh of Kanota (1878–1942). Born and bred a Rajput prince, trained under the prince-regent of the Jodhpur ruling family, officer in the Jaipur State Forces and the British Indian Army, he participated in imperial ventures abroad, helped control the Boxer Rebellion in China, served in Basra during the First World War, and was schooled in English military manners and customs as much as Indian princely mores and rules. Amar Singh wrote a daily diary in English for forty-four years from 1898 to 1942, preserved in eighty-nine bound volumes, about eight hundred pages each, in the Kanota archive. I quote from a diary entry for November 9, 1901. Aged twenty-three, Amar Singh had recently married a young woman from a neighboring princely house, to whom he was greatly drawn from their first meeting at the time of their arranged wedding.

> I was always up talking with my wife until twelve and sometimes one at night. It was *necessary for me to talk to her and try and make her mind on the same level and footing as mine own.* This thing can only be done gradually and to do it one must first grow familiar and win another's confidence and love ...
>
> I am glad to say we do not disagree on anything at all. Of course she has some superstitions still in her head, but they will gradually all die out if I have occasion to stop and talk to her for a long and continuous time ...
>
> ... She is a very mild woman and not at all disposed to mix up and make rows with others. She is very obedient to my will and orders. *I only wish she would continue to behave herself as she has done up to the present all throughout her life.*[29]

Ambedkar provides another example of the role of guide and instructor that progressive men of the later nineteenth and early to mid-twentieth centuries saw as intrinsic to their duties in marriage. In February 1948, a few months before his second marriage, he sent his prospective bride Sharda, renamed Savitabai after the marriage, the highly educated doctor who married him when she was thirty-nine, three designs from the *Illustrated Weekly of India*, illustrating women's sleepwear from three different regions. He recommended the Marwari design—slightly modified—as the most fetching of the three, adding that "Sharu [Sharda] should decide for herself, she is free." However, "If Raja's choice is approved [using the name she often called him by], five or six sleeping dresses should be made." In her own rendition of the dutiful wife, Savitabai adds: "He obviously never imposed his wishes on me, but . . . his choice would be so appropriate that I would always find them acceptable. Needless to say, I did get five or six Marwari-style sleeping dresses stitched."[30]

In another letter a few weeks later, Ambedkar mentioned other items she might want in her bridal attire: "While in the train [from Bombay to Delhi, where he now lived as Law Minister in independent India's first cabinet] I remembered that you had mentioned a dressing gown. I forgot about it. I give you the liberty to buy one. But can you assure me that you can choose a good one in point of colour and material? Better you wait till you come here."[31]

Three brief comments from men of the Partition and Independence generation whom I have discussed earlier demonstrate the persistence of this belief in men's obligation to educate their wives: women and girls always considered "minors" in some fundamental sense, even if they were thought "mature" enough to be wives and mothers. My examples—Harivansh Rai Bachchan, an upper-caste Hindu (b. 1907); Jagjivan Ram, a Dalit (b. 1908); and Akhtar Husain Raipuri, a middle-class Muslim of aristocratic background (b. 1912)—represent the gamut of social backgrounds I have referenced in this study.

I noted that Bachchan's family elders arranged his first marriage in 1926 to help him get over the tragic death of his first love and her husband, his bosom pal and "brother." When Bachchan met the bride Shyama, he first wondered about the brains of his elders, who believed that "this immature child could be an appropriate companion for me." But then, he writes, "another thought struck me—like lightning. If she couldn't rise to my level, I could descend to hers. . . . I became like a child with my child-bride. . . . I made her my playmate. And I was convinced that one day this playmate would become my fellow-sufferer and companion, sharing all my joys and sorrows, hopes and disappointments, peace and struggles."[32] In other words, a large part of the responsibilities of the householder—educating and looking after their wives and dependents—would still be fulfilled. And, who knows, perhaps one day his "child-bride" would grow into a "fellow-sufferer and companion": nothing less. In Shyama's case, as Bachchan's recollections have it, she did just that.

Jagjivan Ram married Indrani Devi in 1935. She was twenty-four, he twenty-seven. He had obtained a bachelor's degree from Calcutta University before becoming a full-time Congress worker and political activist. She was a qualified schoolteacher who left her urbane, politically conscious natal family and her job in the industrial city of Kanpur to live in his village home and wherever else his political career took him after that. Yet his early letters indicate his sense of his appointed duty to educate her. Consider two of these. The first is from the year they married. It relates to the drawing up of constituencies for provincial assembly elections: "I fear that *you will not be able to understand these yet*, and not at all if I put them in a letter. *You will understand some of it when I explain face to face.*" The second is a letter of March 1941, in which he explains the meaning of socialism as he understands it ("when the distribution of wealth can be organized to the benefit of every member of society"), adding, "*As you read more books, your interests will grow, and you will understand everything.*"[33]

The 23-year-old Akhtar Raipuri, who had begun to work on an Urdu dictionary after completing his master's degree, married the fifteen-year-old schoolgirl Hameeda in December 1935. He had greatly admired her spunk and literary interests when they first met a few months earlier. However, his approach after their marriage was very much in line with that of the other men. As she recalled it, he congratulated her for putting down a newspaper she picked up to read during the train journey from her parents' home to his after their wedding, reasoning that his bride, who had read and admired his revolutionary fiction and non-fiction, would not understand the news. There was more in that vein throughout their life together, although since she was already well-schooled and comparatively self-confident on account of her elite background, "education" by her husband seemed to consist more of directing her physical movement—in the home and outside.[34]

Navrapana (Husbandness)

What do the women we have met in the preceding chapters have to say about what men and women brought to a marriage, and how the men saw their role in it? We know that many of them—Swami Harishanand's wife Janaki Devi, Shivrani Devi Premchand, Hameeda Husain Raipuri, Kamala Sankrityayan, Indrani Jagjivan Ram, among others—shared something of their husbands' (and society's) views on the inheritances of men and women. Willingly or unwillingly, they went along with existing arrangements in the making of marriages and homes, and thereby with the existing notions of "husbandness" and "motherhood" underpinning them. Nonetheless, their assessment of the comportment of their husbands, and of men more generally, was mixed.

Though we have no record of her words, Janaki Devi's handling of her husband in the years following their marriage reveals a lot about her thinking. Still in her twenties, she took on the role of the adult in the relationship, indulging and monitoring her husband, a "spoilt child" in his fifties, with endless patience and occasional anger. We know more about what some of our other women protagonists said about their feelings.

I have described the interactions of Kamala and Rahul Sankrityayan in several chapters. In the context of their last years together, when she was stuck inside an endless series of hospital rooms with her mentally incapacitated husband, Kamala repeatedly invoked a "vale of tears" as a description of a woman's life. Her husband could not comprehend the meaning of a woman's tears, she writes, else he would not so easily have abandoned his first wife, a child bride, to her long life of tears.[35] Or, we might add, his more independent second wife, managing alone with their son in Russia through the siege of Leningrad and beyond.[36]

As Kamala sees it, the "vale of tears" came with the bond of marriage—a bond seen by most women until recently as a necessity—and with women's ownership of the responsibilities that marriage implied. Her comments on her husband's "common behavior"—the "torment[ing of] a helpless woman"—are significant. His behavior was especially shocking, she said, coming from a person of his nobility and high standards. Which leads to her sobering judgment: "however educated, rational, learned a man might be, *his nature* [svabhav] *remains that of an ordinary man.*"[37]

What Kamala calls the "nature . . . of an ordinary man" is what Baby Kamble describes as "husbandness"—behavior that smacks of husbandly authority and male entitlement. Ambedkar, more outspoken than most, accepted the charge, in response to some colleagues' comments on how he didn't seem to care for his first wife and their family as much as he did for books and learning: "That's the kind of person I am. . . . I don't express love the way you people do, therefore you think I am heartless. But that is absolutely false." In his natal family, he added, that was the pattern of men's behavior toward their wives: "That is the *baal kadu* [Ayurvedic potion given to children] of our family. It had some effects on the males. That must be the cause of my behavior."[38]

Men's burden of guiding, disciplining, and educating themselves and their worlds was not always expressed in the strictness of Ambedkar, the irritability of Sankrityayan's later years, or the restlessness, poetic suffering, and despondency of Bachchan. Observers noted the camaraderie, the easy conversation and laughter, and the joyous sport with children—and, less commonly, with wives—that marked Sankrityayan's bearing, as it did that of Premchand, Gandhi, Damodar Jadhav, and others discussed in earlier chapters.

Premchand, Sankrityayan, Raipuri and his idol Abdul Haq, Bachchan's grandfather Bholanath, Bachchan himself, and the Dalit men who appear in Valmiki's and Indrani Ram's accounts of proceedings in their rural communities were happy in the homosocial company of friends and admirers who shored up their sense of community, self-worth, and relevance. Many of them also appear to have been concerned heads of household, loving fathers, and caring husbands—even when they were strict disciplinarians. Yet the freedom to roam free, and to make all important decisions, runs through these men's stories.

Men not involved in the kind of public intellectual and political work done by the public figures mentioned above expressed male authority, and their duty to maintain order, in other ways. For Akbar Mirza, the upstanding police officer, administrator, guardian of a new law and order, manly pursuits involved hunting, athletics, motorcycle riding, a proud independence, and being a family man in command of his domestic and wider civic world. Among working-class men (and women) of the late colonial and early postcolonial period, a very different social stratum, there was not only an intense desire to see their children educated like "sahibs" but also a pride in physical labor that saves them from the dissipation and helplessness of the middle and upper classes.

Consequently, Narendra Jadhav told me, his father scoffed at the suggestion that he might occupy his time after retirement in jotting down memories of his life. Despite his desire to educate his sons, the proud working-class person in him did not want to be associated with "soft," "Brahminical" practices. It was only after his death that his children found the set of notebooks they had given him, hidden in a trunk under his bed, with his scattered, repetitive, and telling account of notable incidents in his childhood and youth. This working-class pride went along with an exceptional determination to ensure the educational progress and professional achievements of his sons, suggested in Narendra's comment on his father, cited in chapter 5: "Dada's self-confidence was extraordinary. 'Get me a long enough stick, I'll flatten this circular earth and show you.'"

Kamala Sankrityayan's and Indrani Jagjivan Ram's statements on public and private "jails" echo Sonubai Jadhav's comments to her husband: "It's always you, you, and you.... What about me? I am the insignificant Sonu, always nodding her head to whatever you say and walking behind you like your shadow?"[39] The three women's words also bring to mind Akbar Mirza's handling of his wife Khurshid's independence and initiative.

Early in their marriage, Akbar intercepted and read Khurshid's personal letters. Learning of her interest in films from an intercepted letter, he refused initially to countenance her traveling to Bombay, even with him as chaperone, to speak with people in the film industry. Near the end of his life, after his retirement, his need to be in charge was undiminished. It showed when they were on holiday in England, in his refusal to accompany her to the BBC or to let her travel alone on the London underground. Khurshid was by this time a recognized artist, writer, social worker, and archivist of folklore, in addition to being a mother and grandmother. She comments on these proceedings in the lively autobiography she wrote after his death. Her words are poignant: "How does one explain the selfishness of a beloved husband who has to be reassured all the time that he has the priority in his wife's life, despite her professional commitments?"[40]

In the end, what the women might have said is: "*Educators*, educate yourselves—about the people, animals, and lives around you, and most of all about yourselves." For the thing men did not question at all, in their lives and activities in the domestic arena or the wider public domain, was their right to wander at will and thus fulfill their natural talents. They hardly pondered the historically produced self-image of men as necessarily complex, thinking, many-sided, and independent human beings: so self-evident, so *natural* that it remains pervasive, even though it is widely challenged today. The belief depended, critically, on the assumption that the "self-made man" is beholden to no one outside himself, least of all to wives and other "minor dependents" in an only-occasionally-visible domestic world. To investigate that image might have been a step too far, too risky for men—and for some women, too risky for society as they knew it.

The preceding pages should have shown the gulf that separates the cultural, social, economic inheritances and practices, and day-to-day lives, aspirations, and struggles of the "respectable" castes and classes, the *bade log* or "big people," on the one hand, and of the "masses," *chote log* or "small people," on the other. At the same time, they have indicated the commonality of gendered hierarchies, and of the violence and discrimination attending them, across caste, class, and community divisions. What we encounter here is not just a broadly male-centered and male-dominated society. We encounter an insistently, not to say proudly, patriarchal order that, with all its variations, contradictions, and conflicts, thrives on sharp caste, class, and gender divides. The multiple threads are deeply entrenched and need to be recognized, and combated, accordingly.

This book has also underscored the inextricable intertwining of "World Historical" time, the time of the future, and "everyday" time, the time of the here and now. Perhaps it invites us thereby to reflect a little more carefully on what is classified as "necessary" (the thunder and lightning of "World Historical" events?) and what as "contingent" (the matter of survival and reproduction of the species, of companionship and care, and the accompanying drudgery of everyday domestic life?).

It is my hope that the detail and range of the present inquiry will help open up new questions about the lived experience and multiple meanings of the South Asian modern, and lead to more detailed and resolute exploration of this critical underbelly of modernity in the Indian subcontinent—and elsewhere.

Epilogue

YM YLIMAF

The title of this epilogue is the phrase "my family," somewhat scrambled. The impulse for scrambling the words comes from Samuel Butler's *Erewhon, or Over the Range* (1872). *Erewhon*, the name of the country in which Butler's satirical novel is set, is an anagram for *nowhere*. To the traveler who is the narrator of the story, "Erewhon at first seems utopian in its disregard for money—which lends status but has no purchasing value—and machines—which have been outlawed as dangerous competitors in the struggle for existence." As he gets to know the institutions and procedures of Erewhon better, however, "his illusions of utopia and eternal progress are stripped away."[1] I experienced a parallel sense of dystopia in examining the discourses surrounding the family in modern South Asia—with all the difference in political and cultural context.

In the received discourses, the sacred, fundamentally harmonious family, the self-sacrificing, loving mother, the home were objects of veneration. So much so that even my immediate community of idealistic, leftist, cosmopolitan intellectuals and political activists failed to mount a sustained critique of the domestic order and its pillars: the absent/present father, the presiding matriarch and other elders, the presumed naturalness of the hierarchy and allotted gender roles.

Two centuries of colonial rule and imperialist domination had left deep scars. They led, on the one hand, to an urgent desire to match the material and scientific advances of the West; on the other, to a largely unquestioned investment in what were seen as precious and unassailable Indian inheritances. Social traditions and cultural treasures bequeathed by an ancient civilization, these inheritances, appropriately modified, would serve as the core of the authentic indigenous resources remaining to the colonized, and the recently liberated. Prominent among them were the sacrosanct home and family.

This book is about the larger family, the context, country, and culture in which I grew up. How does my own specific, and narrower, domestic world—my natal family, my marital history and intimate relations—fit into this narrative? Familial arrangements and prescriptions were little discussed when I was growing up. They were an unacceptable subject for a child's or an adolescent's questioning. There were things that children did not need to know, or even think about: the dogma obtained especially in this hallowed space of nurture and care. It was common sense that the loving, caring family and home automatically protected all those within its embrace. The family was still conceived as an extended community of parents, grandparents, children, cousins, aunts and uncles, putative aunts and uncles, servants, and more. Yet, it goes without saying, its loving embrace and protection was extended in different measures to different members. The male of the species was especially favored: more especially, sons, the natural inheritors and guardians of the family's name, honor—and property, in the case of families that had property to pass on.

All of this was magnified for my older brother and myself once we were sent away to a boarding school in the foothills of the Himalayas at the ages of six and five and a half, respectively. We came home from school for the three-month winter vacation. During that time, we were spoiled, given whatever we asked for, and celebrated—as much for speaking English fluently as for anything else! Luckily, our wants were in tune with the times, and in line with those of our lower-middle-class and middle-class neighbors. We craved Mother's delicious home-cooked food, outings to the cinema, jaunts in Father's occasionally available official car (later he bought his first private car, a Morris Minor), and the running around, cricket and football, hopscotch and seven-tiles, with neighborhood kids whose parents, all "Aunties" and "Uncles," spoiled us as much as family elders who were blood relations.

It was, as they say, a more innocent age, when children were meant to be, and told to be, seen and not heard. When we played like children, "without a care in the world," and asked no questions about "adult" matters—like sex and money, politics, and many other things, including sacred spaces like the family and sacred compacts like those between parents and children, and husbands and wives. Call it my innocence, my sheltered upbringing, the cocoon in which my brother and I grew up in our strictly regimented school in the hills and the wild freedom of the three months' winter vacation at home, but it was not until recently that I found out about several hidden parts of my birth family's history.

❀ ❀ ❀

In 2019, seventeen years after my father died, I discovered that my mother was his second wife. The fact of my father's first wife and marriage was a well-kept family secret. My father had never dropped a hint of this earlier history. Nor had my mother, though I guess she knew of it, especially given my father's expressed concern—about which I learned when I learned of his first marriage—that nothing from the earlier marriage should cast a shadow on the home he was making with my mother. When I finally asked my mother, in her nineties, if my father had been married earlier as a child, as so many others were in those times, she said, "I don't know."

I do not know if any of my siblings knew; there were five of us, two boys born three and five years into my parents' marriage, and three girls, born five, seven, and fifteen years after me. My older brother likely did not; my sense is that he would not have let the matter rest, had he got an inkling of it. My two youngest sisters may have heard something about an earlier marriage from my mother; they were continuously with her, and they became her closest, most intimate friends as they grew up. But, if they knew, they too honored our parents' desire to keep the secret a secret.

I may never have learned about my father's first wife and her abandonment, but for the research I began a few years ago on the history of family life and circumstances in colonial and postcolonial India. My investigations quickly revealed the widespread incidence of child marriages, or very early marriages, in respectable middle- and upper-class, middle- and upper-caste circles across much of the country, well into the 1920s and '30s if not later. And with that, a history of abandonment of many of these young wives by their aspiring, ambitious, even idealistic "modern" husbands. The finding made me wonder about the early period of my father's life in a smallholding, upper-caste (Brahmin) household in a Bhumihar/Brahmin-dominated village on the border of Uttar Pradesh and Bihar in northern India. I still didn't ask my mother, fearing that it might be too direct and embarrassing, given the culture of respectability and reticence in our family. And, because my late father had very largely cut us, and himself, off from his village background, I couldn't ask any relatives or associates there.

In the end, an elderly second cousin of mine, fourteen or fifteen years younger than my father and one of his greatest admirers and followers from his childhood in the village to the end of his life, told me about my father's earlier marital history. My cousin worked in a well-established civil engineering firm in northern India from the mid-1950s until 1970. He then moved to the United States to pursue his engineering career, before branching off into some not-so-successful business ventures in North Carolina. I came to know him in my schooldays, when he visited my parents' home every now and then during our winter vacations, and we met on several occasions between my move to the United States in 1998 and his passing in 2023.

The first piece I published out of my research on the history of the modern Indian family was a long essay in Hindi centered on the marital histories of three leading public figures from Uttar Pradesh and Bihar, from districts neighboring the area where my father and my cousin grew up.[2] In the essay, I discussed in some detail the three protagonists' child marriages, and the abandonment of their young brides by two of them. My cousin read the essay with much interest, and began reminiscing about life in the village, and how men and women were married and lived—or did not live—together. In the course of those nostalgic ruminations, he said to me, assuming I already knew or had surmised somehow, that my father had married and lived for a decade with *"Badi Chachi"* (that is, "Older Aunt"; my mother was *"Chachi,"* "Aunt").

Here is a summary of what my cousin told me. My father's first marriage occurred sometime in the early 1930s, when he was in his midteens, his bride a little younger. Though "unschooled," she was an attractive woman, gentle, loving, caring—interested in the well-being of all around her ("much like your mother"). She was greatly liked in my father's village home. Unfortunately, she had ovarian problems, sexual intercourse was painful for her (so my cousin had gathered as a child), and she never had children. Nevertheless, Chachaji (my father, "Respected Uncle" to my cousin)—who was away from the village much of this time, initially as a student in Calcutta and Allahabad, and later, at the start of World War II, as a short-term emergency commission officer in the Indian army—was deeply attached to her. "You could see this in all their interactions."

Then, misfortune struck. My father heard a rumor that one of his uncles, a notorious philanderer, had taken advantage of his young bride when she and a younger female family member with her own health issues accompanied him to the big city of Patna for medical consultation. They stayed in an ashram in Patna managed by a priest whom the family knew, and slept on the floor in one of its rooms. The family would probably not have expected the male elder, accompanying the women to the city, to molest girls/women of his own family. Whether he did or not in this instance, the suspicion was enough. My father made surreptitious inquiries about who had slept next to whom, believed "something" must have happened, and abandoned his wife. She returned to her parents' village in a neighboring district, never married again (upper-caste women were rarely if ever allowed to do so), and resumed occasional visits to my father's ancestral home only several years later. This followed entreaties from her in-laws, who remained fond of her and treated her as a member of the family. However, her husband, my father, never saw her again. (The uncle, whom my father abused to his face, stayed on comfortably in his part of the ancestral home.)

How much the fact of her childlessness had to do with my father's abandonment of his first wife, I do not know. Before this incident, my cousin said, my father had not contemplated a second marriage, despite the pleas of some elders. He did it on the rebound, as it were, in bitterness and anger—and (I might add) perhaps some reinvigorated sense of independence and idealism. He arranged his second marriage on his own, advertising for an educated girl of appropriate caste background and family, and refusing any dowry and other unnecessary expenditure. As part of the agreement, he promised his prospective new in-laws that the shadow of his first, childhood wedding would never be allowed to fall on this, his chosen marriage.

There was an additional twist to my cousin's tale. My father's father, a tall, well-built, well-respected Deputy Inspector of Schools, who was regularly posted to districts some distance from his home, had established a second family with a lower-caste woman who cleaned and cooked for him when he worked in Hazaribagh, in southern Bihar. This was while his first wife, my father's mother, was still living in grandfather's village: she died shortly after the birth of her only child, my father, in 1917. Grandfather treated his common-law wife honorably, and looked after the four children they had together (two daughters older than my father, and two sons, younger than him) in the ways he thought best for them. The daughters attended school for several years before they were married into comfortable Brahmin homes in the countryside; the sons graduated from the prestigious Banaras Hindu University and had fairly successful careers.

Because of my grandfather's standing in the village and beyond, his kith and kin accepted the children as part of his family. My father also showed no resentment toward them, according to my cousin. He did, however, insist that they have nothing to do with his new "nuclear" family. Later in life, when he decided to sell his share of the little ancestral land his family owned in the village, my father visited his stepbrothers and instructed them strictly to steer clear of the proceedings. As a senior civil servant, he said, he would help them as much as he could in other ways. Their father, also my father's father, had already made it clear to them and to their mother that they were never to make any claims on the family's ancestral property—and they never did.

❋ ❋ ❋

My father thought of himself very much as a self-made man. The first graduate from his village, with a further master's degree in English literature. The first from the village to become an officer in the British Indian Army and then (after

World War II) the prestigious civil service. The first to wear English-style trousers, and speak in English with British colleagues. He was a lover of poetry in English, Hindi, and Urdu and of the classical and semi-classical music of north India, and, in time, a well-published novelist in Hindi.

As I remember him, he was a man of two (or more) parts that sat together somewhat uneasily. A proud Indian: proud of his ancient Hindu roots and, paradoxically, given the chauvinist Hindu views he expressed on many occasions, of India's plural culture, the sitar and *shehnai*, the *kathak* dance, and the Urdu *ghazal*—all part of the rich Indo-Muslim heritage that India's current Hindu right-wing regime is bent on destroying. At the same time, he flaunted a commitment to what he thought of as modern ("English") ways. A traditional head of household, concerned to preserve and perpetuate his family and community's name and heritage, he also had the self-image of a man-about-town, who enjoyed parties and drinking and dancing, and was something of a flirt—a trait that my mother, but not my cousin, referred to in passing comments over the years.

My mother grew up in a more urban milieu than my father. Her father, a science teacher and school principal in various small and large towns in Uttar Pradesh, sent her to school, and then to a prestigious girls' college in Banaras (named Besant College, after Annie Besant). There she read up to First Arts, the first year of the B A, before she was married. At the same time, she grew up under the strict discipline imposed at home by a censorious, demanding schoolmaster father and a strong-willed, well-educated young stepmother who herself became a teacher later; my mother's own mother died when my mother was still a little girl. The discipline was especially punishing for a girl, and often even more so for a stepchild—something that is noticeable across castes and communities.

While her stepmother spoiled her younger blood brother and her stepbrothers—getting up, even late at night, my mother recalled, to cook sweets that they asked for—my mother learned to eat whatever she was given. In addition to schoolwork and homework, washing and looking after her clothes and personal things, she helped with cooking and other household chores and, no doubt, with attending to the needs of her younger siblings. Unlike the boys, she was prohibited from running around with friends in the neighborhood or leaving the house unless directed and accompanied by someone else, especially once she had reached puberty. Like other adolescent girls, she left the confined space of home and neighborhood only to go to school. (Her younger sister, the youngest child, may have escaped the rigors of this discipline somewhat, at least while she was little.)

As a result of this upbringing, as my mother told me and as we, her children, observed, my mother was a diffident person, especially in unfamiliar settings and interactions. She carried the handicap into her marriage with my father. They married when she was eighteen and he twenty-eight. She became an apparently timid and traditional homemaker, comfortable only in her home, with relatives, servants, and itinerant salespersons she knew. Ill at ease with dealings outside this circle, she skirted things that required independent, public decision-making. Moving with my father from one official posting to another, one district to another, she did what he asked her to do, while performing the duties of a civil servant's wife and a mother. Her inner strength and resources were reserved, it seemed, for the fulfillment of her children's desires. That strength appeared largely behind the scenes, in unseen encouragement or quiet permission for the children to do what they wanted, even when Father disapproved.

My parents had us five children, as I've mentioned, and a sixth who died as an infant. It was only once she had children, and the children grew up and became her friends, that my mother began to enjoy her life as a married woman. This is something my elderly cousin noted and I had registered faintly as a schoolchild. Since my father's death in 2002, or perhaps a little earlier—once retirement, old age, and declining health had reduced his swagger—she had come more into her own.

During this later stage, she lived largely with my older brother, in his turn a senior civil servant, but also spent long periods of time in the homes of her other children. My parents had begun the practice after my father's retirement, as so many elders in middle- and lower-middle-class families do. The arrangement has become more common with the erosion of traditional rural and urban neighborhood communities. The situation is compounded by the absence of institutional facilities for the care of the elderly, and the cultural disapproval that attaches to any proposals for such "impersonal" care, whatever the costs and burdens of multiple generations living together and the considerable tensions that arise in consequence. Difficult inheritances that we continue to live with.

For over two decades, until she passed away in 2024, my mother lived as the family elder. Quietly, without making an exhibition of her authority, almost without it being noticed, she became the center of the family, presiding over the desires and needs of her children, grandchildren, and latterly great-grandchildren. However, her authority remained wrapped in hesitancy and diffidence—sometimes even within the intimate circle made up by her and her children. Publicly, and formally, my elder brother remained head of household until his untimely passing in 2018. However, my mother was the axis of the wide network of kith and kin, dependents and servants who kept in touch and passed through my brother and sister-in-law's "open house"; she doled out love and benevolent kindness to all in the "family," and gained intensified attention from her children.

The one countervailing circumstance is that several of her children travel a great deal, in India and overseas, and I now live in America. All of us have established an independence in our work and our marriages, but we have also tried to be devoted sons and daughters, honoring and looking after our elderly parents in such a way that we have sometimes compromised on the needs of our partners (and perhaps ourselves).

❀ ❀ ❀

How different has it been in the lives of my own generation? Should I not say something about my own history? That, coming of age in the 1970s and '80s, I have loved and been loved by several remarkable women. That I have married twice—with two successful, accomplished, world-traveling academics, now teaching at universities in the United States and Britain. That I have a son from my first marriage, now a musician in Berlin. That my parents and siblings accepted my second marriage, but continued to treat my former wife as their "true" daughter- and sister-in-law. Perhaps this flows in part from the fact that she is the mother of their grandchild (or, for my siblings, nephew). But also perhaps because of a sense that my life partner for the last quarter of a century is too "individualistic" and "Westernized," too insistent on her independence, and too dogmatic in her challenging of the mores and expectations of the traditional/modern Indian family.

Should I not say something about my own shortcomings as a husband and partner, despite my best intentions? One small illustration may make the point. Since we moved to the United States, my partner and I have visited India practically every winter for research and family reasons—until the coronavirus disrupted all our lives in unprecedented ways. On more than one occasion, when we had been there a few weeks, she would ask me whether I missed our home in the States. I would reply, lightheartedly, "Why should I? You're here with me." To this, she would respond, simply, "I miss it." The exchange serves to highlight how I still thought of the physical structure, the space of our home, as *background*: a roof and walls that provided the context and location for what really mattered, a couple, a family's being together and building a life together. I was slow to recognize the emotional investment she had in the physical space of our home: its layout, its low lighting and arrangement of furniture, its aesthetic pleasures, comforts, and joys—the things that make it a sanctuary, a *home*.

I could add further notes: about how the women I married have said, at different times, to different people, that I do not discuss feelings easily, evade conversations on "difficult" personal subjects—and that I often didn't let them speak. My second wife has also criticized my refusal to openly discuss or think decisively about another vital matter: her ambivalence about having, yet in her view (at least in retrospect), her clear desire to have, a child.

There is more, but this essay is not an autobiography. I hope the fragments in this epilogue suffice to indicate how much I am a part of the history outlined in this book.

❀ ❀ ❀

One last word. It has not been easy to write about people and families I already knew before I began research for this study, or people and families I came to know later through exploration of their writings and through interviews. There is understandable sensitivity regarding information on many of the issues addressed here, even where friends or family themselves provided the information, often in published work. I know it feels different—it *is* different—when that very information appears in the writings of others who do not have the same rights or investments in the particular lives and experiences under discussion. All of this has made me hesitate. The hesitation is not reduced in reflecting on my own natal family, or my personal relationships, given the exposures that come with public statement, the secrets it may reveal, the sensibilities it might hurt.

At one juncture, a couple of decades ago, I began making mental (and graphic) notes on the middle-class mores revealed in bizarre comments and behavior I encountered in family circles I knew to some extent from childhood. Comments and behavior that spoke of unquestioned hierarchies, hypocrisy, and male conceit. Some of the things I saw and heard aroused in me a sense of shame and outrage. Discussing them with my brother-in-law, a prominent historian and commentator on India's recent past and contemporary condition, I asked whether we might consider jointly writing a history of the modern Indian family. He thought a few moments before responding, "I'd be too scared."

Two decades on, I understand more fully what he meant. Such a history of domestic morals and practices is dangerously close to the bone; its investigation is liable to lacerate the flesh, the self and self-image, in unexpected ways. It is, however, a close-to-the-bone investigation that we must undertake if we are not to remain a somewhat complacent, politically radical, yet socially conservative, people. That is a position in which, regretfully, some of the most progressive sections of India's intellectuals and political activists have found themselves, even in the face of the endlessly humiliating practices of caste, class, and gender intolerance that continue to plague India's everyday.

Acknowledgments

A few lines at the end or beginning of a book are paltry acknowledgment of all the people and institutions whose presence, collaboration, and generosity have made the work possible. The following words can scarcely convey my immense gratitude to the scholars, friends, colleagues, and well-wishers who have contributed to the making of this book.

Let me begin with my current home institution. Sincere thanks to Emory University, the Emory College of Arts and Sciences, and staff and members of the history department and of the Emory library for their support through the years of my research and writing.

Among individuals: Ruby Lal, companion, colleague, copilot, critic, was the first to identify this inquiry as more than worthwhile: rather, as vital, crucial. And to insist, gently but forcefully, at every stage when other actors or concerns or enthusiasms tempted me to stray into other paths, that I retain sharp focus on *men* as denizens of the domestic world. Rajeswari Sundar Rajan, Tanika Sarkar, Partha Chatterjee, and David Nugent have been other major interlocutors over the years of my concentrated work on this book. I do not have the words to acknowledge the value of their collective comradeship and criticism. Other colleagues whose responses greatly clarified my thinking, pointed me to additional sources and contacts, and saved me from many errors include Mrinalini Sinha, Lynne Huffer, Chowdhury Muhammad Naim, Kamran Asdar, Maya Pandit, and Jaya Sankrityayan.

Deep gratitude to members of several reading groups who worked through rough-and-ready drafts and provided critical feedback over many years. One, made up of two uncommon "specialists," Ruby Lal and V. Narayana Rao, constant in their simultaneous generosity, inspiration, criticism, cautioning, and insights; a second, of three highly engaged "non-specialist" readers, Mary Odem,

Ralph Gilbert, and Ruby in another guise, who provided equally abundant doses of questions, encouragement, nourishment, and cheer; a third, consisting of Jonathan Prude, a historian of untapped visual archives of American labor in the nineteenth century, Donald Reitzes, an urban sociologist working on the homeless and on questions of belonging in Atlanta and other US cities, and myself, a student of South Asian affairs and colonial/postcolonial histories (an unexpected and productive combination); and last but not least, one constituted by an anthropologist and a historian, David Nugent and myself, both thinking of themselves as perpetual students, engaged in writing books that can never have an ending. Other colleagues at Emory who need to be singled out include Laurie Patton, Shalom Goldman, Clifton Crais, Adriana Chira, Carla Freeman, Anna Grimshaw, Kristin Mann, Yanna Yannakakis, Brajesh Samarth, and two outstanding South Asia librarians, Gautham Reddy and Tim Bryson. So do some wonderful students, several of them now established academics, who helped with their comments and research assistance along the way: Adeem Suhail, Emma Meyer, Navyug Gill, Pankhuree Dube, Shreyas Srinath, and most recently Hansen Hugo, first-rate student and research assistant.

I have to thank other colleagues and friends, near and far, for their responses and contributions. In North America, Swapna Banerjee, to whom I give additional thanks for her generosity in sharing with me a proof copy of her book *Fathers in a Motherland* when it was not yet published; Arjun Appadurai, Anjali Arondekar, Akeel Bilgrami, Indrani Chatterjee, Swati Chattopadhyay, Wendy Doniger, Katherine Ewing, Ania Loomba, Gail Minault, Gayatri Spivak, Anne Stoler, and Ashwini Tambe for comments and questions; Anne Murphy and other organizers and participants in the South Asia Conference of the Pacific Northwest held at the University of British Columbia in February 2018; Lisa Trivedi, Thomas Wilson, Sabrina Datoo, Donald Carter, Rebecca Gruskin, Chao Ren, Nick Tackes, Arathi Menon, and other faculty and students for an extraordinary two days of discussion at a lecture and workshop at Hamilton College, New York, in February 2023; Razi Raziuddin and his co-organizers of the Indian Diaspora Washington DC Forum, and subtle commentators Arjun Appadurai and Tanika Sarkar, for their responses at a Zoom event in November 2023. Special thanks also to a range of scholars, activists, and friends on other continents: Romila Thapar, Gopal Guru, Sukhadeo Thorat, Ashok Vajpayee, Ashok Maheshwari, Abhay Dube, Anand Teltumbde, Anand Patwardhan, Simanthini Dhuru, Anuradha Kumar, Flavia Agnes, Indu Agnihotri, and the much-missed Sharmila Rege in India; Bruce and Sally Cleghorn, David Hardiman, David Page, Ruth Kirkwilson, Rajyashree Gokhale, Sushrut Jadhav,

Margrit Pernau, Biplab Basu, Nishad Pandey, Nariaki Nakazato, and other interlocutors in Europe and farther afield.

Heartfelt gratitude for their generosity in providing invaluable information on different families, communities, and histories in India and Pakistan: to Jaya Sankrityayan, Sara Rai, Kamran Asdar, Navina Haidar and her family, Javeed Alam and his extended family, Maya Pandit and her contacts in Baby Kamble's family, Narendra Jadhav and his family, S. Anand (of Navayana), Vijay Surwade and his family, Vasant and Meenakshi Moon's family, Urmila Pawar, Kumud Pawde, Sanjay Kumar, and other well-wishers too numerous to name in Allahabad, Banaras, Lucknow, Delhi, Dehradun, Nagpur, Aurangabad, Pune, Bombay, Kolkata, London, and elsewhere.

Special thanks to Kamil Khan Mumtaz saheb and his daughter Samiya Mumtaz sahiba for their kindness in providing the cover photograph and obtaining the permission of other members of the family of Begum Hameeda Husain Raipuri (née Omar) for its use in this book—and to Kamran, once more, for facilitating all of this. Also, to my wonderfully professional editors at Duke University Press, Ken Wissoker and Ryan Kendall, and their anonymous readers, who all asked for "more"—and to Liz Smith, Dave Rainey, and the entire production team at Duke, who have been a pleasure to work with.

I will end with a few more personal acknowledgments: To my mother, Shree Kumari, my sisters, Geetanjali, Jayanti, and Gayatri, my brother-in-law Sudhir, and my son Nishad, for their lasting interest and indulgence. To Ramlal Pandey (Ramnath bhaiya to me and my generation), for his remarkable reminiscences of life in the remote north Indian village where he grew up, and on from there. And, finally, my deepest gratitude to four women who would prefer not to be named here—partners and comrades at various times, for various lengths of time—without whom this book, and my life, would be far poorer.

Notes

PRELUDE

1 Louis Althusser uses the phrase "an answer to a question that is nowhere posed"; Althusser, *Reading Capital*, 29. For an explication of my usage of "fragment," see Pandey, *Routine Violence*, chap. 2, "In Defense of the Fragment." A slightly different articulation appeared in the original version published with the same title in *Representations* 37 (Winter 1992).

2 I refer to important scholarly writings on several of these themes in the section titled "Historiography" in chapter 1.

3 Cf. Guha, *History at the Limit of World History*.

4 Shivrani Premchand, *Premchand Ghar Mein*.

5 Madan, *Premchand*, 20.

6 Baby Kamble, *Jina Amucha*; English translation by Maya Pandit, *The Prisons We Broke*. *Dalit* is the name that Dalit activists give to the depressed castes and classes formerly known as Untouchables.

7 Kamble, *Prisons We Broke*, 147, 155, 156.

8 One scholar makes the point about the crisscrossing axes that determine gender power in South Asian homes as follows: a woman's place depends on "the status of her husband, her possession of sons, her fertility, looks, health and capacity for domestic labour. The middle-aged mother of grown-up sons could be a powerful matriarch and elderly mothers-in-law could command and oppress young [daughters-in-law]." T. Sarkar, *Hindu Wife, Hindu Nation*, 21.

9 It is worth noting that this applied to Baby Kamble's husband: an unemployed young man in a house full of elders, whose enterprising wife (Baby Kamble) comes up with an idea that allows him to contribute to the family's income, he is still someone from whom she has to hide her writing for twenty years.

10 Another term that may well come from the same root (route?) is *nivri* in Kutchi, which refers to girls or young women sitting around idling, as a young bride might be allowed to do briefly! I am grateful to Sabrina Datoo for drawing my attention to this term and its meaning.

Epigraph: M. K. Gandhi, "Indian Home Rule or *Hind Swaraj*," 35.

1   Tagore, *Home and the World*, 19, 23. *Ghare Baire* was written in the wake of the turn-of-the-century Swadeshi Movement, calling for a boycott of British manufactures and the use of local, *swadeshi* products, a moment of inspiration and fervor among progressive nationalist youth in Bengal. It was translated into English by the author's nephew, Surendranath Tagore, and published under the title *The Home and the World* in 1919. The translator's explanation of *purdah* may be helpful for readers unfamiliar with the term and its implications: "The seclusion of the zenana [the women's domain], and all the customs peculiar to it, are designated by the general term *Purdah*, which means Screen." Tagore, *Home and the World*, 23n.

2   Tagore, *Home and the World*, 31.

3   Tagore, *Home and the World*, 38, 44.

4   Bama, *Sangati*, 69, 70. The theme of *Sangati*, says the author, is "the growth, decline, culture, and liveliness of Dalit women. . . . To bounce like a ball that has been hit became my deepest desire, and not to curl up and collapse because of the blow" (vii). The title, *Sangati*, refers to a word or phrase of a song sung in different ways without deviating from the central raga or melody, variations on a theme. Bama's book is part of a surge in Dalit (ex-Untouchable) women's autobiographical writings, an important new stage in the intellectual and political upheaval that came with the rise of the militant Dalit movement of the 1970s and '80s.

5   Hosain, *Sunlight on a Broken Column*. The novel was written against the backdrop of the unprecedented dislocation, uncertainty, and anguish that accompanied the partition of the Indian subcontinent into the new nation-states of India and Pakistan, especially for youth who challenged traditional mores and witnessed the uprooting of their "minority" Muslim (or, elsewhere, Sikh and Hindu) families and community. The quotations that follow are from pages 28 and 38.

6   Bachchan, *Atmakatha*, I:96–97.

7   R. Sankrityayan, *Meri Jivan Yatra*, III:49.

8   Chughtai, *Kaagazi hai Pairahan*, 141.

9   Chughtai, *Kaagazi hai Pairahan*, 7–8.

10   Baisantri, *Dohra Abhishaap*, 32–33, 68.

11   The phrase in this section's subheading comes from Gayatri Spivak, for whom "feudality" signifies a mode of production where the value-form is taken by "loyalty." Spivak, "More Thoughts on Cultural Translation"; Spivak and Baer, "Redoing Marxism at the Gigi Café."

12   B. R. Ambedkar, "The Hindu and His Belief in Caste," in *Writings and Speeches*, vol. 5 (1989), 100. See also B. R. Ambedkar, "Castes in India."

13   Valmiki, *Joothan*, 11, 12.

14   *Times of India*, "Over 30% Women from 14 States, UT Justify Beating by Husbands."

15   I take the conceptualization from Lal, *Coming of Age*.

16   Snell, *Autobiographical Writing in Hindi*, chap. 12. (Translation from the Hindi mine.)

17 T. Sarkar, *Hindu Wife, Hindu Nation*, 192, 194, 198, 228. Sarkar makes the argument for Bengal, but the "revivalism" was apparent among upper castes across the land. I discuss other analyses of the conundrums in other parts of India in the section titled "Historiography" below.

18 Swapna Banerjee, *Fathers in a Motherland*, provides a recent example. Like other scholars, Banerjee questions the assumption of any simple demarcation between these domains.

19 There has been considerable pathbreaking work on Dalit life and struggles relating to gender and family issues as well; see, among many others, Rege, *Writing Caste, Writing Gender*; Geetha, *Patriarchy*; Guru, "Dalit Women Talk Differently." However, this work has typically appeared in studies devoted primarily to Dalit conditions and histories. What might we gain if we juxtapose the very different histories of the elite and the subaltern, and examine them as part of the same struggle to forge a new society? Rege, *Writing Caste*, and Arya, "Dalit or Brahmanical Patriarchy," may be making a similar proposition.

20 See Burnett-Hurst, *Labour and Housing*, 20–22 and passim; Purcell and Hallsworth, *Labour Conditions in India*, 8.

21 Pradhan, *Untouchable Workers*, 13.

22 Cf. Guha, *History at the Limit of World History*.

23 Yadav, *Autobiography of Dayanand Saraswati*, 8; K. M. Sen, *Hinduism*, 110. Babasaheb Ambedkar, to take a rather different example, declared that his idea of *tapasya* (asceticism) did not mean retiring to a forest for meditation: "My idea of [*tapasya*] implies (1) extreme power of enduring suffering, and (2) extreme power of working." Yusufji, *Ambedkar*, 143. Let me add, in parentheses, that childhood, missing in the classical description of life stages, emerged as a clearly demarcated phase in life in the context of new debates on child marriage and child labor, the welfare of women and children, and formal education from childhood onward.

24 On how classical notions of human development came to be inflected by discourses of Western science, see Botre and Haynes, "Brahmacharya," 163–85; Pande, "Time for Sex," 279–302; Pande, "Sorting Boys and Men," 332–58.

25 Thompson, *Making of the English Working Class*, 1.

26 See Chatterjee, "Nationalist Resolution"; T. Sarkar, *Hindu Wife, Hindu Nation*; and on the "imperial social formation," Sinha, *Specters of Mother India*.

27 Chatterjee, "Nationalist Resolution"; Sumit Sarkar, "'Kaliyuga,' 'Chakri,' and 'Bhakti'"; Walsh, *Domesticity in Colonial India*; Minault, *Secluded Scholars*; Lal, *Coming of Age*; T. Sarkar, *Hindu Wife, Hindu Nation*; Sreenivas, *Wives, Widows and Concubines*; Majumdar, *Marriage and Modernity*; Swapna Banerjee, *Fathers in a Motherland*. For more general surveys, see Uberoi, *Family, Kinship and Marriage*; Chatterji, *Unfamiliar Relations*; Loomba and Lukose, *South Asian Feminisms*.

28 T. Sarkar, *Hindu Wife, Hindu Nation*, 43–44.

29 The quotation is from Lal, *Coming of Age*, 126. See also Swapna Banerjee, *Fathers in a Motherland*; Minault, *Secluded Scholars*; Walsh, *Domesticity in Colonial India*.

30 Sreenivas, *Wives, Widows and Concubines*, 6. See also Newbigin, *Hindu Family*; Buettner, *Empire Families*.

31 Sinha, "Global Perspective on Gender," 365.

32 Ghosh, *Gentlemanly Terrorists*; Sinha, *Colonial Masculinity*; Rosselli, "Self-Image of Effeteness."

33 See, for example, Alter, "Somatic Nationalism"; Alter, "Indian Clubs and Colonialism"; Chowdhury, *Frail Hero*; Srivastava, *Constructing Post-colonial India*; Sikata Banerjee, *Make Me a Man!*; S. Sen, *Colonial Childhoods*; R. Chopra, Osella, and Osella, *South Asian Masculinities*.

34 Alter, "Masculinities and Culture," 298.

35 Srivastava, "Introduction," 15.

36 Kishwar, "Gandhi on Women"; Hardiman, *Gandhi in His Time*; G. Gandhi and Suhrud, *Scorching Love*; Erikson, *Gandhi's Truth*.

37 Sinha (citing Andrea Cornwell), "A Global Perspective on Gender," 359.

38 The few examples in the historical literature on the nineteenth century where women's writing figures prominently have been eye-opening. See, for example, T. Sarkar, *Words to Win*; Chandra, *Enslaved Daughters*; B. Ray, *Early Feminists of Colonial India*; Raychaudhuri and Forbes, *Memoir of Dr. Haimabati Sen*; Chakravarti, *Rewriting History*.

39 On "performance," see Goffman, *Presentation of Self.* Whereas Goffman is concerned with performance in daily social interaction, I am concerned also with the performance of the self in textual representation, which foregrounds the question of audience—both existing and anticipated.

40 Spiegel, "Memory and History," 157. For an introduction to the extensive debate on memory and history, see Nora, "Between Memory and History"; Nora, *Conflicts and Divisions*, "General Introduction"; Novick, *The Holocaust in American Life*. I discuss some of this literature in my *Remembering Partition*, 8–12.

41 The Indian constitution listed particularly marginalized and stigmatized castes and subcastes in two categories of Scheduled Castes and Scheduled Tribes, which constituted 16.6 percent and 8.6 percent respectively of the total Indian population according to the census of 2011. The term Dalits encompasses both, though it is used mostly for Scheduled Caste groups, and among them, especially for those more educationally advanced and politically active.

42 Men and women who remain manual workers, performing hard physical labor for a living, have little time for autobiographical or any other kinds of writing, far less writings that deal with their domestic lives. This is what one would expect, given the widespread poverty and illiteracy in India, and the constant, grinding labor necessary to keep working people alive. Yet, autobiographies by working people dealing with the political aspects of working-class lives and struggles did start appearing in Hindi at least from the 1920s onward; see C. Joshi, *Lost Worlds*.

43 I refer to Ambedkar's comment at his first meeting with Gandhi in August 1931: "Gandhiji, I have no homeland.... How can I call this land my own ... wherein we are treated worse than cats and dogs, wherein we cannot get water to drink?" Keer, *Ambedkar*, 166.

44 Shaw, *What Women Ought to Be.*

45 Pandey, *History of Prejudice*, 2. On the question of touch and its significance for sociological/historical analysis, see Guru, "Power of Touch"; Guru, "Archaeology of Un-

touchability"; discussion of the latter piece by Sundar Sarukkai and Balmurli Natrajan in *Economic and Political Weekly* 44, nos. 37 (2009), and 44, no. 51 (2009).

2. HOMES OUR FATHERS BUILT

Epigraph: Hosain, *Sunlight on a Broken Column*, 38.

1 Snell, "Hindi Poet," 425. The phrase "the legendary and the observed" that I refer to below also comes from this article.

2 Bachchan, *Atmakatha*, I:85 and 82.

3 Bachchan, *Atmakatha*, II:196–97.

4 Bachchan, *Atmakatha*, II:233–34, 256.

5 Jadhav, *Aamcha Baap aan Aamhi*. The memoir appears in interestingly altered form in editions following the original 1993 version. I have used the 1994 second edition and 2007 fifth "people's edition," along with the author's transcreation of the story in English, published in India as *Outcaste: A Memoir* and in the United States as *Untouchables: My Family's Triumphant Escape from India's Caste System*. For a discussion of its various incarnations, see my *History of Prejudice*, chap. 6.

6 Jadhav, *Aamcha Baap*, 5th ed., 14–15.

7 Jadhav, *Untouchables*, 245–48; quotation from page 248.

8 Bachchan, *Atmakatha*, I:21.

9 Bachchan, *Atmakatha*, I:70.

10 Bachchan, *Atmakatha*, I:89.

11 Bachchan, *Atmakatha*, I:173–74.

12 The information in this and the following two paragraphs comes from the condensed version of the eighty-nine volumes of Amar Singh's diary: Kanota, Rudolph, and Rudolph, *Reversing the Gaze*, part 5, "Private Lives in Patriarchal Space." Quotations in this paragraph are from page 358.

13 Kanota, Rudolph, and Rudolph, *Reversing the Gaze*, 358, 362.

14 See Hosagrahar, *Indigenous Modernities*.

15 *A Gazetteer of Delhi*, part A, "Gazetteer of the Delhi District (1912)."

16 For nineteenth- and twentieth-century developments in small towns and old pilgrimage, trade, and cultural centers, see, for example, Bayly, *Rulers, Townsmen and Bazaars*, esp. chaps. 9 and 12; Oldenberg, *Colonial Lucknow*; N. Kumar, *Artisans of Banaras*; Freitag, *Culture and Power*; Hasan, *From Pluralism to Separatism*; Glover, *Making Lahore Modern*. The literature on the new metropoles of Bombay and Calcutta is large. For a few recent interventions, see Chattopadhyay, *Representing Calcutta*; P. Chopra, *Joint Enterprise*; N. Rao, *House*; Chhabria, *Making the Modern Slum*; Shaikh, *Outcaste Bombay*.

17 Cf. Glover, *Making Lahore Modern*, 48–52. The quotes are from V. Jacquemont's 1831 notes on the Punjab. Glover also cites Rudyard Kipling's parallel comments from the turn of the twentieth century.

18 Oldenberg, *Colonial Lucknow*, xv.

19 Kashi Ram, *Notes and Suggestions on Sanitation in Punjab* (1884), 10, cited in Glover, *Making Lahore Modern*, 133–34.

20 Glover, *Making Lahore Modern*, 135, 140–41.

21 Glover, *Making Lahore Modern*, 141–42.

22 Tandon, *Punjabi Century*, 18, 19.

23 Glover, *Making Lahore Modern*, 147, 149. The population of Lahore and the canton-
ment area grew from 149,396 in 1881 to 429,727 in 1931; see *Statistical Abstract*, "No.
24—Population of Principal Towns, Alphabetically Arranged"; Hutton, *Census of India*, 54.

24 Glover, *Making Lahore Modern*, 151–53.

25 Tandon, *Punjabi Century*, 237, 238; also cited in Glover, *Making Lahore Modern*, 153.

26 For Gujarat, see Desai, "Bungalow," 355–62; for cities in other regions, see references in
note 16 above.

27 Gopal, *A Part Apart*, 486.

28 S. Rai, *Raw Umber*, 38–39. For another autobiographical account that notes the same
kind of division of space to meet the household head's (official/business) needs, on the
one hand, and the rest of the family's (domestic) needs, on the other, see Azra Kidwai's
reminiscences of the aristocratic and middle-class homes she grew up in, in Lucknow,
Bara Banki, and Delhi, summarized in Lal, *Coming of Age*, 1–31.

29 Edwardes, *Gazetteer*, 199. Also cited in N. Rao, *House*, 98.

30 N. Rao, *House*, 99–100.

31 See N. Rao, *House*, 103, 120, 132–33.

32 Bachchan, *Atmakatha*, I:171.

33 Bachchan, *Atmakatha*, I:173–74.

34 Bachchan, *Atmakatha*, I:159.

35 Bachchan, *Atmakatha*, II:254. I have used Snell's translation for the phrases quoted in
this paragraph; Bachchan, *Afternoon of Time*, 339.

36 Bachchan, *Atmakatha*, II:250.

37 Valmiki, *Joothan*, 11.

38 For one early collection, see Marriott, *Village India*; for a recent one, Banerjee-Dube,
Caste in History. See also P. Sainath's powerful report, *Everybody Loves a Good Drought*.

39 Lewis, "Peasant Culture," 148, 155, 156.

40 Kamble, *Jina Amucha*, 13; *Prisons We Broke*, 7, 8, 82, and Gopal Guru's "Afterword," 166.

41 Bama, *Karukku*.

42 Quoted in Edwardes, *Gazetteer*, 195.

43 See Gopal, *A Part Apart*, 110, 190; Keer, *Dr. Ambedkar*, 65. I discuss Ambedkar's family
life more fully in chapter 3.

44 While Ahmedabad, Calcutta, and Delhi were equally crowded in some parts, the
greater availability of land for horizontal expansion made for different architectural
possibilities. Ahmedabad experienced a commercial and industrial boom like Bombay's
in the later nineteenth and twentieth centuries, and also became known for its workers' tenements. The following account of Bombay tenements draws largely on Burnett-
Hurst, *Labour and Housing*; Pradhan, *Untouchable Workers*; R. Kumar, "City Lives";
and Finkelstein, *Archive of Loss*.

45 Finkelstein, *Archive of Loss*, 89.

46 R. Kumar, "City Lives," 47, 48.

47 Cited in R. Kumar, "City Lives," 49. For Ahmedabad parallels, see McGowan, "Ahmedabad's Home Remedies," 411.

48 Purcell and Hallsworth, *Labour Conditions in India*, 8. The figure for number of inhabitants is surely an underestimate.

49 The information in the preceding paragraphs comes from Baisantri, *Dohra Abhishaap*, 27, 43, 44, 48.

50 Jadhav, *Untouchables*, 106, 107.

51 Jadhav, *Untouchables*, 243.

52 Finkelstein, *Archive of Loss*, 108, 109.

3. DUTY

Epigraph: Dhritarashtra to Gandhari, in Irawati Karve's reconstruction of these two pivotal characters of the *Mahabharata*: Karve, *Yuganta*, 38.

1 I owe thanks to Chaudhuri Mohammed Naim for emphasizing the importance of this distinct history as revealed in its linguistic register.

2 *Bhadralok* in the subheading refers to worthy, respectable people—of "good" family. Of the examples presented here, Rahul Sankrityayan as a Brahmin ranked high in the traditional caste order. Many from Prasad and Premchand's scribal caste of Kayasthas, as in Gandhi's merchant (Bania) background, were traditionally ranked lower, but now qualified for the rank of respectable folk, having done well under regional princely states and under British colonial rule, through new economic and service opportunities from the sixteenth century onward; Carroll, "Caste"; O'Hanlon, "Social Worth of Scribes"; Bellenoit, "Between Qanungos and Clerks."

3 See M. K. Gandhi, *Autobiography*, 5. See also the excellent discussion in Hardiman, *Gandhi in His Time*, chap. 5.

4 R. Sankrityayan, *Meri Jivan Yatra*, I:53. The first four volumes of the six-volume autobiography are dated 1944, 1950, 1951, and 1967 (the last published posthumously). Volumes V and VI were compiled, edited, and published later by Kamala Sankrityayan. All six volumes were reprinted by Radhakrishna Prakashan in the 1990s (Delhi: Radhakrishna Prakashan, 1994–96). I have used the third paperback reprint, 2014. Cited hereafter as R. Sankrityayan, *Jivan Yatra*, followed by volume and page number.

5 R. Sankrityayan, *Kanaila ki Katha*, dedication.

6 Prasad, *Atmakatha*, 23.

7 Prasad, *Atmakatha*, 23. The distinguished Hindi poet and educationist Mahadevi Varma noted another physical effect that Prasad's wife suffered: "She had to sit for hours on end with head bent [and covered] in unchanging posture: in consequence, her spine curved in such a way that she couldn't stand straight even in youth": Varma, *Sansmaran*, 92–93.

8 Prasad, *Atmakatha*, 24, 33.

9 Prasad, *Autobiography*, 23; Prasad, *Atmakatha*, 72.

10 The literature on this theme is large: see Rich, *Of Woman Born*; McClintock, *Imperial Leather*; S. Ray, *En-gendering India*; Boehmer, *Stories of Women*; Ramaswamy, *Goddess*.

11 Prasad, *Atmakatha*, 614. For further discussion of the equation of woman with mother, see chapter 6 below.

12 Premchand, "Nari-jati ke adhikar," 249.

13 P. Joshi, *Gandhi on Women*, 17–18, and M. K. Gandhi, *Women and Social Justice*, 29, 161, respectively.

14 See, among others, Chakravarti, "Whatever Happened to the Vedic *Dasi*?"; Chatterjee, "Nationalist Resolution"; Roy, *Indian Traffic*; T. Sarkar, *Hindu Wife, Hindu Nation*; Pandey, "Men in the Home."

15 Men far removed from public, political, and intellectual pursuits articulated the same kind of argument, as middle-class comfort, nuclear households, salaried work for men (outside the home), and domestic work as the responsibility of women (inside the home) were naturalized as the norm, in India and across the globe, around the middle decades of the twentieth century.

16 A. Rai, *Premchand*, 34.

17 Bigamy was not prohibited in Hindu law until the revision of the Hindu Code in the mid-1950s. Marriage and inheritance laws in colonial and postcolonial India are framed in light of custom, defined separately for different religious communities, though some alternatives are available under a set of uniform, nonreligious laws. Hence the reform of the Hindu Code. For the British colonial and Indian national reform of customary law on marriage, inheritance, and associated matters, see Derrett, *Introduction to Modern Hindu Law*; Parashar, *Women and Family Law*; Agarwal, *A Field of One's Own*; Nair, *Women and Law*; Flavia Agnes, *Law and Gender Inequality*; Sturman, *Government of Social Life*.

18 Premchand called her a "warrior woman," and another noted Hindi writer and friend, Banarsidas Chaturvedi, described her as "Premchand's dictator"; S. Rai, *Raw Umber*, 43.

19 Shivrani Premchand, *Premchand Ghar Mein*; Madan, *Premchand*; A. Rai, *Premchand*; Swan, *Munshi Premchand*.

20 Shivrani Premchand, *Premchand Ghar Mein*, 189.

21 Shivrani Premchand, *Premchand Ghar Mein*, 97–98.

22 Madan, *Premchand*, 168, emphasis added.

23 Shivrani Premchand, *Premchand Ghar Mein*, 29.

24 Shivrani Premchand, *Premchand Ghar Mein*, 33.

25 Shivrani Premchand, *Premchand Ghar Mein*, 45.

26 Shivrani Premchand, *Premchand Ghar Mein*, 295–96.

27 Shivrani Premchand, *Premchand Ghar Mein*, 190.

28 The limited information I have found on Yelena (Lola) Kozerovskaya's life comes from Rahul Sankrityayan's autobiography and an essay on his mother by Rahul and Lola's son Igor; Igor Sankrityayan, "Meri Yashodhara ma Yelena Sankrityayan."

29 R. Sankrityayan, *Jivan Yatra*, II:280. He gave up the robes of a Buddhist monk when he first reached Soviet soil in 1935. A fictionalized version of his idealistic relationship with Lola (Yelena), written in a Bihar jail just after he learned of the birth of his son in March 1939, appears in R. Sankrityayan, *Jeene ke Liye*. The dedication in the first edition reads, "An offering of love to Lola."

30 R. Sankrityayan, *Jivan Yatra*, III:192–93.

31 R. Sankrityayan, *Jivan Yatra*, IV:393, 397.

32 R. Sankrityayan, *Jivan Yatra*, IV:397–98.

33 R. Sankrityayan, *Jivan Yatra*, IV:426.

34 R. Sankrityayan, *Jivan Yatra*, V:134–35.

35 See Snapshot 4 in chapter 1.

36 Srivastava, "Ghumakkads," 395.

37 R. Sankrityayan, *Ghumakkad Shastra*, 9, 10.

38 R. Sankrityayan, *Ghumakkad Shastra*, 12.

39 R. Sankrityayan, *Ghumakkad Shastra*, 17.

40 The author was perhaps thinking of himself and the child marriage he managed to escape when he was still a teenager. Yet, his argument is facile. The point about controlling the population is an odd "scientific" reason for abandoning marriage, and the overall message appears stranger, in view of his recognition of the emotional and sexual needs of men and women—as well as his own marital history.

41 R. Sankrityayan, *Jivan Yatra*, VI:342, 357–58, 361, 368, and passim.

42 For further details, see Pandey, "Hindustani Aadmi Ghar Mein."

43 R. Sankrityayan, *Jivan Yatra*, VI:378–79, 382.

44 For the following account, I have used Khairmode, *Ambedkar*; Gopal, *A Part Apart*; Keer, *Dr. Ambedkar*; Omvedt, *Ambedkar*; Savita Ambedkar, *Dr. Ambedkaranchya Sahvaasaat*; among other studies. Some details vary in the different accounts, but not in the substance of the life story.

45 Khairmode, *Ambedkar*, 2:117–18, cited in Gopal, *A Part Apart*, 232–33.

46 Gopal, *A Part Apart*, 176; cf. 233.

47 Khairmode, *Ambedkar*, 2:67–68, cited in Gopal, *A Part Apart*, 100.

48 Gopal, *A Part Apart*, 101.

49 Gopal, *A Part Apart*, 214.

50 By the 1930s and '40s, when he moved into his new house in Dadar, Ambedkar had one of the largest private libraries in India, with over 45,000 books. Gopal, *A Part Apart*, 68; Yusufji, *Ambedkar*, 135, 146.

51 Keer, *Dr. Ambedkar*, 43, 44; cf. 248.

52 Gopal, *A Part Apart*, 101.

53 Cited in Savita Ambedkar, *Babasaheb*, 79.

54 Letter of February 1, 1948, to Savita Ambedkar, added by Vijay Surwade in Appendix 1, Savita Ambedkar, *Babasaheb*, 316.

55 Letter to Kamalakant Chitre, cited in Keer, *Dr. Ambedkar*, 441.

56 Rege cites one Dalit song: *"Baba mhanto samaj mala—lagna konashi karu?"* (The community calls me Father—who can I marry [from my own daughters]?); see Rege, *Writing Caste, Writing Gender*, 62. See also Omvedt, *Ambedkar*, 119–20.

57 Savita Ambedkar, *Babasaheb*, translator's note, x–xiii, and epilogue (pieced together from Vijay Surwade's introductions to the second and fourth editions), 297–324.

58 Cf. Akbar S. Ahmed, *Jinnah, Pakistan and Islamic Identity: The Search for Saladin* (London: Routledge, 1997); Faiz Rahman Siddiqui, "To Evade Marriage, Atal Bihari Vajpayee Locked Himself up for 3 Days," *Times of India*, August 18, 2018; N. P. Ullekh,

The Untold Vajpayee: Politician and Paradox (Gurgaon: Penguin Random House India, 2017); Nilanjan Mukhopadhyay, *Narendra Modi: The Man, the Times* (Delhi: Westland, 2013).

59 Indrani Jagjivan Ram, *Dekhi, Suni*, I–III; Indrani Jagjivan Ram, *Milestones*, condensed one-volume English translation of her three-volume memoir. I have supplemented Indrani Devi's account with information from an extended 1978 interview with Jagjivan Ram (J. Ram, interview) and Sharma, *Jagjivan Ram*.

60 As his daughter, Meira Kumar, put it, "Babuji [Father] was born amidst poverty and untouchability . . . in Chandwa, a small, backward village in Bihar in a country reeling under the shame of being a British colony." M. Kumar, "My Father's Childhood," 34.

61 Someone from his low-caste background could never become prime minister in "this god-forsaken [*kambakht*] land," he noted at the time, adding that it was more consequential for a cobbler in India to become a lower-rank government official than a millionaire shoe-manufacturer; S. Venkat Narayan and Prabhu Chawla, interview, "I Wish Harijans Had Become Brahmins—Jagjivan Ram," *IndiaToday.in*, September 15, 1979 (updated July 6, 2018), https://www.indiatoday.in/magazine/interview/story /19790915-i-wish-harijans-had-become-brahmins-jagjivan-ram-822581-2014-02-21; Vir Sanghvi, *Mandate: Will of the People* (New Delhi: Westland, 2015).

62 Indrani Jagjivan Ram, *Dekhi, Suni*, I:18–20.

63 Indrani Jagjivan Ram, *Dekhi, Suni*, I:43–44.

64 J. Ram, interview.

65 Indrani Jagjivan Ram, *Dekhi, Suni*, I:42.

66 Indrani Jagjivan Ram, *Dekhi, Suni*, I:45.

67 Indrani Jagjivan Ram, *Dekhi, Suni*, I:46–47.

68 Indrani Jagjivan Ram, *Dekhi, Suni*, I:91.

69 She was to be Jagjivan Ram's true intellectual and political heir. Highly educated, she joined the prestigious Indian Foreign Service, later resigning to become a Congress leader, member of the central government, and the first woman speaker of India's lower house of Parliament.

70 Indrani Jagjivan Ram, *Dekhi, Suni*, I:149. Jagjivan's mother was with her son and daughter-in-law in Patna to help with the child and supervision of the endless housework in a major public figure's home.

71 S. C. Bose, *Indian Pilgrim*; N. K. Bose, *Parivrajak ki Diary*.

4. DISCIPLINE

Epigraph: Hartman, *Lose Your Mother*, 88.

1 Khurshid Mirza began and gave up a career as an actress early in her marriage, returning to it fully only after her husband's passing; Hameeda Raipuri established herself as a writer, lauded for her storytelling abilities and use of everyday language, with the autobiography she wrote after her husband's death. She went on to write two other memoirs, a novel, and stories for children, as well as a cookbook.

2 Hameeda Raipuri, *Humsafar*, 333–34.

3 Hameeda Raipuri, *Humsafar*, 11.

4 A. Raipuri, *Gard-e-Raah*, 69, 82, 274, 276. Emphasis added in last quote.

5 For a summary of Akhtar's career and contributions to progressive literature, see Jalil, *Liking Progress, Loving Change*, 404 and passim.

6 A. Raipuri, *Gard-e-Raah*, 17.

7 I refer to a cultural, as much as an economic, aristocracy that provides the ground for a move into new educational institutions and its rewards in independent, middle-class professions.

8 See facsimile of letters between Hameeda's father and Abdul Haq, in Hameeda Raipuri, *My Fellow Traveller*, photo gallery preceding page 69.

9 Hameeda Raipuri, *Humsafar*, 42–43, emphasis added.

10 Hameeda Raipuri, *Humsafar*, 59, emphasis added. Hameeda completes the story by reporting a song the bridegroom's party, consisting of Haq and a small group of younger leftist intellectuals, sang on arrival at the railway station in Orai, where the wedding took place: *"Layak dulha layen hain / anpadh larki le lenge / le lenge, bhai le lenge"* (We've brought an accomplished bridegroom / We'll take back an illiterate girl / Yes, we'll take her, we'll take her); *Humsafar*, 48. She quotes the song at several points in her autobiography and in other writings, adding that it was bound to have an effect on her psyche. *Humsafar*, 11; *My Fellow Traveller*, xvi; *Nayab Hain Hum*, 15.

11 Hameeda Raipuri, *Humsafar*, 63.

12 Hameeda Raipuri, *Humsafar*, 113, emphasis added.

13 Hameeda Raipuri, *Humsafar*, 177.

14 Hameeda Raipuri, *Humsafar*, 185, emphasis added.

15 See Hameeda Raipuri, *Humsafar*, 193–203, 211–12, 250–51. Akhtar declares he could never choose England after all the racism and oppression Indians had suffered under British colonial rule. Though he does not provide the details, he confirms other points of Hameeda's account, including her father's and her intervention in helping obtain their passports: "One day she suddenly came up with the idea of their going to Europe," he writes. "We had been married a year, and while she was as unworldly as I, she was also a courageous spirit like me." A. Raipuri, *Gard-e-Raah*, 94, 95.

16 Hameeda Raipuri, *Humsafar*, 254. I return to the question of men's discontent and impatience in chapter 6 below.

17 Hameeda Raipuri, *My Fellow Traveller*, 32–33, emphasis added.

18 Hameeda observes that Akhtar modeled himself on Abdul Haq so closely that he adopted his daily routine and his idiosyncrasies, including using a bitter neem twig to brush his teeth every morning! Hameeda Raipuri, *Humsafar*, 329.

19 I use Amina Azfar's translation here: A. Raipuri, *Dust of the Road*, 54.

20 A. Raipuri, *Gard-e-Raah*, 85. The Urdu/Hindi word for owl, *ullu*, is used metaphorically for an idiot.

21 A. Raipuri, *Gard-e-Raah*, 82. When the Urdu dictionary was ultimately published, Haq refused to acknowledge Akhtar's part in its preparation, in the manner of a jilted lover or a father betrayed by his son, apparently because Akhtar had left Hyderabad against his wishes.

22 Hameeda Raipuri, *Humsafar*, 47. Hameeda quotes her sister's words several times, as a comment she often recalled in the early days of her marriage; cf. *Humsafar*, 82, 98.

23 Hameeda Raipuri, *Humsafar*, 256.

24 This is Azfar's translation; A. Raipuri, *Dust of the Road*, 157.

25 The evidence, available in autobiographical, ethnographic, and fictional accounts, published and unpublished, is massive. But more than multiplication of examples, the point is to reflect on new tendencies at work that refashioned domestic lives in subtle ways, while leaving ideas of male entitlement and women's dependence very much in place.

26 Hameeda Raipuri, *Humsafar*, 284. Akhtar uses the exact same phrase, *chappa-chappa*, for his travels and knowledge of Iran; A. Raipuri, *Gard-e-Raah*, 188.

27 Hameeda Raipuri, *Humsafar*, 324, 326, 332.

28 Hameeda Raipuri, *Humsafar*, 265.

29 Hameeda Raipuri, *Humsafar*, 320–21. Her preface to the 1992 edition of Akhtar's *Dust of the Road* gives slightly different timings (xv).

30 Hameeda's preface to A. Raipuri, *Dust of the Road*, xviii.

31 Hameeda Raipuri, *My Fellow Traveller*, 359.

32 Hameeda Raipuri, *Humsafar*, 298, 321.

33 A. Raipuri, *Gard-e-Raah*, 275; cf. Hameeda Raipuri, *Humsafar*, 298–99.

34 Khurshid Mirza, *Woman of Substance*, 11. I cite this 2005 Indian edition in the following pages. The text is the same as that of the earlier Pakistani edition, Khurshid Mirza, *Modern Muslim Woman*. However, the introductory and end matter, and the photographs included, are changed. Both the Pakistani and Indian publishers have retained the date "Karachi, 1983" at the end of the book, though it is clear the last few pages were written after Khurshid's move to Lahore in 1985; see *Woman of Substance*, 230.

35 Salman Haider, Zoom interview, August 24, 2020.

36 Khurshid Mirza, *Woman of Substance*, 105–106; Khurshid Mirza, interview by Lutfullah Khan, LAL, 1975.

37 Khurshid Mirza, *Woman of Substance*, 106.

38 Khurshid Mirza, *Woman of Substance*, 108.

39 Khurshid Mirza, *Woman of Substance*, 111, 112.

40 Khurshid Mirza, *Woman of Substance*, 116, 119.

41 Khurshid Mirza, *Woman of Substance*, 114.

42 Khurshid Mirza, *Woman of Substance*, 116.

43 Khurshid Mirza, *Woman of Substance*, 116, 139, emphasis added.

44 Khurshid Mirza, *Woman of Substance*, 151.

45 "The Uprooted Sapling" was the title Khurshid chose when her memoir was first published in monthly installments in the Lahore newspaper, *Herald*, August 1982–April 1983. Siobhan Lambert-Hurley notes that the title explicitly refers to Khurshid's father, a "young sapling uprooted from a green hilly Bhantani hamlet [in Kashmir] and transplanted [to] the fertile soil of Aligarh"; *Elusive Lives*, 146. I suggest that, consciously or unconsciously, it refers also to Khurshid's own life: a sapling uprooted more than once to live and grow in other soils.

46 Khurshid Mirza, *Woman of Substance*, 169–70, 172.

47 See Pandey, *Remembering Partition*; Zamindar, *Long Partition*.

48 Khurshid Mirza, *Woman of Substance*, 227.

49　Khurshid Mirza, *Woman of Substance*, 175, 185.

50　A huge sum at the time, when well-placed police officers earned a few hundred rupees a month, far short of a thousand even if one added subsidized accommodation, servants, and other perks the government provided; Mirza, *Woman of Substance*, 164–65; cf. 115.

51　Khurshid Mirza, *Woman of Substance*, 175, 176.

52　Khurshid Mirza, *Woman of Substance*, 178. Hameeda expressed the same sentiment in her autobiography: "With what determination and enthusiasm every individual undertook to build the homeland." Like Khurshid, she also joined the National Guard; Hameeda Raipuri, *Humsafar*, 269–70.

53　The words are those of her nephew Salman Haider, the Indian Foreign Service officer they stayed with in London. Khurshid's greatest fame came with her role as Akka Bua in the T V serial *Zer Zabar Pesh* (1974); she also won numerous national awards for her acting.

54　In interviews with me, Salman Haider underlined Akbar ("Daddy Mirza")'s rather strict and aloof manner.

55　Khurshid Mirza, *Woman of Substance*, 185, 190, 212.

56　Khurshid Mirza, *Woman of Substance*, 206.

57　Vasudha Dalmia, review of Rupert Snell's abridged translation of Bachchan's four-volume autobiography, *In the Afternoon of Time: An Autobiography*, in *Bulletin of the School of Oriental and African Studies, University of London* 64, no. 1 (2001): 138–40.

58　Bachchan, *Atmakatha*, II:119.

59　Bachchan, *Atmakatha*, II:144; cf. II:184.

60　I have left out another encounter that Bachchan writes about at some length, since the woman's career as a revolutionary married to another revolutionary, and in hiding when he met her, prevents Bachchan from placing her so squarely within the mainstream of his ruminations on marriage and motherhood. For a discussion of this revolutionary, and Bachchan's claimed romance with her, see Loomba, *Revolutionary Desires*, 87–91 and passim.

61　Bachchan, *Atmakatha*, I:159.

62　Bachchan, *Atmakatha*, I:158, 169.

63　The phrase in quotation marks is my translation of Bachchan's delicate explanation in Hindi: Bachchan, *Atmakatha*, I:161.

64　Bachchan, *Atmakatha*, I:165.

65　Bachchan, *Atmakatha*, I:169, 171.

66　Percy Bysshe Shelley, "To a Skylark," 1820, https://www.poetryfoundation.org/poems /45146/to-a-skylark.

67　Bachchan, *Atmakatha*, I:191, 192. I return to the theme of men's naturalization of women's suffering in chapter 7 below.

68　She struck him, he wrote, "as a quintessential Hindu woman, who could not escape the hold of her father even when far away from him." Bachchan, *Atmakatha*, II:141.

69　Bachchan, *Atmakatha*, II:154, 156–57.

70　Bachchan perhaps reads too much into the response of his large fan following, excited by his sonorous recitation of his poems, especially the famous *"Madhushala"* (Drinking house).

71 Bachchan, *Atmakatha*, II:184.

72 Bachchan, II:176; Robert Louis Stevenson, "On Falling in Love," *Cornhill Magazine* 35 (1877): 216, https://digital.nls.uk/rlstevenson/browse/archive/78693235.

73 Bachchan, *Afternoon of Time*, 299–300.

74 Bachchan, *Atmakatha*, II:212, 221–22. I discuss the theme of woman as mother further in chapter 7 below.

75 Bachchan, *Atmakatha*, II:215–16.

76 Bachchan, *Atmakatha*, I:192.

77 Bachchan, *Atmakatha*, II:216, 218.

78 I should add that many of the contradictory tendencies underscored here are noticeable even where marriage practices and family life appear more traditional. For one fascinating "traditional" marriage, in which romantic desire and attachment to spouse and children were candidly expressed in diaries and letters, along with the man's desire to be on the move all the time, see Robinson, *Jamal Mian*.

5. DIGNITY

Ambedkar's address at the All-India Depressed Classes conference, Nagpur, July 18–20, 1942; B. R. Ambedkar, *Writings and Speeches*, vol. 17, pt. 3 (2003), 276.

1 The statement applies even to non-kin communities, people from multiple places who come together in one destinations. See, for example, the community of the poor inhabiting an urban village on the outskirts of a big city, which is at the heart of Premchand's novel *Rangbhumi*; and Chatterjee, *Politics of the Governed*, 57–58 and passim.

2 For one evocative discussion of Bhakti *sants* and the *warkari sampraday*, see Zelliot, *Untouchable to Dalit*, chap. 2. For peasant protest and the growth of the Sikh community as an example of lower-class assertions, see Irfan Habib, *The Agrarian System of Mughal India* (1963; 2nd ed., Delhi: Oxford University Press, 1999); J. S. Grewal, *The Sikhs of the Punjab* (Cambridge: Cambridge University Press, 1990); Oberoi, *Construction of Religious Boundaries*.

3 Nagaraj, *Flaming Feet*, 162.

4 For just one other striking example, a mass conversion to Islam by Dalits in Tamilnadu in the 1980s carefully deliberated and led by educated youth in the village of Meenakshipuram and its vicinity, see Mujahid, *Conversion to Islam*. For the mass conversion of Dalits along with Ambedkar in 1956 and those that followed after, see, among others, Omvedt, *Dalit Visions*; Jondhale and Beltz, *Reconstructing the World*; A. Rao, *Caste Question*. Scholars have noted that the Buddhist conversion inspired by Ambedkar was preceded by Iyothee Thoss (Iyothee Dass)'s late nineteenth- and early twentieth-century focus on Buddhism in his efforts to mobilize the Parayas and other low castes against the Brahmins of Tamilnadu, in what is now seen as a progenitor of the influential Self-Respect Movement in southern India in later decades; see Pandian, *Brahmin and Non-Brahmin*, 106, 111, 116, 120; Aloysius, *Religion as Emancipatory Identity*.

5 For Sanskritization and Westernization, see Srinivas, *Religion and Society among the Coorgs*. For one example of contrasting Sanskritizing and Westernizing attempts among

higher and lower castes in a north Indian village in the 1950s, see Cohn, "Changing Status of a Depressed Caste," 53–77.

6   Nagaraj, *Flaming Feet*, 162.

7   Prelude and chapters 1 and 2.

8   Moon, *Vasti*. English translation by Gail Omvedt: Moon, *Growing Up*.

9   B. R. Ambedkar, *Writings and Speeches*, vol. 17, pt. 2 (2003), 395.

10 Cf. Eleanor Zelliot's list of "Ambedkar's Guiding Principles," no. 6, in "The Leadership of Babasaheb Ambedkar," in her *From Untouchable to Dalit*, 62.

11 B. R. Ambedkar, *Writings and Speeches*, vol. 2 (1982), 44.

12 See B. R. Ambedkar, *Essential Writings*, 10, 16, and passim.

13 *Report of Depressed Class Conference, Nagpur Session* (Nagpur: G. T. Meshram, 1942), 28–29, cited in Zelliot, *From Untouchable to Dalit*, 131.

14 B. R. Ambedkar, *Essential Writings*, 48–49.

15 For a couple of striking examples, see Yusufji, *Ambedkar*, 74, 120–21.

16 For studies from two very different locations, see Frazier, *Black Bourgeoisie*; Vicziany and Mendelsohn, *Untouchables*. See also Marion Kaplan's compelling account of the ways in which European Jewry sought to acculturate to gentile society in nineteenth- and twentieth-century Europe, with the Jewish home as a key site in the process: Kaplan, *Making of the Jewish Middle Class*.

17 M. K. Gandhi, *Young India*, 460, emphasis added. See also M. K. Gandhi, *Thoughts on National Language*, 97–98 and passim. For some striking nineteenth-century examples from Bengal, see Nandy, *Intimate Enemy*, 87, 89. Also, Susobhan Sarkar, *On the Bengal Renaissance*; Sumit Sarkar, *Critique of Colonial India*.

18 The proposal of a young Dalit activist to install English as the Dalit mother-goddess provides a quixotic illustration as late as the first decade of the twenty-first century. Dalits, he and his associates argued, should not be deprived of the gifts of modernity, which Lord Macaulay bestowed on India in the nineteenth century through his promotion of English education. Chandrabhan Prasad, "The English Day," October 25, 2006, Chandrabhanprasad.com/party/English_Day.pdf.

19 B. R. Ambedkar, *Writings and Speeches*, vol. 17, pt. 3 (2003), 276. Compare D. R. Nagaraj's comment that, for Ambedkar, "the Dalit is primarily a humiliated person and other dimensions of a Dalit's personality are secondary"; Nagaraj, *Flaming Feet*, 78.

20 Rege translates numerous examples in her collection of Dalit women's autobiographies; Rege, *Writing Caste, Writing Gender*. See also my *History of Prejudice*, chaps. 2 and 6.

21 Kamble, *Jina Amucha*, 99; the translation is Maya Pandit's, in Kamble, *Prisons We Broke*, 122. Cf. the parallel argument by Alice Walker: "What good was the Civil Rights Movement? . . . It broke the pattern of black servitude in this country. . . . It gave us hope for tomorrow. It called us to life"; Walker, "The Civil Rights Movement: What Good Was It?" (1967), repr. in Alice Walker, *In Search of Our Mothers' Gardens: Womanist Prose* (New York: Harvest Book Harcourt, 1983), 128–29; also Nikki Giovanni, *The Prosaic Soul of Nikki Giovanni* (New York: Perennial, 2003), 406–7.

22 Kamble, *Jina Amucha*, 52–54.

23 Note, in this context, the title of Narendra Jadhav's English rendition of his family memoir in its American incarnation, *Untouchables: My Family's Triumphant Escape from India's Caste System*. I have outlined the family's story in chapter 2 above.

24 Vidyut Bhagwat, "Ek streevadi vatsan," in *Aamcha Baap aan Aamhi: Svarup ani Sameeksha*, ed. Shailesh Tribhuvan (Mumbai: Granthali, 2008), 229.

25 Jadhav, *Aamcha Baap*, 14–15.

26 Jadhav, *Outcaste*, 228–30. The American edition uses slightly different phrasing; *Untouchables*, 257–60.

27 Valmiki, *Joothan*, 12.

28 Valmiki, *Joothan*, 16

29 There were jibes about an Untouchable wanting to be like a Brahmin, learning to read and write. Om wasn't allowed to drink the water other students drank; nor could the village washerman's son, Om's classmate, persuade his father to iron Om's uniform even for a special occasion; Valmiki, *Joothan*, 28, 40, 77.

30 For a somewhat different use of the title *Munshi* to distinguish lower-caste teachers (*Munshi* or mere "writer") from higher-caste ones (teacher or *Master ji*), see Cohn, "Changing Status," 74. More generally, however, *Munshi* is used to acknowledge special learning and expertise.

31 See Valmiki's story about this demeaning practice, "Salaam," published originally in *Hans* in 1973, reproduced in his short-story collection, *Salaam*.

32 Valmiki, *Joothan*, 57–59.

33 Valmiki, *Joothan*, 14.

34 This and the quotations in the following paragraphs come from Valmiki, *Joothan*, 45–48.

35 Moon, *Growing Up*.

36 Moon, *Growing Up*, 1, 2. The details of life in the *vasti* come from Moon's autobiography and from several interviews I had with his daughter and son-in-law in Nagpur in 2012.

37 Moon, *Growing Up*, 2. Compare Baisantri's very similar description of conditions in a neighboring workers' *basti*, cited in the last section of chapter 2 above.

38 Moon, *Growing Up*, 22.

39 Moon, *Growing Up*, 118.

40 Moon, *Growing Up*, 77; cf. 74.

41 Moon, *Growing Up*, 52.

42 When Vasant told her of his desire to complete an MA and his nervousness about leaving his job in order to do so, she said, "As long as I have my hands and feet there's no anxiety"; Moon, *Growing Up*, 157.

43 Moon, *Growing Up*, 172.

44 Kamble, *Jina Amucha*, 39, 43, 83, for quotations in this and next paragraph.

45 The memoir was published in book form four years later: Kamble, *Jina Amucha*.

46 See obituaries in *The Hindu*, April 23, 2012; *Maharashtra Times*, April 28, 2012, https://maharashtratimes.com/editorial/manasa/-/articleshow/12904269.cms; Tina Das, "Babytai Kamble: The Mahar Icon Who Was 'Reborn' to Write about Dalit Women's Subjugation," *The Print*, April 21, 2022, https://theprint.in/theprint-profile/babytai-kamble-the-mahar-icon-who-was-reborn-to-write-about-dalit-womens-subjugation/924436/.

47 Sunaina Arya surveys the debate and stresses the need to distinguish between the idea of a Brahmin and a Brahmanical patriarchy; see Arya, "Dalit or Brahmanical Patriarchy," 217–28, and the references she cites. Also, Geetha, *Patriarchy*; Chakravarti, *Gendering Caste*; Rege, "'Real Feminism' and Dalit Women"; Guru, "Dalit Women Talk Differently"; Omvedt, "Downtrodden among the Downtrodden."

48 For inheritance rules in middle- and upper-caste and class Hindu families, under the alternative *mitakshara* and *dayabhag* systems, and in Muslim families under Muslim law, see Nair, *Women and Law*; Parashar, *Women and Family Law Reform*; Agnes, *Law and Gender Inequality*; Sturman, *Government of Social Life*.

49 Baisantri, *Dohra Abhishaap*, 43, 48, 49.

50 Baisantri, *Dohra Abhishaap*, 50, 51.

51 Moon, *Growing Up*, 118.

52 Moon, *Growing Up*, 55, 118, 119.

53 Valmiki, *Joothan*, 91.

54 Moon, *Growing Up*, 10, 172. As in the grandfather's statement of aspirations, "Saheb" was the honorific the mother used for her educated, middle-class son.

55 Moon, *Growing Up*, 172. The marriage was conducted following Hindu customs and rituals. The mass conversion of Mahars and other Dalits to Buddhism, initiated by Ambedkar, occurred a few years later in 1956. Vasant Moon was among the youth who enthusiastically embraced Buddhism then, and his mother quietly did so too.

56 The subtitle of the American edition; Jadhav, *Untouchables*.

57 Leela and Tusha did their work in the home, as homemakers, though the latter also had a clerical position for a time in the Public Works Department, Government of Maharashtra. In Narendra Jadhav's reckoning, it was only with his own and his children's generation that girls'/women's horizons, aspirations, and abilities changed. He makes the point in an addendum to his work, by foregrounding his daughter Apoorva Jadhav's very different view of the world in her eloquent reflections on growing up in Bombay and the United States at the turn of the twenty-first century; Jadhav, *Untouchables*, 291–95.

58 Interview with Maya Pandit, in Kamble, *Prisons We Broke*, 147.

59 Interview with Maya Pandit, in Kamble, *Prisons We Broke*, 147, 155, 156, 157.

60 Kamble, *Prisons We Broke*, 5, 107; cf. Kamble, *Jina Amucha*, 12, 85. The last quote comes from Maya Pandit's interview in *Prisons We Broke*, 144.

61 Kamble, *Prisons We Broke*, 156.

62 Kamble, *Prisons We Broke*, 147, 155.

6. THE THINGS MEN TOUCHED

Epigraph: Baldwin, *Evidence of Things Not Seen*, xvii.

1 Pandey, *History of Prejudice*, 2, cited in chapter 1 above.

2 Yusufji, *Ambedkar*, 141.

3 Chughtai, *Kaagazi*, 102–3.

4 Chughtai, *Kaagazi*, 7. M. Asaduddin's translation differs slightly from mine; Chughtai, *Life in Words*, 1–2.

5   Individual cases of course varied. Ismat and her husband, married in 1942, had two children. Akhtar and Hameeda Raipuri, married in 1935, had five. My parents, married in 1946, had six, of whom one died in infancy. I met colleagues and friends of my parents who had eight or ten children, not counting infant deaths. The burdens of continuous birthing, and of mortality among infants and mothers, were greater among the poorer working classes; I discuss the matter later in this section.

6   See chapter 2.

7   The next two paragraphs recapitulate information I have provided in chapters 2 and 4.

8   For one incisive, yet nostalgic, discussion of *adda*, see Chakrabarty, *Provincializing Europe*, chap. 7.

9   See chapter 5 above for this and the following example.

10   Indrani Jagjivan Ram, *Dekhi, Suni*, I:39.

11   Valmiki, *Joothan*, 32.

12   Jadhav, *Untouchables*, 209, 211. I have added the emphasis and shifted the last sentence from the middle to the end of the paragraph.

13   Cf. Amia Srinivasan, writing about advanced capitalist countries of the West: "It is striking, though unsurprising, that . . . men tend to respond to sexual marginalization with a sense of entitlement to women's bodies." Women protesting against their sexual marginalization, on the other hand, "typically do so with talk not of entitlement but empowerment." Srinivasan, *Right to Sex*, 90.

14   Chughtai, *Kaagazi*, 257–58; Khurshid Mirza, *Woman of Substance*, 98, for Rashid Jahan's comments.

15   Chughtai, *Kaagazi*, 258–59.

16   Baisantri, *Dohra Abhishaap*, 11, 50, 51, 104.

17   Kamble, *Jina Amucha*, 65.

18   Snapshot 3a in chapter 1.

19   Nasreen Munni Kabir, *Guru Dutt: A Life in Cinema* (Delhi: Oxford University Press, 1996), 113.

20   See chapter 5.

21   The term she uses is *poojniya*, "deserving of worship"; R. Sankrityayan, *Jivan Yatra*, VI:315, 342. See also 378 and passim. *He, him*, and *you* are in the elevating *vous* form throughout. Emphases added.

22   See chapter 3.

23   See letters cited in Indrani Jagjivan Ram, *Dekhi, Suni*, I:41, 44, 45, as well as Appendices 2 and 3 on pages 175 and 176–77, respectively.

24   See chapter 3.

25   For just one striking example, in line with several others quoted in the last two volumes of his autobiography put together by Kamala after his death, see his letter of November 25, 1956, from the Buddhist pilgrimage center of Kusinara (Kusinagar) in northern India on his way to Nepal: R. Sankrityayan, *Jivan Yatra*, VI:335–36.

26   Savita Ambedkar, *Babasaheb*, 316. The next three quotations are from pages 61, 69, and 92, respectively.

27   See chapter 4.

28   Bachchan, *Atmakatha*, I:192; II:195, 240.

29 For a fuller discussion of this theme, see chapter 7, section on "*Navrapana* (Husbandness)."

30 Gopal, *A Part Apart*, 233, citing Khairmode, *Ambedkar*, 2:117–18.

31 Varle, *Matoshree Ramabai Ambedkar Yaancha Sahavasat*, 49, cited in Gopal, *A Part Apart*, 100.

32 R. Sankrityayan, *Jivan Yatra*, VI:338. At another place, she describes the role of a young homemaker and mother like herself through the Hindi adage "*pir, bavarchi, bhishti, khar*"—someone who is teacher, cook, water-carrier, and mule, all in one.

33 Kamala to Rahul, Mussoorie, January 11, 1955, emphasis added. (I owe thanks to Jaya Sankrityayan for allowing me to consult the original letters, kept in her files in Dehradun).

34 The phrase I have translated as "common behavior" has a sharper edge: the word *saamanya* also translates as "vulgar." Quotations from R. Sankrityayan, *Jivan Yatra*, VI:361, 382; see also 378.

35 R. Sankrityayan, *Jivan Yatra*, VI:604, 605. The history of this period in their lives must be a chapter of another story. For a few more details, see my "Hindustani Aadmi Ghar Mein."

36 Hameeda Raipuri, *Humsafar*, 254, 271. On another occasion, Akhtar expressed displeasure at her getting land allotted for them to build their own house, a development about which he was later rather pleased; Hameeda Raipuri, *Humsafar*, 271–72, 277.

37 Kamble, *Jina Amucha*, 70.

38 Gopal Guru, "Afterword," in Kamble, *Prisons We Broke*, 166.

39 Kamble, *Jina Amucha*, 12, 78, and passim; *Prisons We Broke*, 155. See also chapter 5 above.

40 Jadhav, *Untouchables*, 209, 210.

41 Jadhav, *Untouchables*, 213. Her husband's diktat had to hold sway, although in their working-class home, there were obvious departures from upper-caste and middle-class norms and practices. There is little evidence, for instance, of the use of flattering terms like *swami* (lord and master) or *devata* (god) for men by women in working-class households. Though this would seem to defy the norm, even among the laboring poor, her son suggests that Sonubai regularly addressed her husband as "Jadhav."

42 Jadhav, *Untouchables*, 284.

43 R. Sankrityayan, *Jivan Yatra*, VI:293. The sentiment is expressed again on page 357.

7. THE NATURE OF MEN

Epigraph: Beauvoir, *Second Sex*, 442.

1 Kamble, *Prisons We Broke*, 156.

2 Tagore, *Home and the World*, 40.

3 I heard this usage regularly in my years in Calcutta in the 1980s. Partha Chatterjee confirmed its use among Muslim Bengalis in an email communication, August 25, 2021.

4 Prasad, *Atmakatha*, 614; Premchand, "Nari-jati ke adhikar," 249; M. K. Gandhi, *Women and Social Justice*, 161, cited in chapter 3 above.

5 Bachchan, *Atmakatha* I:170; II:117.

6 Bachchan, *Atmakatha* I:169. See chapter 4 above.

7 Bachchan, *Atmakatha* I:175. His in-laws also bought him a bicycle when they discovered he had to walk over four miles to and from the university, in addition to the various homes where he tutored children; *Atmakatha* I:180.

8 Bachchan, *Atmakatha* I:238.

9 Bachchan, *Atmakatha* I:191.

10 See chapters 4 and 5.

11 Quotations in this and the next paragraph are from Bachchan, *Atmakatha* II:179, 185, 196, 197, 212, 221–22.

12 Literally, "like that of a swimmer who can go on no longer, using his last ounce of energy to reach the shore." Bachchan, *Atmakatha*, III:162.

13 Bachchan, *Atmakatha*, III:162–65.

14 I take the formulation "work, work, work" from Premchand's brief autobiographical statement, cited in Madan, *Premchand*, 168, and in chapter 3 above.

15 R. Sankrityayan, *Ghumakkad Shastra*, 9, 10, 52, 60. Parts of these quotations appeared in chapter 3. *Purush*, literally "men," appears to be used here and other places in the text as the universal male form for human beings, and Sankrityayan suggests it applies to women too. But all the examples he names are men.

16 R. Sankrityayan, *Ghumakkad Shastra*, 90; see 89–91.

17 R. Sankrityayan, *Ghumakkad Shastra*, 53, 55. In the new chapter added in 1956, he adds, "Young women wanderers should carry a small pistol with them" (92).

18 R. Sankrityayan, *Ghumakkad Shastra*, 9.

19 R. Sankrityayan, *Ghumakkad Shastra*, 52–53.

20 R. Sankrityayan, *Ghumakkad Swami*.

21 R. Sankrityayan, *Ghumakkad Swami*, 71, 89–92, 94, 106–10.

22 R. Sankrityayan, *Ghumakkad Swami*, 104, emphasis added.

23 R. Sankrityayan, *Ghumakkad Swami*, 105; cf. 109.

24 R. Sankrityayan, *Jivan Yatra*, V:180.

25 Ambedkar's self-characterization is discussed in chapters 3 and 6; Akhtar Raipuri's of himself and Abdul Haq in chapter 4. These examples, like those of Rahul Sankrityayan, Harishanand, and others, point to a problem that has baffled progressive activists and thinkers in colonial and postcolonial South Asia. To this day, countries in the region lack a proper structure of public institutional care for the aged and the seriously ill. There is continued societal investment in, and demand for, family support for elders. At the same time, any idea of older people withdrawing from this world in preparation for transition to another has become increasingly irrelevant—given the emphasis of the modern, and of modern sages and reformers, on deliverance ("progress") in the here and now. The irreconcilability of adventurous men's and (if the thought is even entertained for them) women's will to be free, and their need for family, community, and daily sustenance remains profound.

26 Cf. Swapna Banerjee's proposition about the "new leadership role of fathers" as teachers in the nineteenth and twentieth centuries. Ideas of masculinity, she notes, shifted from "physical strength to moral education"; Swapna Banerjee, *Fathers in a Motherland*, 13, 21, and passim.

27 M. K. Gandhi, *Autobiography*, 7, 9, 208. Cf. Hardiman, *Gandhi in His Time*, 95–98.

28 M. K. Gandhi, *Autobiography*, 208–9.

29 Kanota, Rudolph, and Rudolph, *Reversing the Gaze*, 227–28. The English is his own; emphases mine.

30 Savita Ambedkar, *Babasaheb*, 70, 71.

31 Savita Ambedkar, *Babasaheb*, 320. "He would pay attention to everything related to me," Savitabai observes. "Particularly in the matter of clothes, the choice would always be his"; *Babasaheb*, 71. For another striking example of guidance on a rather different subject, see his reference to books on "married life" by Tolstoy and Disraeli that he thought she might profitably read: *Babasaheb*, 75.

32 Bachchan, *Atmakatha*, I:169, 170. I have translated this passage more literally, and perhaps less idiomatically, than necessary, in order to convey what I see as the precise tenor of Bachchan's thinking.

33 Indrani Jagjivan Ram, *Dekhi, Suni*, I:184, 202, emphases added.

34 See chapters 5 and 6.

35 R. Sankrityayan, *Jivan Yatra*, VI:357, 361; see also 383.

36 See Igor Sankrityayan, "Meri Yashodhara ma Yelena Sankrityayan."

37 R. Sankrityayan, *Jivan Yatra*, VI:357, emphasis added.

38 Khairmode, *Ambedkar*, 2:108 and 3:224, cited in Gopal, *A Part Apart*, 214, 102.

39 Jadhav, *Untouchables*, 209, 210, also cited in chapter 6, above.

40 Khurshid Mirza, *Woman of Substance*, 151, cited in chapter 4, above.

EPILOGUE

1 "Erewhon," *Encyclopedia Britannica*, March 27, 2018, https://www.britannica.com/topic/Erewhon.

2 Pandey, "Hindustani Aadmi Ghar Mein."

Bibliography

PRIMARY SOURCES

Ambedkar, B. R. *Babasaheb Ambedkar Writings and Speeches*. Vols. 1–21. Bombay/Mumbai: Government of Maharashtra, 1979–2006.

Ambedkar, B. R. "Castes in India: Their Mechanism, Genesis and Development." *Indian Antiquary* 41 (May 1917): 81–95.

Ambedkar, B. R. *The Essential Writings of B. R. Ambedkar*. Edited by Valerian Rodrigues. Delhi: Oxford University Press, 2002.

Ambedkar, Savita. *Dr. Ambedkaranchya Sahvaasaat*. 1990. 4th ed. Mumbai: Tathagat Prakashan, 2020. Translated into English by Nadeem Khan. *Babasaheb: My Life with Dr. Ambedkar*. Gurugram: Penguin Random House, 2020.

Bachchan, Harivanshrai. *Atmakatha, Volume I: Kya Bhulun, Kya Yaad Karun*. 1969. Repr., Delhi: Rajpal and Sons, 2015.

Bachchan, Harivanshrai. *Atmakatha, Volume II: Nir ka Nirman Phir*. 1971. Repr., Delhi: Rajpal and Sons, 2019.

Bachchan, Harivanshrai. *Atmakatha, Volume III: Basere se Dur*. 1978. Repr., Delhi: Rajpal and Sons, 2014.

Bachchan, Harivanshrai. *Atmakatha, Volume IV: Dashdwar se Sopan Tak*. 1991. Repr., Delhi: Rajpal and Sons, 2014.

Bachchan, Harivansh Rai. *In the Afternoon of Time: An Autobiography*. Translated by Rupert Snell. Gurgaon: Penguin India, 2001.

Baisantri, Kausalya. *Dohra Abhishaap*. Delhi: Parmeshwari Prakashan, 1999.

Bama. *Karukku*. 1992. Translated by Lakshmi Holmstrom. Chennai: Macmillan India, 2000.

Bama. *Sangati: Events*. 1994. Translated by Lakshmi Holmstron. Delhi: Oxford University Press, 2005.

Bose, Nirmal Kumar. *Parivrajak ki Diary*. Translated by Manoj Kumar Mishra. Delhi: Vani Prakashan, 1997.

Bose, Subhas Chandra. *An Indian Pilgrim, or Autobiography of Subhas Chandra Bose*. Calcutta: Thacker, Spink & Co., 1948.

Burnett-Hurst, A. R. *Labour and Housing in Bombay.* London: P. S. King and Son, 1925.

Chughtai, Ismat. *Kaagazi hai Pairahan.* 1992. Nagari transcription by Iftikhar Anjum, 1998. Delhi: Rajkamal Paperbacks, 2016.

Chughtai, Ismat. *A Life in Words: Memoirs.* Translated by M. Asaduddin. Delhi: Penguin Books, 2012.

Edwardes, S. M. *The Gazetteer of Bombay City and Island.* Vol. 1. Bombay: Times Press, 1909.

Gandhi, Gopalkrishna, and Tridip Suhrud. *Scorching Love: Letters from Mohandas Karamchand Gandhi to His Son Devadas.* Delhi: Oxford University Press, 2022.

Gandhi, M. K. *An Autobiography, or The Story of My Experiments with Truth.* Translated by Mahadev Desai. Ahmedabad: Navajivan, 1927.

Gandhi, M. K. "Indian Home Rule or *Hind Swaraj.*" 1910. In *Hind Swaraj and Other Writings,* edited by Anthony J. Parel. Cambridge: Cambridge University Press, 1997.

Gandhi, M. K. *Thoughts on National Language.* Ahmedabad: Navajivan, 1956.

Gandhi, M. K. *Women and Social Justice.* 3rd ed. Ahmedabad: Navajivan, 1947.

Gandhi, M. K. *Young India, 1919–1922.* New York: B. W. Huebsch, 1924.

A Gazetteer of Delhi. 1913. Gurgaon: Vintage, 1992.

Hosain, Attia. *Sunlight on a Broken Column.* 1961. Delhi: Penguin, 1992.

Hutton, J. H. *Census of India, 1931.* Delhi: Government of India, 1931.

Jadhav, Narendra. *Aamcha Baap aan Aamhi.* 1993. 2nd ed. Mumbai: Granthali, 1994; 5th people's ed. Mumbai: Granthali, 2007.

Jadhav, Narendra. *Outcaste: A Memoir.* Delhi: Viking, 2003. Published in the United States as *Untouchables: My Family's Triumphant Escape from India's Caste System.* Berkeley: University of California Press, 2005.

Kamble, Baby. *Jina Amucha.* 1986. Repr., Pune: Sugava Prakashan, 1990; 3rd ed., 2008.

Kamble, Baby. *The Prisons We Broke.* 2008. Translated by Maya Pandit. Hyderabad: Orient Longman, 2008.

Kanota, Mohan Singh, Susan H. Rudolph, and Lloyd I. Rudolph, eds. *Reversing the Gaze: Amar Singh's Diary, A Colonial Subject's Narrative of Imperial India.* Delhi: Oxford University Press, 2000.

Kumar, Meira. "My Father's Childhood." In *Babu Jagjivan Ram in Parliament: A Commemorative Volume,* 34–38. http://jagjivanramfoundation.nic.in/pdf/Speeches%20in%20Parliament/JAGJIVAN%20RAM-PROFILE.pdf.

Mirza, Khurshid. Interview by Lutfullah Khan. LAL, 1975. Accessed January 19, 2019. YouTube video, 51:12. https://www.youtube.com/watch?v=-OZSxBbVaZs.

Mirza, Khurshid. *The Making of a Modern Muslim Woman: Begum Khurshid Mirza (1918–1989).* Edited by Lubna Kazim. Lahore: Brite, 2003.

Mirza, Khurshid. *A Woman of Substance: The Memoirs of Begum Khurshid Mirza (1918–1989).* Edited by Lubna Kazim. New Delhi: Zubaan, 2005.

Moon, Vasant. *Growing Up Untouchable in India: A Dalit Autobiography.* Translated by Gail Omvedt. Lanham, MD: Rowman and Littlefield, 2000.

Moon, Vasant. *Vasti.* Mumbai: Granthali, 1995.

Pradhan, G. R. *Untouchable Workers of Bombay City.* Bombay: Karnatak, 1938.

Prasad, Rajendra. *Atmakatha.* Patna: Sahitya Sansar, 1947.

Prasad, Rajendra. *Autobiography*. Bombay: Asia Publishing House, 1957.

Premchand. "Nari-jati ke adhikar." In *Vividh Prasang*, vol. 3, edited by Amrit Rai, 249–50. Allahabad: Hans Prakashan, 1980.

Premchand. *Rangbhumi*. 1927. Allahabad: Sarasvati, 1965.

Premchand, Shivrani Devi. 1944. *Premchand Ghar Mein*. Delhi: Atmaram and Sons, 2012.

Purcell, A. A., and J. Hallsworth. *Report on Labour Conditions in India*. London: Trades Union Congress General Council, 1928.

Raipuri, Akhtar Husain. *The Dust of the Road. A Translation of "Gard-e-Raah."* Translated by Amina Azfar. Karachi: Oxford University Press, 2000.

Raipuri, Akhtar Husain. *Gard-e-Raah*. Karachi: Maktaba-e-Danyal, 1984.

Raipuri, Hameeda Akhtar Husain. *Humsafar*. Karachi: Maktaba-e-Danyal, 2008.

Raipuri, Hameeda Akhtar Husain. *My Fellow Traveller: A Translation of "Humsafar."* Translated by Amina Azfar. Karachi: Oxford University Press, 2007.

Raipuri, Hameeda Akhtar Husain. *Nayab Hain Hum*. Karachi: Maktaba-e-Danyal, 1999.

Ram, Indrani Jagjivan. *Dekhi, Suni, Beeti Baatein*. Volumes I–III. Delhi: Jagjivan Vidya Bhavan, 1994–97.

Ram, Indrani Jagjivan. *Milestones: A Memoir*. Translated by Tara Joshi. New Delhi: Penguin, 2010.

Ram, Jagjivan. Interview. "Oral History Transcript." New Delhi: Nehru Memorial Museum, no. 504.

Rao, Raja. *Kanthapura*. 1938. 2nd ed. New Delhi: Oxford University Press, 1974.

Report of Depressed Class Conference, Nagpur Session. Nagpur: G. T. Meshram, 1942.

Sankrityayan, Igor Rahulovich. "Meri Yashodhara ma Yelena Sankrityayan." 2001. Translated from the Russian by Jitendra Raghuvanshi. *Abhinavkadam* 11, nos. 16–17 (2006–2007): 295–307.

Sankrityayan, Kamala. *Mahamanav Mahapandit*. Delhi: Radhakrishna, 1995.

Sankrityayan, Rahul. *Ghumakkad Shastra*. 1949. Rev. 1956. Delhi: Kitab Mahal, 2014.

Sankrityayan, Rahul. *Ghumakkad Swami*. 1958. Delhi: Kitab Mahal, 2019.

Sankrityayan, Rahul. *Jeene ke Liye*. 1940. Allahabad: Kitab Mahal, 2016.

Sankrityayan, Rahul. *Kanaila ki Katha*. 1957. Patna: Kitab Mahal, 2015.

Sankrityayan, Rahul. *Meri Jivan Yatra*. Volumes I–IV, 1944, 1950, 1951, 1967. Volumes V–VI, compiled and edited by Kamala Sankrityayan, n.d. Delhi: Radhakrishna Prakashan, 1994–96; 3rd paperback reprint, 2014.

Saraswati, Dayanand. *The Autobiography of Dayanand Saraswati*. Autobiographical fragments, edited and rendered into English by K. C. Yadav. Delhi: Manohar, 1987.

Statistical Abstract Relating to British India from 1876/7 to 1885/6. London: Her Majesty's Stationary Office, 1887.

Tagore, Rabindranath. *The Home and the World*. 1916. Translated by Surendranath Tagore. London: Penguin, 2005.

Tandon, Prakash. *Punjabi Century, 1857–1947*. London: Chatto and Windus, 1961.

Times of India. "Over 30% Women from 14 States, UT Justify Beating by Husbands: NFHS." November 28, 2021. https://timesofindia.indiatimes.com/india/over-30-women -from-14-states-ut-justify-beating-by-husbands-hs/articleshowprint/87961478.cms.

Valmiki, Omprakash. *Joothan*. Delhi: Radhakrishna Prakashan, 1997.

Valmiki, Omprakash. *Salaam*. Delhi: Radhakrishna Prakashan, 2000.

Varma, Mahadevi. *Sansmaran*. Delhi: Rajpal and Sons, 1984.

SECONDARY SOURCES

Agarwal, Bina. *A Field of One's Own: Gender and Land Rights in South Asia*. Cambridge: Cambridge University Press, 1994.

Agnes, Flavia. *Law and Gender Inequality: The Politics of Women's Rights in India*. Delhi: Oxford University Press, 1999.

Aloysius, G. *Religion as Emancipatory Identity: A Buddhist Movement among the Tamils under Colonialism*. Delhi: New Age International, 1998.

Alter, Joseph S. "Indian Clubs and Colonialism: Hindu Masculinity and Muscular Christianity." *Comparative Studies in Society and History* 46, no. 3 (2004): 497–534.

Alter, Joseph S. "Masculinities and Culture." In *Critical Themes in Indian Sociology*, edited by Sanjay Srivastava, Yasmeen Arif, and Janaki Abraham, 298–312. Delhi: Sage, 2019.

Alter, Joseph S. "Somatic Nationalism: Indian Wrestling and Militant Hinduism." *Modern Asian Studies* 28, no. 3 (1994): 557–88.

Althusser, Louis. *Reading Capital*. Translated by Ben Brewster. New York: Pantheon, 1970.

Arya, Sunaina. "Dalit or Brahmanical Patriarchy? Rethinking Indian Feminism." *Caste: A Global Journal on Social Exclusion* 1, no. 1 (February 2020): 217–28.

Baldwin, James. *The Evidence of Things Not Seen*. New York: Henry Holt and Co., 1985.

Banerjee, Sikata. *Make Me a Man! Masculinity, Hinduism, and Nationalism in India*. Albany: SUNY Press, 2005.

Banerjee, Swapna. *Fathers in a Motherland: Imagining Fatherhood in Colonial India*. Delhi: Oxford University Press, 2022.

Banerjee-Dube, Ishita. *Caste in History*. Delhi: Oxford University Press, 2008.

Bayly, C. A. *Rulers, Townsmen and Bazaars: North Indian Society in the Age of British Expansion*. Cambridge: Cambridge University Press, 1983.

Beauvoir, Simone de. *The Second Sex*. Translated by H. M. Parshley. London: Jonathan Cape, 1953.

Bellenoit, Hayden. "Between Qanungos and Clerks: The Cultural and Service Worlds of Hindustan's Pensmen, c. 1750–1850." *Modern Asian Studies* 48, no. 14 (July 2014): 872–910.

Boehmer, Elleke. *Stories of Women: Gender and Narrative in the Postcolonial Nation*. Manchester: Manchester University Press, 2005.

Botre, Shrikant, and Douglas E. Haynes. "Understanding R. D. Karve: Brahmacharya, Modernity, and the Appropriation of Global Sexual Science in Western India, 1927–1953." In *A Global History of Sexual Science, 1880–1960*, edited by Veronika Fuechtner, Douglas E. Haynes, and Ryan Jones, 163–85. Berkeley: University of California Press, 2018.

Buettner, Elizabeth. *Empire Families: Britons and Late Imperial India*. Oxford: Oxford University Press, 2004.

Carroll, Lucy. "Caste, Social Change, and the Social Scientist: A Note on the Ahistorical Approach to Indian Social History." *Journal of Asian Studies* 35, no. 1 (November 1975): 63–84.

Chakrabarty, Dipesh. *Provincializing Europe: Postcolonial Thought and Historical Difference*. Princeton, NJ: Princeton University Press, 2000.

Chakravarti, Uma. *Gendering Caste: Through a Feminist Lens*. Calcutta: Stree, 2003.

Chakravarti, Uma. *Rewriting History: The Life and Times of Pandita Ramabai*. Berkeley: University of California Press, 1998.

Chakravarti, Uma. "Whatever Happened to the Vedic *Dasi*?" In *Recasting Women: Essays in Indian Colonial History*, edited by Kumkum Sangari and Sudesh Vaid, 27–87. Delhi: Kali for Women, 1989.

Chandra, Sudhir. *Enslaved Daughters: Colonialism, Law and Women's Rights*. Oxford: Oxford University Press, 1998.

Chatterjee, Partha. "The Nationalist Resolution of the Women's Question." In *Recasting Women: Essays in Indian Colonial History*, edited by Kumkum Sangari and Sudesh Vaid, 233–53. Delhi: Kali for Women, 1989.

Chatterjee, Partha. *The Nation and Its Fragments: Colonial and Postcolonial Histories*. Princeton, NJ: Princeton University Press, 1993.

Chatterjee, Partha. *Politics of the Governed: Reflections on Popular Politics in Most of the World*. Delhi: Permanent Black, 2004.

Chatterji, Indrani, ed. *Unfamiliar Relations: Family and History in South Asia*. New Delhi: Permanent Black, 2004.

Chattopadhyay, Swati. *Representing Calcutta: Modernity, Nationalism and the Colonial Uncanny*. London: Routledge, 2005.

Chhabria, Sheetal. *Making the Modern Slum: The Power of Capital in Colonial Bombay*. Seattle: University of Washington Press, 2019.

Chopra, Preeti. *A Joint Enterprise: Urban Elites and the Making of British Bombay*. Minneapolis: University of Minnesota Press, 2011.

Chopra, Radhika, Caroline Osella, and Filippo Osella, eds. *South Asian Masculinities: Context of Change, Sites of Continuity*. Delhi: Women Unlimited, 2004.

Chowdhury, Indira. *The Frail Hero and Virile History: Gender and the Politics of Culture in Colonial Bengal*. Delhi: Oxford University Press, 1998.

Cohn, Bernard S. "The Changing Status of a Depressed Caste." In *Village India: Studies in the Little Community*, edited by McKim Marriott, 53–77. Chicago: University of Chicago Press, 1955.

Derrett, J. D. M. *Introduction to Modern Hindu Law*. London: Oxford University Press, 1963.

Desai, Madhavi. "The Bungalow in the Colonial and Postcolonial Twentieth Century: Modernity, Dwelling and Gender in the Cultural Landscape of Gujarat, India." In *The Routledge Companion to Modernity, Space and Gender*, edited by Alexandra Staub, 350–66. London: Routledge, 2018.

Du Bois, W. E. B. *The Souls of Black Folk*. 1903. New York: Signet Classic, 1969.

Erikson, Erik. *Gandhi's Truth: On the Origins of Militant Nonviolence*. London: Faber and Faber, 1970.

Finkelstein, Maura. *The Archive of Loss: Lively Ruination in Mill Land Mumbai*. Durham, NC: Duke University Press, 2019.

Frazier, E. Franklin. *Black Bourgeoisie*. New York: Free Press, 1957.

Freitag, Sandria B., ed. *Culture and Power in Banaras: Community, Performance, and Environment, 1800–1980*. Berkeley: University of California Press, 1992.

Geetha, V. *Patriarchy*. Calcutta: Stree, 2009.

Ghosh, Durba. *Gentlemanly Terrorists: Political Violence and Colonial State in India, 1919–1947*. Cambridge: Cambridge University Press, 2017.

Glover, William. *Making Lahore Modern: Constructing and Imagining a Colonial City*. Minneapolis: University of Minnesota Press, 2007.

Goffman, Erving. *The Presentation of Self in Everyday Life*. 1956. Rev. ed. New York: Anchor Books, 1959.

Gopal, Ashok. *A Part Apart: The Life and Thought of B. R. Ambedkar*. New Delhi: Navayana, 2023.

Guha, Ranajit. *History at the Limit of World History*. New York: Columbia University Press, 2003.

Guru, Gopal. "Archaeology of Untouchability." *Economic and Political Weekly* 44, no. 37 (2009): 49–56.

Guru, Gopal. "Dalit Women Talk Differently." *Economic and Political Weekly* 30, no. 41/42 (October 1995): 2548–50.

Guru, Gopal. "Power of Touch." *Frontline* 23, no. 25 (December 16–29, 2006). https://frontline.thehindu.com/cover-story/article30212003.ece.

Hardiman, David. *Gandhi in His Time and Ours: The Global Legacy of His Ideas*. Ranikhet: Permanent Black, 2004.

Hartman, Saidiya. *Lose Your Mother: A Journey along the Atlantic Slave Route*. New York: Farrar, Straus and Giroux, 2007.

Hasan, Mushirul. *From Pluralism to Separatism: Qasbas in Colonial Awadh*. Delhi: Oxford University Press, 2004.

Hosagrahar, Jyoti. *Indigenous Modernities: Negotiating Architecture and Urbanism*. London: Routledge, 2005.

Jalil, Rakhshanda. *Liking Progress, Loving Change: A Literary History of the Progressive Writers' Movement in Urdu*. Delhi: Oxford University Press, 2014.

Jondhale, Surendra, and Johannes Beltz, eds. *Reconstructing the World: B. R. Ambedkar and Buddhism in India*. Delhi: Oxford University Press, 2004.

Joshi, Chitra. *Lost Worlds: Indian Labour and Its Forgotten Histories*. London: Anthem, 2003.

Joshi, Pushpa. *Gandhi on Women*. Delhi: Centre for Women's Development Studies, 1988.

Kaplan, Marion. *The Making of the Jewish Middle Class: Women, Family, and Identity in Imperial Germany*. New York: Oxford University Press, 1991.

Karve, Irawati. *Yuganta: The End of an Epoch*. 1969. Hyderabad: Orient Blackswan, 2008.

Keer, Dhananjay. *Dr. Ambedkar, Life and Mission*. 1954. Bombay: Popular Prakashan, 2005.

Khairmode, C. B. *Dr. Bhimrao Ramji Ambedkar*. 12 vols. Pune: Sugava Prakashan, 1952–92.

Kishwar, Madhu. "Gandhi on Women." *Economic and Political Weekly* 20, no. 40 (October 5, 1985): 1691–702; and 20, no. 41 (October 12, 1985): 1753–58.

Kumar, Nita. *The Artisans of Banaras: Popular Culture and Identity, 1880–1986*. Princeton, NJ: Princeton University Press, 1988.

Kumar, Radha. "City Lives: Workers' Housing and Rent in Bombay, 1911–1947." *Economic and Political Weekly* 22, no. 30 (July 1987): 47–56.

Lal, Ruby. *Coming of Age in Nineteenth-Century India: The Girl-Child and the Art of Play-fulness*. New York: Cambridge University Press, 2013.

Lambert-Hurley, Siobhan. *Elusive Lives: Gender, Autobiography and the Self in Muslim South Asia*. Palo Alto, CA: Stanford University Press, 2018.

Lewis, Oscar. "Peasant Culture in India and Mexico: A Comparative Analysis." In *Village India: Studies in the Little Community*, edited by McKim Marriott, 145–70. Chicago: University of Chicago Press, 1955.

Loomba, Ania. *Revolutionary Desires: Women, Communism, and Feminism in India*. Abingdon, UK: Routledge, 2019.

Loomba, Ania, and Ritty A. Lukose, eds. *South Asian Feminisms*. Durham, NC: Duke University Press, 2012.

Madan, Indar Nath. *Premchand: An Interpretation*. Lahore: Minerva, 1946.

Majumdar, Rochona. *Marriage and Modernity: Family Values in Colonial Bengal*. Durham, NC: Duke University Press, 2009.

Marriott, McKim, ed. *Village India: Studies in the Little Community*. Chicago: University of Chicago Press, 1955.

McClintock, Anne. *Imperial Leather: Race, Gender and Sexuality in the Colonial Contest*. London: Routledge, 1995.

McGowan, Abigail. "Ahmedabad's Home Remedies: Housing in the Re-making of an Industrial City, 1920–1960." *South Asia: Journal of South Asian Studies* 36, no. 3 (September 2013): 397–414.

Minault, Gail. *Secluded Scholars: Women's Education and Muslim Social Reform in Colonial India*. New York: Oxford University Press, 1998.

Mujahid, Abdul Malik. *Conversion to Islam: Untouchables' Strategy for Protest in India*. Chambersburg, PA: Anima, 1989.

Nagaraj, D. R. 1993. *The Flaming Feet and Other Essays: The Dalit Movement in India*. Rev. ed. Edited by Prithvi Datta Chandra Sobhi. Ranikhet: Permanent Black, 2010.

Nair, Janaki. *Women and Law in Colonial India: A Social History*. Delhi: Kali for Women, 1996.

Nandy, Ashis. *The Intimate Enemy: Loss and Recovery of Self under Colonialism*. Delhi: Oxford University Press, 1983.

Newbigin, Eleanor. *The Hindu Family and the Emergence of Modern India: Law, Citizenship and Community*. Cambridge: Cambridge University Press, 2013.

Nora, Pierre. "Between Memory and History: *Les lieux de mémoire*." *Representations* 26 (1989): 7–25.

Nora, Pierre, ed. *Conflicts and Divisions*. Vol. 1 of *Realms of Memory: Rethinking the French Past*. New York: Columbia University Press, 1996.

Novick, Peter. *The Holocaust in American Life*. New York: Houghton Mifflin, 1999.

Oberoi, Harjot. *The Construction of Religious Boundaries: Culture, Identity, and Diversity in the Sikh Tradition*. Delhi: Oxford University Press, 1994.

O'Hanlon, Rosalind. "The Social Worth of Scribes: Brahmins, Kāyasthas and the Social Order in Early Modern India." *Indian Economic and Social History Review* 47, no. 4 (December 2010): 563–95.

Oldenberg, Veena. *The Making of Colonial Lucknow*. Princeton, NJ: Princeton University Press, 1984.

Omvedt, Gail. *Ambedkar: Towards an Enlightened India.* New Delhi: Penguin, 2004.

Omvedt, Gail. *Dalit Visions: The Anti-caste Movement and the Construction of an Indian Identity.* New Delhi: Orient Longman, 1995.

Omvedt, Gail. "The Downtrodden among the Downtrodden: An Interview with a Dalit Agricultural Laborer." *Signs: Journal of Women in Culture and Society* 4, no. 4 (Summer 1979): 763–74.

Pande, Ishita. "Sorting Boys and Men: Unlawful Intercourse, Boy-Protection, and the Child Marriage Restraint Act in Colonial India." *Journal of the History of Childhood and Youth* 6, no. 2 (Spring 2013): 332–58.

Pande, Ishita. "Time for Sex: The Education of Desire and the Conduct of Childhood in Global/Hindu Sexology." In *A Global History of Sexual Science, 1880–1960*, edited by Veronika Fuechtner, Douglas E. Haynes, and Ryan Jones, 279–302. Berkeley: University of California Press, 2018.

Pandey, Gyanendra. *History of Prejudice: Race, Caste, and Difference in India and the United States.* New York: Cambridge University Press, 2013.

Pandey, Gyanendra. "Hindustani Aadmi Ghar Mein: Tab—aur Ab?" *Pratimaan* 6, no. 11 (January–June 2018): 196–231.

Pandey, Gyanendra. "Men in the Home: Everyday Practices of Gender in Twentieth–Century India." *Feminist Studies* 46, no. 2 (2020): 403–30.

Pandey, Gyanendra. *Remembering Partition: Violence, Nationalism, and History in India.* New York: Cambridge University Press, 2001.

Pandey, Gyanendra. *Routine Violence: Nations, Fragments, Histories.* Palo Alto, CA: Stanford University Press, 2006.

Pandian, M. S. S. *Brahmin and Non-Brahmin: Genealogies of the Tamil Political Present.* Delhi: Permanent Black, 2007.

Parashar, Archana. *Women and Family Law Reform in India: Uniform Civil Code and Gender Equality.* Delhi: Sage, 1992.

Rai, Amrit. *Premchand: Kalam ka Sipahi.* 1962. Allahabad: Hans Prakashan, 2013.

Rai, Sara. *Raw Umber: A Memoir.* Chennai: Westland, 2023.

Ramaswamy, Sumathi. *The Goddess and the Nation: Mapping Mother India.* Durham, NC: Duke University Press, 2010.

Rao, Anupama. *The Caste Question: Dalits and the Politics of Modern India.* Berkeley: University of California Press, 2009.

Rao, Nikhil. *House, but No Garden: Apartment Living in Bombay's Suburbs, 1898–1964.* Minneapolis: University of Minnesota Press, 2013.

Ray, Bharati. *Early Feminists of Colonial India: Sarala Devi Chaudhurani and Rokeya Sakhawat Hossain.* Oxford: Oxford University Press, 2012.

Ray, Sangeeta. *En-gendering India: Woman and Nation in Colonial and Postcolonial Narratives.* Durham, NC: Duke University Press, 2000.

Raychaudhuri, Tapan, and Geraldine Forbes, eds. *The Memoir of Dr. Haimabati Sen: From Child Widow to Lady Doctor.* Translated by Tapan Raychaudhuri. Berkeley: University of California Press, 2000.

Rege, Sharmila. "'Real Feminism' and Dalit Women: Scripts of Denial and Accusation." *Economic and Political Weekly* 35 no. 6 (February 2000): 492–95.

Rege, Sharmila. *Writing Caste, Writing Gender: Reading Dalit Women's Testimonios.* New Delhi: Zubaan, 2006.

Rich, Adrienne. *Of Woman Born: Motherhood as Experience and Institution.* 1976. New York: W. W. Norton, 1986.

Robinson, Francis. *Jamal Mian: The Life of Maulana Jamaluddin Abdul Wahab of Farangi Mahall, 1919–2012.* Karachi: Oxford University Press, 2018.

Rosselli, John. "The Self-Image of Effeteness: Physical Education and Nationalism in Nineteenth-Century Bengal." *Past and Present* 86, no. 1 (February 1980): 121–48.

Roy, Parama. *Indian Traffic: Identities in Question in Colonial and Postcolonial India.* Berkeley: University of California Press, 1998.

Sainath, P. *Everybody Loves a Good Drought: Stories from India's Poorest Districts.* Delhi: Penguin, 1996.

Sarkar, Sumit. *A Critique of Colonial India.* Calcutta: Papyrus, 1985.

Sarkar, Sumit. "'Kaliyuga,' 'Chakri,' and 'Bhakti': Ramakrishna and His Times." *Economic and Political Weekly* 27, no. 9 (July 1997): 1543–59 and 1561–66.

Sarkar, Susobhan. *On the Bengal Renaissance.* Calcutta: Papyrus, 1979.

Sarkar, Tanika. *Hindu Wife, Hindu Nation: Community, Religion, and Cultural Nationalism.* Delhi: Permanent Black, 2001.

Sarkar, Tanika. *Words to Win: The Making of a Modern Autobiography.* Chicago: University of Chicago Press, 1999.

Sen, K. M. *Hinduism.* Baltimore, MD: Penguin, 1967.

Sen, Satadru. *Colonial Childhoods: The Juvenile Periphery of India, 1850–1945.* London: Anthem, 2005.

Shaikh, Juned. *Outcaste Bombay: City Making and the Politics of the Poor.* Seattle: University of Washington Press, 2021.

Sharma, Nalin Vilochan. *Jagjivan Ram: A Biography.* Patna: Sanjivan Press, ca. 1950s.

Shaw, Stephanie. *What Women Ought to Be and to Do: Black Professional Women Workers during the Jim Crow Era.* Chicago: University of Chicago Press, 1996.

Sinha, Mrinalini. *Colonial Masculinity: The "Manly Englishman" and the "Effeminate Bengali" in the Late Nineteenth Century.* Manchester: University of Manchester Press, 1995.

Sinha, Mrinalini. "A Global Perspective on Gender: What's South Asia Got to Do with It?" In *South Asian Feminisms,* edited by Ania Loomba and Ritty A. Lukose, 356–74. Durham, NC: Duke University Press, 2012.

Sinha, Mrinalini. *The Specters of Mother India: The Global Restructuring of an Empire.* Durham, NC: Duke University Press, 2006.

Snell, Rupert. "A Hindi Poet from Allahabad: Translating Harivansh Rai Bachchan's Autobiography." *Modern Asian Studies* 34, no. 2 (May 2000): 425–47.

Snell, Rupert, ed. *Autobiographical Writing in Hindi: A Reader.* Delhi: Rajkamal Prakashan, 2023.

Spiegel, Gabrielle M. "Memory and History: Liturgical Time and Historical Time." *History and Theory* 41, no. 2 (May 2002): 148–62.

Spivak, Gayatri Chakravorty. "More Thoughts on Cultural Translation." *Transversal* 6 (2008). https://transversal.at/transversal/0608/spivak/en.

Spivak, Gayatri Chakravorty, and Ben Conisbee Baer. "Redoing Marxism at the Gigi Café: A Conversation." *Rethinking Marxism: A Journal of Economics, Culture and Society* 20, no. 4 (2008): 631–43.

Sreenivas, Mytheeli. *Wives, Widows and Concubines: The Conjugal Family in Colonial India.* Bloomington: Indiana University Press, 2008.

Srinivas, M. N. *Religion and Society among the Coorgs of South India.* Oxford: Clarendon Press, 1952.

Srinivasan, Amia. *The Right to Sex: Feminism in the Twenty-First Century.* New York: Farrar, Straus and Giroux, 2021.

Srivastava, Sanjay. *Constructing Post-colonial India: National Character and the Doon School.* London: Routledge, 1998.

Srivastava, Sanjay. "Ghumakkads, a Woman's Place, and the LTC-walas: Towards a Critical History of 'Home,' 'Belonging' and 'Attachment.'" *Contributions to Indian Sociology* (n.s.) 39, no. 3 (2005): 375–405.

Srivastava, Sanjay. "Introduction." In *Sexual Sites, Seminal Attitudes: Sexualities, Masculinities and Culture in South Asia*, edited by Sanjay Srivastava, 11–47. Delhi: Sage, 2004.

Sturman, Rachel. *The Government of Social Life in Colonial India: Liberalism, Religious Law, and Women's Rights.* New York: Cambridge University Press, 2012.

Swan, Robert O. *Munshi Premchand of Lamhi Village.* Durham, NC: Duke University Press, 1969.

Thompson, E. P. *The Making of the English Working Class.* London: Victor Gollancz, 1963.

Uberoi, Patricia, ed. *Family, Kinship and Marriage in India.* Delhi: Oxford University Press, 1993.

Varle, Radhabai. *Matoshree Ramabai Ambedkar Yaancha Sahavasat.* 1991. Aurangabad: Kaushalya Prakashan, 2011.

Vicziany, Marika, and Oliver Mendelsohn. *The Untouchables: Subordination, Poverty and the State in Modern India.* Cambridge: Cambridge University Press, 1998.

Walsh, Judith. *Domesticity in Colonial India: What Women Learned When Men Gave Them Advice.* Delhi: Oxford University Press, 2004.

Yusufji, Salim, ed. *Ambedkar: The Attendant Details.* New Delhi: Navayana, 2017.

Zamindar, Vazira. *The Long Partition and the Making of Modern South Asia: Refugees, Boundaries, Histories.* New York: Columbia University Press, 2007.

Zelliot, Eleanor. *From Untouchable to Dalit: Essays on the Ambedkar Movement.* 1992. 2nd rev. ed. Delhi: Manohar, 1996.

Index

Note: Page numbers in italics indicate maps. Page numbers in bold indicate references to extensive family history narratives.

Baisantri, Kausalya, x, 16, **54–55**, 127–28, 140, 142

Baluchistan, *xv*

Bama, 13, 51, 184n4

Banaras, *xiv, xv*, 44–45, 66, 79, 174

Banaras Hindu University, 173

Bangladesh (East Bengal, East Pakistan from 1947 to 1971), *xv*, 1, 86, 154

Bannerjee, Swapna, 24

Baroda, *xiv, xv*

Bengal, *xiv, xv*, 12, 18, 129, 154, 184n1, 185n17, 197n17

Bengali (language), 20

Bengali people, 122, 141, 201n3

bhadralok. See respectable castes and classes

Bholanath (grandfather of Bachchan), 35, 37–38, 138, 166

Bihar, *xiv, xv*, 41, 63–64, 70, 78–79, 81, 89, 172–73

Bismil, Ram Prasad, 18

Bombay, x–xi, *xiv, xv*, 35, 46, 49, 51–53, 55–56, 71, 75–77, 100, 107, 115–16, 118, 124, 129, 131, 152, 164, 167, 188n44; Dadar (district), 44; Parel (neighborhood), 52, 56; Siddharth College, 116; Sydenham College, 76; Wadala (neighborhood), 55–56, 129

Bombay films, xi, 49, 100

Bombay Improvement Trust, 44, 52

Bombay Legislative Council, 46, 115

Bose, Nirmal, 82

Bose, Subhas, 82, 158

Brahmin (caste), 36, 52, 64, 77, 160, 173. *See also* caste order

British Trades Union Congress Delegation (1927), 53

Calcutta, *xiv, xv*, 53, 63, 74, 79, 150, 164, 172, 187n16, 188n44, 201n3

caste order, 14–15, 16–18, 39, 42, 46, 49–51, 59–60, 80, 104, 112–15, 119–20, 123, 126, 135, 192n61, 198n29; inter-caste marriage in, 77–78, 104, 173; upward mobility and, 28, 35, 113, 127. *See also* Dalit classes; Dalit struggle; housing; sanitation, as boundary between classes; upper castes and classes

Chamar (caste), 14, 16, 50. *See also* caste order

Champa (Bachchan's first love), 105, 155–56

Champaran, 64

Chatterjee, Partha, 24

chawl/tenement, 21, 52, 55–56, 75–76, 112, 149. *See also* housing: of lower classes

Chhapra, *xiv, xv*, 63

child labor, 18, 119–21, 127, 142–43, 185n23. *See also* laboring people

child marriages, 19, 47, 61–63, 66, 70, 73, 75, 79, 97, 104–5, 125, 155, 162, 164–65, 171, 185n23

child rearing, 23–24; among lower classes, 14–16, 21, 51, 116, 119, 121, 140; among middle classes, 34, 46, 107–9, 127–29, 141; among upper classes and elites, 73, 94–95, 97, 129, 137–38, 140, 144, 170, 175

child widows. *See* widows: children as

Chughtai, Ismat, 15, 138, 142

Churha (caste), 17–18, 50. *See also* caste order

civil law, 19, 190n17, 199n48

colonial/imperial formation: and construction of family ideals, 23–25, 126; contradictions of, 21–23, 41–42; working people's struggles and, 112–13, 124

colonial state: changing structure and authority of, 37, 101, 138–39; laws of, 19, 190n17

conjugality, 3, 19, 24–26, 87, 136, 141, 144, 147. *See also* child marriages; marriages, types of

Dalit classes, 28, 30, 33, 151, 166, 183n6, 184n4, 185n19, 186n41; Ambedkar and, *xiv*, 7, 17, 74–78, 114–17; aspirations of, 113, 112–26, 192n61; daily routines of, 50–52; discrimination against, 17–18, 78, 121; oppression of, 14–15, 17–18, 51, 62, 112, 119–21, 123, 131, 141, 197n19; patriarchy and, 35, 126–27, 130–32, 142–43, 151; physical labor and, 16, 23, 27, 29, 30, 35, 76, 94, 99, 117–18, 119–21, 140, 167; writings of, 28, 33, 35, 117–18, 184n4. *See also* Ambedkarite movement; caste order; Dalit struggle; housing: of lower classes; laboring people; sanitation, as boundary between classes

Dalit struggle: cleanliness and dress, importance of, 2, 80, 115–19, 123; dignity and respectability, quest for, 28, 30, 112–25, 131–32; education and, 113, 116–19, 122–23, 196n4; military service, importance of, 75, 79, 108, 148, 157, 163; Promised Land and, 113; religious conversion and, 113, 196n4, 199n55. *See also* Ambedkarite movement; Untouchables; visceral register of history

gender: construction of, 6, 129–30, 183n8; hierarchies and violence of, 3, 11, 17, 18–20, 31, 36, 40, 65–66, 125, 126–32, 135, 143–47, 154, 168–69, 177, 190n15. *See also* domestic work of men; domestic work of women; husbandness; manliness/manhood; motherhood; woman

Ghare Baire (The home and the world) (Tagore, 1915), 12, 20, 154, 184n

ghumakkadi. See wandering, philosophy of

Ghumakkad Shastra (Treatise on wandering) (Sankrityayan, 1949), 72–73, 158–59. *See also* wandering, philosophy of

Ghumakkad Swami (The wandering religious mendicant) (Sankrityayan, 1958), 159. *See also* Harishanand (Swami)

girl-child/woman, 18–19, 23, 44. *See also* motherhood; woman

Glover, William, 41–43

Gorakhpur, 99

Goregaon, 116

Gujarat, *xiv, xv,* 41, 44, 80

Gujrat, *xiv, xv,* 42, 44

Haq, Maulvi Abdul, 90–91, 93, 162, 166, 193n10, 193n21

Harishanand (Swami), **159–61**, 165. *See also* Janaki Devi; wandering, philosophy of

Hazaribagh, 173

Hindi (language), ix–xiii, 5–7, 14, 17, 20, 59, 60, 71, 74, 89, 92, 94, 119, 121, 143, 146, 156, 172, 174,

Hindu Code. *See* civil law

Hindustan Socialist Republican Army (formerly Hindustan Republic Association), 18

historiography, 8, 12, 24–26, 29, 41, 183n2, 185n17; archive, 26–27, 31, 78, 102, 114, 135, 163, 179; "fragment" as archive, 1, 183n1; history of the everyday, 7, 22, 26, 102, 110, 112, 118, 149, 168, 177; memory as source of history, 27, 36, 86, 90–91, 145, 186n40. *See also* autobiographies and memoirs, importance as source material; visceral register of history; World History

Home and the World, The (Ghare Baire) (Tagore, 1915), 12, 20, 154, 184n1

homosociality, 4, 46, 95, 166. *See also* housing: physical barriers of class and gender

honor: of family, 3, 14–15, 16, 17, 31, 33, 49,

100, 111, 115, 132, 151, 170; of nation, 3, 28, 31, 115–16

housing: of lower classes, 16, 20–21, 49–56, 121–22, 141–42; of middle classes, upper classes, and elites, 35–51; physical barriers of class and gender, 38–47, 51–52, 91, 112, 132, 139, 188n28; reform of, 41–42, 45. *See also* chawl/tenement; domestic space

Humsafar (Raipuri, 2008), 89

husbandness, 5–7, 154, 165–68. *See also* Kamble, Baby

Hyderabad (Deccan, in Hyderabad State, later Andhra Pradesh), *xiv, xv,* 91–93, 193n21

Hyderabad (Sindh Province), *xiv, xv,* 101

Independence, of India/Pakistan, xi, 20, 30, 47, 50, 69, 85–86, 109, 144–45, 164. *See also* Pakistan

Indian Administrative Service, 131

Indian Civil Service, 99, 131

Indian National Congress, xi–xii, 60, 70, 81, 164, 192n69

Indian Pilgrim, An (Bose, 1948), 82

industrial age, time/space of, 2, 21–23, 66, 110, 112. *See also* everydayness/everyday time, of domestic life; modernity; World History

infanticide, 18–19

infant mortality, 14, 62, 75–77, 81, 142–43, 149, 200n5

inheritances, of tradition and knowledge, 2–3, 17, 19–20, 27–30, 109, 112, 148–49, 156, 165, 169, 175

"inner" vs. "outer" worlds. *See* domestic space: home vs. world, dichotomy of

Jadhav, Damodar, x, 129, 152, 166

Jadhav, Narendra, x, **35**, 55–56, **118**, 121, **129–30**, 141, 152, 167, 199n57, 201n41

Jadhav, Sonubai, x, 55, 152, 167

Jahan, Begum Waheed (also known as Ala Bi), 15, 142

Jaipur, xii, *xiv, xv,* 39

Jamuna River, 36

Janaki Devi (wife of Harishanand), 160–61, 165–66, 208

Jat (caste), 50. *See also* caste order

Jinnah, Muhammad Ali, 78

Kabir, Sharda. *See* Ambedkar, Savitabai

Kalimpong, *xiv, xv*, 74

Kamble, Baby, x, 5–7, **50–51**, 117–18,
   124–26, 131–32, 142–43, 151–52, 154, 166,
   183n9. *See also* Ambedkarite movement;
   husbandness

Kanaila ki Katha (Sankrityayan, 1957), 62

Kanpur, *xiv, xv*, 53, 79–81, 145, 164

Kapadia, Kasturba. *See* Gandhi, Kasturba

Karachi, *xiv, xv*, 94, 101–3, 151

Karukku (Bama, 1992), 188n41

Kashi Ram, 42

Kolhapur, 52

Kozerovskaya, Yelena (Lola) Narvertovna, 70,
   83, 190n29

Kumar, Radha, 53

laboring people, 21, 23, 27–28, 30, 49, 51, 53, 55, 59,
   76, 79, 111–12, 115, 117–21, 124, 126–27, 140,
   142, 158, 167, 186n42, 201n41. *See also* child labor; Dalit classes; Dalit struggle; domestic servants; domestic work of men; domestic work
   of women; Untouchables

labor migration, x, 35, 51, 53–54, 75, 78–79,
   112–13, 118, 124–25, 129–30

labor protests, 35, 86. *See also* Ambedkarite movement; Dalit struggle

Lahore, x, *xiv, xv*, 41, 104, 106–7, 148; Model
   Town (neighborhood), 43–44

Lal, Ruby, 24

language, as signifier of men's domestic role. *See*
   visceral register of history: language and

Leningrad, 15, 70–72, 166

Lewis, Oscar, 50

London, 52, 75–77, 103, 167

Lucknow, *xiv, xv*, 42, 80–81, 98

Lucknow University, 67, 69–70

Madhya Pradesh, *xv*, 41

Madras (now Chennai), *xiv, xv*, 91, 93

Mahar (caste), 51, 54, 113, 117, 121–22, 124–25,
   129, 131. *See also* caste order

Maharaj, Shahu, 52

Maharashtra, xi, *xiv, xv*, 18, 114, 116, 118, 124

Majumdar, Rochona, 24

male entitlement. *See* domestic work of men;
   patriarchy

male privilege. *See* domestic work of men;
   patriarchy

Mang (caste), 16. *See also* caste order

manliness/manhood, 34, 85, 154; ego and insecurity in, 151; "new man," 6–7, 23–24, 109–10,
   158–59, 202n26. *See also* domestic work of
   men; husbandness; patriarchy

marriages, dissolution of: by abandonment, 19,
   61, 69, 73, 83, 166, 171–73, 191n40; by divorce,
   19, 62, 66

marriages, types of: child/infant, 19; common
   law, 61, 173; of convenience (in old age),
   71–72, 77–78, 160–61; idealistic, 66–69; love
   and companionate, 19, 24, 30, 31, 70, 107. *See
   also* child marriages; conjugality

Marwaris, 122, 163–64

masculinity, 8, 24–25, 202n26. *See also* domestic
   work of men; husbandness; manliness/
   manhood; patriarchy; visceral register of history; World History

Mehta, Hansa, 46

Meira Kumar, 81

memory, 27, 36, 85–86, 90, 91. *See also* autobiographies and memoirs, importance as source
   material; everydayness/everyday time, of domestic life; historiography; World History

Meri Jivan Yatra (Sankrityayan, 1944), xii, 71,
   189n4

middle classes, x, 14, 20–21, 35, 52, 60–61,
   85, 103, 116, 155, 164, 170, 175, 177, 188n28,
   190n15, 193n7; education and, 28–30, 86,
   114–16, 123–24, 130–31, 144, 167, 199n54;
   men of, 30, 48–49, 64–68, 72–73, 76–82,
   86, 94, 96–97, 109–10, 137, 146, 148–49,
   151, 201n41; modernity and, 24, 41–47, 86,
   114–18, 130, 197n18; women of, 16, 64–66,
   69, 86, 96–97, 109, 127, 139, 142, 156–58,
   167–68, 201n41. *See also* child rearing:
   among middle classes; housing: of middle
   classes, upper classes, and elites

Milestones (Jagjivan Ram, Indrani, 2010), xii,
   192n59

Milind College, Aurangabad, 116

Minault, Gail, 24

Mirza, Akbar, xi, **87–88, 96–103**, 167. *See also*
   Mirza, Khurshid

Mirza, Khurshid (née Jahan), xi, **87–88, 96–103**,
   109, 145, 156, 167–68, 192n1, 195nn52–53

modernity, 2, 4, 11–17, 22–25, 27, 39, 41–44, 86, 114–19, 197n18. *See also* Dalit struggle; everydayness/everyday time, of domestic life; industrial age, time/space of; postcolonial debates; World History

Modern Muslim Woman (Mirza, 1985), xi, 194n45

Modi, Narendra, 75, 78

Moon, Malti (sister of Moon, Vasant), 128, 130

Moon, Purnabai, xi, 121, 124, 128, 130, 144

Moon, Vasant, xi, 114, **121–24**, 128, 130, 140, 199n55

Moscow, 74, 150

motherhood, 23, 165, 195n60; veneration of, 6, 12, 18, 64–65, 105–6, 154–57, 169. *See also* child rearing; domestic work of women; woman

Mumbai. *See* Bombay

Muzaffarnagar, *xiv, xv*

Nagaraj, D. R., 113

Nagpur, x–xi, *xiv, xv*, 16, 53–55, 114, 122–23, 128, 130, 140; Empress Mills, Nagpur, 55; Khalasi Lines (neighborhood), 16, 54

Narain, Pratap (Bachchan's father), 34, 37–38, 139

"Nari-jati ke adhikar" (Premchand, 1931), 65, 154

Nasik, x, *xiv, xv*, 35, 56, 116

National Family Health Survey (2021), 18

nationalism, 47, 64–65, 154. *See also* anti-colonial movement; postcolonial debates

National Planning Commission, 35

navrapana. See husbandness

Nehru, Jawaharlal, 49, 81

Nepal, 71

"new man." *See under* manliness/manhood

new woman, 7, 24, 159

New York, 45, 52, 75–76

nuclear family. *See under* family

Oldenberg, Veena, 42

Pakistan (formerly West Pakistan), *xi, xv*, 1, 86–88, 94, 97–98, 101–3, 151, 184n5

Pandey, Kedarnath. *See* Sankrityayan, Rahul

Pandit, Maya, 131–32

Paraya (caste), 51, 196n4. *See also* caste order

Parel, 52, 56

Pariyar, Kamala. *See* Sankrityayan, Kamala

Partition, of British India, 20, 30, 48, 85–86, 97, 101, 144, 164

Patna, *xiv, xv*, 64, 78, 81, 89, 172

patriarchy, 5–6, 80–81, 87–88, 91–93, 99–100, 103, 105, 109–10, 126–27, 130–32, 135, 139–44, 148–52, 161–68, 177, 189n7, 194n25. *See also* caste order; Dalit classes; Dalit struggle; domestic work of men; duty; husbandness; manliness/manhood

Poona (now Pune), *xiv, xv*, 50, 116, 124, 148

postcolonial debates, 1, 4, 19, 23–24, 30–31, 41, 70, 112–13, 144, 167. *See also* anti-colonial movement; colonial/imperial formation; Dalit struggle; patriarchy; woman; work

Prasad, Rajendra, xi, **60–64**, 66, 78, 82, 154, 189n7

Pratapgarh, 36

Pratap Narain (Bachchan's father), 34, 37–39, 139

Premchand (Rai, Dhanpat), x, 5, **45, 60–62**, 65, **66–70**, 78, 82–83, 137, 154, 166. *See also* Premchand, Shivrani Devi

Premchand, Shivrani Devi (wife of Premchand), 5, 45, 62, **66–69**, 87–88, 144–45, 165

Premchand Ghar Mein (Premchand in the home) (Premchand, Shivrani, 1944), 62, 67

Prisons We Broke, The (Kamble, 1986), 5

professional classes. *See* middle classes

"Promised Land," 113. *See also* Dalit struggle

"public" vs. "private" world. *See* domestic space: home vs. world, dichotomy of

Pune. *See* Poona

Punjab, *xiv, xv*, 41–44, 48, 79

purdah, 12, 50, 61, 63–64, 83, 89–90, 96, 97–98, 126, 132, 151, 184n1. *See also* domestic work of women; patriarchy; woman

Quetta, *xiv, xv*, 97, 102–3

Quit India, 81, 108

Radio Pakistan, 97, 102

Rai, Dhanpat. *See* Premchand

Rai, Sripat, 45

Raipur, *xiv, xv*, 89

Raipuri, Akhtar Husain, xi, 4n, 86n, **87–96**, 103, 139–40, 150–51, 162, 164–66, 193n15, 193n18. *See also* Raipuri, Hameeda Akhtar Husain

www.ingramcontent.com/pod-product-compliance
Lightning Source LLC
Chambersburg PA
CBHW020857270326
41928CB00006B/754